Colonial Jerusalem

Contemporary Issues in the Middle East
Mehran Kamrava and Carol Fadda-Conrey, *Series Advisers*

COLONIAL JERUSALEM

The Spatial Construction of Identity and
Difference in a City of Myth, 1948–2012

THOMAS PHILIP ABOWD

SYRACUSE UNIVERSITY PRESS

Copyright © 2014 by Syracuse University Press

Syracuse, New York 13244-5290

All Rights Reserved

First Paperback Edition 2016

16 17 18 19 20 21   6 5 4 3 2 1

All photographs courtesy of Thomas Philip Abowd unless otherwise indicated.

Parts of chapter 5 originally appeared as "National Boundaries, Colonized Spaces:
The Gendered Politics of Residential Life in Contemporary Jerusalem," *Anthropological
Quarterly* (Fall 2007): 1027–1064. Reprinted with permission.

∞ The paper used in this publication meets the minimum requirements of the American National Standard
for Information Sciences—Permanence of Paper for Printed Library Materials, ANSI Z39.48–1992.

For a listing of books published and distributed by Syracuse University Press,
visit www.SyracuseUniversityPress.syr.edu.

ISBN: 978-0-8156-3348-8 (cloth)   978-0-8156-3469-0 (paperback)   978-0-8156-5261-8 (e-book)

Library of Congress has catalogued the cloth edition as follows:

Abowd, Thomas Philip, 1967– author.
Colonial Jerusalem : the spatial construction of identity and difference in a city of myth, 1948–2012 /
Thomas Philip Abowd. — First edition.
pages cm. — (Contemporary issues in the Middle East)
Includes bibliographical references and index.
ISBN 978-0-8156-3348-8 (cloth : alk. paper) — ISBN 978-0-8156-5261-8 (ebook) 1. Jerusalem—
History—20th century.   2. Jerusalem—History—21st century.   3. Jerusalem—Ethnic relations—
History—20th century.   4. Jerusalem—Ethnic relations—History—21st century.   5. Jerusalem—Politics
and government—20th century.   6. Jerusalem—Politics and government—21st century.   7. Palestinian
Arabs—Jerusalem—Social conditions—20th century.   8. Palestinian Arabs—Jerusalem—Social conditions—
21st century.   9. Jews—Jerusalem—History—20th century.   10. Jews—Jerusalem—History—
21st century.   11. Arab-Israeli conflict—Jerusalem—Influence. I. Title.
DS109.93.A64 2014
956.94′4205—dc23   2014011261

Manufactured in the United States of America

To my family and to all those in Palestine/Israel
who were for me what anthropologists like to call "essential kin"

THOMAS PHILIP ABOWD teaches in the Departments of Anthropology and American Studies at Tufts University. He received his PhD in Cultural Anthropology from Columbia University. He has been involved for two decades in scholarly projects related to Palestine, Israel, and the Middle East and is the recipient of awards from the Fulbright Hays, the Fulbright Doctoral Dissertation Research Abroad (DDRA), the Palestinian American Research Center, and the Social Science Research Council.

There is no document of civilization which is not at the same time a document of barbarism. And just as such a document is not free of barbarism, barbarism taints also the manner in which it was transmitted from one owner to another.

—WALTER BENJAMIN,
Theses on the Philosophy of History

Contents

Illustrations

MAPS

Acknowledgments

This book was inspired by many friends, mentors, colleagues, and teachers in the United States and Palestine/Israel. First, let me thank those in Jerusalem and throughout Palestine/Israel who made this project possible through their generosity, hospitality, and solidarity. Some of them must remain anonymous but let me thank the following by name: Ala Alazza, Albert Algazerian, Suad Amiry, George Azar, Gabriel Baramki, Dianna Buttu, Catherine Cook, Tom Dallal, Ibrahim Daoud, Manal Diab, Nabil Feidy, Julie Gallegos, Toufiq Haddad, Jeff Halper, Rema Hammami, Mahmoud Hawari, Tikva Honig-Parnass, Kamal Jafari, Demetri Karkar, Delia Khano, Gabriel Khano, Mark Khano, Issam Nassar, Alex Pollack, Nidal Rafa, Abaher Sakka, Mariam Shaheen, Arabiya Shawamreh, Salim Shawamreh, Magid Shehade, Raja Shehadeh, Lisa Taraki, and Graham Usher.

My interests in Palestine/Israel and the Middle East more broadly were generated during my undergraduate years at the University of Michigan in Ann Arbor. My thanks, therefore, go to several teachers, advisers, and intellectual mentors who not only helped shape my project but also taught me then and since about intellectual rigor and the joys of teaching. First and foremost has been Salim Tamari, whose scholarly and intellectual example has been immense. I also wish to thank Carol Bardenstein, Juan Cole, Luis Sfeir-Younis, Anton Shammas, and Ann Stoler. Though I never had the pleasure of taking a course with Alan Wald, he has been for me and innumerable other younger scholars and activists a true exemplar of what it means to be a politically committed intellectual of the highest order.

At Columbia University my incredible dissertation committee provided further inspiration. Along with Salim Tamari, let me thank Nick Dirks,

Steven Gregory, Brinkley Messick, and Timothy Mitchell. During my time in New York I was also deeply influenced through seminars, independent studies, and conversations with other wonderful thinkers. A special thanks to Bassam Abed, Talal Asad, Lila Abu Lughod, Manning Marable, Premilla Nadasen, Edward Said, Ella Shohat, and Michael Taussig.

A number of people read chapters of this book over the last several years. Among them are: Julie Peteet, Eva Moseley, and Aseel Sawalha, who read the entire manuscript; and Mary Abowd, Paul Abowd, Dianna Downing, and Salim Tamari, who read much of the manuscript in different phases of its development. Paul's assistance, poise, and intelligence was what finally pushed me through to the end of this project. But his keen political mind challenged me along the way to turn the critical gaze back on myself. All of these individuals read the manuscript with generosity and patience. Others who read chapters and helped me enormously define and refine this project include Samar Alatout, Ala Alazza, Barbara Aswad, Carol Bardenstein, Moshe Behar, Amahl Bishara, Elaine Hagopian, Nubar Hovsapian, Loren Lybarger, Nadine Naber, Issam Nasser, and Sandy Sufian. I have benefited from the patience, skill, and encouragement of amazing editors at Syracuse University Press, as well, particularly Deanna McCay, Mary Selden Evans, Marcia Hough, and their terrific staffs.

In addition to those mentioned above, the following friends have been sources of inspiration, encouragement, love, and playful banter: Ishmael Ahmed, Deborah Al-Najjar, Evelyn Alsultany, Anan Ameri, Siva Arumugam, Moshe Behar, Glenn Bowman, Ethel Brooks, Lori Brooks, Leila Buck, Louise Cainkar, Eugenia Casielles-Suárez, Yogesh Chandrani, Pamela Crespin, Molly Doane, Patrick Dodd, Anne Duggan, Noura Erakat, Nergis Erami, Elizabeth Esch, Amal Fadlalla, Hussein Fancy, Leila Farsakh, Reem Gibreel, Nadia Guessous, Pamela Gupta, Shah Hanafi, Barbara Harvey, Emily Jacir, Randa Jarrar, Mark Keller, King Alfonso XIII, David Levin, Barbara Logan, Jane Lynch, Lucy Mair, Sunaina Maira, Sofian Merabet, Jonathan Metzl, Khaled Muttawa, Sana Odeh, Benefo Ofosu-Benefo, Nima Paidipaty, Luisa Quintero, Kevin Rashid, Shira Robinson, Mabel Rodriguez, Brad Roth, Greg Rowe, Atef Said, Lisa Schwartzman, May Seikely, Fran Shor, Heike Schotten, Larry LaFontaine Stokes, Shahla Talabi, Miriam Ticktin, Hap Veezer, and Laura Wernick.

I would also like to thank Susan Akram, Nidal al-Azraq, Zeina Azzam, Paul Beran, Jim Bowley, Mark Buchan, Deirdre de la Cruz, Lara Deeb, Corey Dolgon, Leila Farsakh, Ilana Feldman, Mona El Ghobashy, Jude Glubman, Sangeetha Gopalakrishnan, Nelson Hancock, Doug Ierly, John Jackson, Anupama Jain, Amira Jarmakani, Munir Jirmanus, Naila Saba Jirmanus, Andrew Kadi, Rhoda Kanaaneh, Aida Khan, Andrew Kurban, Gina Kurban, Darla Linville, Nergis Mavavala, John Mikhail, Deborah Milbauer, Lisa Mitchell, Minoo Moallem, Yousef Munayyer, Hubert Murray, Nancy Murray, Dard Neuman, Sana Odeh, Kate Ramsey, Hilary Rantisi, Marilynn Rashid, Sima Rizvi, Loren Ryter, Dana Sajdi, Hieke Schotten, Sara Shohat, John Stoner, Bob Vitalis, Antina von Schnitzler, Sima Shakhsari, Eric Wakin, David Watson, and Kate Wilson.

Let me also thank colleagues at Tufts for their support over the last few years. Along with Amahl Bishara, they include Hosea Hirata, Lisa Lowe, Sarah Pinto, Hugh Roberts, Nadim Rouhana, Rosalind Shaw, Jean Wu, and Adriana Zavala.

I have been extremely fortunate to have had so many fabulous students at various schools over the last several years. They are too numerous to list individually and their impact on me too great to even remotely describe. They *alone* are worth the sacrifices that this profession requires. When I think about just how much I have learned from these young minds, how they have so consistently challenged my own cultural assumptions, I am affirmed in my choice to be a teacher.

Finally, I would like to thank my very expansive and all-consuming family, who offered immense support and love over the years—not to mention an abundance of drama. Thanks to my grandmother, Rachel Nader Dwaihy, whose belief in me has meant everything. A special tribute, also, to the loving memory of David Barr and Elizabeth Dwaihy Barr, whose love and devotion I will always cherish and without whose belief in me this project would not have been completed. I have been beyond fortunate to have had such incredible siblings, each remarkable in their own distinct ways: Mary, Michael, Gabriele, Elizabeth, and Paul. And finally thanks to my parents, Anne Marie and Thomas, for their examples of decency and their endless concern for others both within our "essential kin" and far beyond.

Colonial Jerusalem

1

Jerusalem, a Colonial City under Construction

I have often noted that the deprivations of the colonized are the almost direct result of the advantages secured to the colonizer. . . . To observe the life of the colonizer and the colonized is to discover rapidly that the daily humiliation of the colonized, his objective subjugation, are not merely economic. Even the poorest colonizer thought himself to be—and actually was—superior to the colonized. This too was part of colonial privilege.

—ALBERT MEMMI, *The Colonizer and the Colonized*, 1965

This is a bleeding process with a vengeance.

—KARL MARX, "Letter to Nikolai Danielson," 1881

In 2004, in a festive ceremony, Israeli authorities broke ground on the Museum of Tolerance (MOTJ) in Jerusalem. The $100-million initiative is sponsored by the Los Angeles–based Simon Wiesenthal Center and is supported by funds raised internationally. This enormous cultural project is currently under construction in the center of Jerusalem, a city Israel has claimed an exclusive right to govern against the weight of world opinion and the historical claims of the indigenous Palestinians. The museum's website features the structure's varied facets and celebrates the purported contributions it will make to "healing" this divided and conflict-ridden urban landscape. Dedicated, as its literature announces, to "human dignity," the MOTJ's founders declare that this elaborate representational space will serve as "a great landmark promoting the principles of mutual respect and social responsibility."[1]

The stated aims of this place of "tolerance" have certainly appeared innocent, even deeply humane, to many Israeli Jews and their supporters abroad. However, this initiative has proven anything but innocuous since plans for it were first unfurled a decade ago. For one, this structure of glass and polished stone is beginning to emerge just a short distance from a string of former Palestinian neighborhoods in West Jerusalem, whose inhabitants were expelled by the new Israeli state in 1948. Further, and perhaps most critically, the museum is being established atop a segment of the Ma'mam Allah (or Mamilla) Islamic Cemetery, a centuries-old Arab burial ground.

Despite lofty assertions about this institution's peaceful character, as construction commenced Israeli building crews were compelled to acknowledge that they had dug up the bones of those buried in the cemetery. Soon thereafter, an embarrassing international scandal arose as news of the violation of these tombs drew predictable responses of protest and indignation from Los Angeles to Lahore, including from thousands of Israeli-Jews dismayed by their government's actions.[2]

1. See the MOTJ's website: http://www.wiesenthal.com/site/pp.asp?c=lsKWLbP JLnF&b=5505225#. Access date November 20, 2013. If one acknowledges, as I do, the force of Zizek's (2010) and Brown's (2006) critiques of the liberal discourse of "tolerance," the name of the Wiesenthal Center's museum is less ironic than it might initially appear.

2. For a trenchant critique of the MOTJ see Khalidi (2011). The Wiesenthal Center answered protests in curious ways. One standard response claimed that the locale was not that of a cemetery at all but rather a parking lot. A picture of the parking lot accompanied this explanation and was meant to assert, in one of the most effective ideological ploys, a claim to the self-evident: "Look, there is obviously only a parking lot here." "Cemetery? What cemetery?" For more on such ideological tactics, see Zizek (1994, 11–12). One problem confronting those who deny the burial site and its Palestinian, Arab, and Muslim heritage is the fact that it is noted on innumerable pre-1948 cartographic and textual representations of Jerusalem—British, Ottoman, Palestinian, and even those of Zionist organizations. The nascent Jewish state paved the parking lot over one segment of the

Who, many demanded, justifies the despoiling and disturbing of graves? Of all the places to establish a cultural center with the avowed aim of documenting the history of anti-Semitism, why had the Israeli government and its American affiliates insisted on the burial ground of another people? And yet, despite these desecrations, digging continued implacably, applauded by U.S. and Israeli politicians and a slew of celebrity endorsers. The project has been bolstered since 2008 by the legal sanction of an Israeli Supreme Court ruling supporting the museum's organizers and affirming their right to build at this locale. This, while voices within the Israeli press and government have questioned whether the graves were even part of a "real" cemetery at all.[3]

Facing mounting international condemnation, the Jewish state erected a symbolic, seamless ten-foot wall around the construction site's perimeter in recent years to block the monitoring of what might yet be disinterred. A series of surveillance cameras has been placed atop this enclosure, directing their panoptic gaze outward at those who wish to observe what is happening within. As with innumerable other battles over land, memory, and the past that have arisen in Jerusalem since the beginning of the Palestinian-Israeli conflict, this one has intensified in emblematic ways. The case of a museum purportedly about remembrance effacing the histories of another people is a striking metaphor for the struggle over this city waged between religious and national communities in the last century.

---

burial ground in the early 1960s and established "Independence Park" (*Gan Ha'atzmaut*) on much of the rest of this several-acre site in the late 1950s.

3. The unanimous Israeli Supreme Court ruling asserted that "for almost 50 years the compound has not been a part of the cemetery, both in the normative sense and in the practical sense." In the wake of this decision, a spokesperson for the Wiesenthal Center was quoted as saying that "attempts to declare the land on which this lot is built a holy place has no grounding in common sense" (*Ha'aretz*, January 7, 2009). For another defense of the MOTJ, see the article in the *Jerusalem Post*, August 15, 2010, titled "Fake Graves Cleared from Jerusalem Cemetery." http://www.jpost.com/Israel/Fake-graves -cleared-from-Jlem-cemetery. Access date November 28, 2012.

COLONIAL JERUSALEM: EXPANSION AND EXCLUSION

This book explores the spatial construction of identity and difference in contemporary Jerusalem, a deeply divided urban center at the core of the sixty-seven-year Palestinian-Israeli conflict. I analyze the political uses of myth, meaning, and memory across an urban landscape integral to the national identities of both Palestinian Arabs and Israeli Jews and highly significant to hundreds of millions of others the world over. Writing a study of this sort requires asking three interrelated questions: First, who, since 1948, has possessed the capacity to regulate, redefine, and reconfigure Jerusalem? Second, how have arrangements of enforced separation (*hafrada* in Hebrew, *infisaal* in Arabic) here and elsewhere in Palestine/ Israel shaped the lives of Arabs and Jews since the rise of this national struggle?[4] And third, who—in the words of urban theorist Henri Lefebvre (1968)—has "the right to the city" and what does social justice demand in contemporary Jerusalem?

In each of the chapters that follow, I detail how borders between (and among) Palestinians and Israelis have been constituted in this most contested of places. This book argues that the Jewish state's attempts to sustain sole control over Jerusalem have been as much about guarding the past as they have been about fortressing the contemporary city with separation walls, checkpoints, and military emplacements. I contend that the frontiers that have dominated and defined Jerusalem have included not simply serpentine ramparts of concrete or electrified fences, but also the ossified boundaries of the imagination and the fortified divides of the mind.

The result has been a prescribed social order of apartness between Palestinians and Israelis across the entire country. This arrangement has made Jerusalem one of the most segregated cities in the world. However, among my central arguments is that this urban space represents not

---

4. I refer to this site of national conflict throughout the book as Palestine/Israel. I do so to acknowledge the fact that two distinct national groups reside today in what had been known internationally before 1948 as Palestine. I also do so to call attention to the reality that these quite heterogeneous communities are bound up together spatially and culturally in important, though often unacknowledged, ways.

simply a severely divided place within a broader *national* struggle but also a colonized space at the heart of a *colonial* conflict. In analyzing Jerusalem within a colonial framework, my book diverges from the bulk of scholarly and nonscholarly writings on the contemporary city and the larger landscape of Palestine/Israel in which it is embedded.[5]

Approaching Palestine/Israel as a site of colonial governance and Jerusalem as a colonial city might appear anything but self-evident to some readers. It certainly has seemed so to a range of Western commentators on the contemporary Middle East. Even those for whom the Jewish state's military occupation of East Jerusalem and the rest of the West Bank is understood to be illegal under international law are commonly averse to define Israeli authority as colonial authority. This reluctance, I assert, has partially to do with a failure to grasp with perhaps enough precision the character of Israeli policy since 1948, particularly its spatial designs and racial assumptions. But beyond misconceptions of, for instance, the discriminatory features of Israeli land law or the exclusionary bylaws of Jewish-only kibbutzim, neighborhoods, or settlements, there are also widely held beliefs about colonialism more generally that contribute to these analyses.

Crucially, there persists a taken-for-granted belief among scholars, politicians, and journalists that colonialism is something that humanity has, in a sense, "progressed" beyond.[6] Colonialism and postcolonialism are all too often regarded as stages in a teleological unfolding of history. And we today—all of us—are said to reside in the latter period. Consequently, the notion of a "colonial present" has not informed the majority of scholarly work on this conflict or on Jerusalem specifically.[7]

5. Among the important exceptions are the scholarly works of Abu El-Haj (2001), Makdisi (2010), Shafir (1989), Honig-Parnass (2011), Davis (2004), Pappe (2007), Rodinson (1973), and Shihade (2011).

6. For superb analyses of the problems associated with the term "postcolonialism" and the theorization of colonialism see McClintock (1995), Stoler (2006), and Comaroff and Comaroff (1991).

7. For more on these themes written from slightly different perspectives, see Gregory (2004) and Mamdani (2004).

Writing about Israel as a colonial state is not simply about leveling a sterner rebuke of its policies and formation. Rather, the importance of doing so pertains to the ways in which Israel (as the dominant power in the country and the region) has organized, made available, and denied the use of land and housing to Arabs and Jews since 1948. Underlying colonial governance, whether in Algeria, North America, South Africa, or Palestine/Israel, has been a relentless territorial expansion, accompanied by methods of racial exclusion and confinement imposed on subjugated and racialized communities. A prodigious and refined ideological machinery has typically also been at work, justifying, normalizing, and vindicating policies of conquest while defining the colonized as dangerous and inferior—when they are even acknowledged at all.

But why, one might still ask, are these acts of expropriation and exclusion expressions of *colonial* power? Conquest and mass expulsions are, after all, as old as human civilization itself. The answer lies primarily in the transformative quality of this distinctly modern exercise of domination. Describing the capacity of colonialism to radically remake captured lands and regulate populations, Talal Asad (1991) explains that "the conditions of reinvention were increasingly defined by a new scheme of things—new forms of power, work and knowledge" (314). These dimensions of rule—legal, cultural, and military—should be seen, he adds, not simply "as a temporary repression of subject populations but as an irrevocable process of transmutation, in which old desires and ways of life were destroyed and new ones took their place" (ibid).[8]

Colonial alterations in Palestine began with greatest force under British rule (1917–1948). A few of these changes and modes of control have persisted as part of Israeli governance (in West Jerusalem from 1948 to the present and in East Jerusalem since 1967).[9] However, despite these

8. For other perceptive works on colonial knowledge production and the imperial imagination, see Mitchell (1988, 1991, 2002), Cohn (1996), Comaroff and Comaroff (1991), Cooper and Stoler (1997), Stoler (1995, 2002), and Dirks (1996).

9. In the years since its establishment in 1948, the Israeli state has adopted some of the most draconian British colonial policies and practices of regulating space, while devising a range of additional ones. Among these colonial continuities include the Israeli

continuities, there was one fundamental rupture in the rule of Palestine in the twentieth century: British authority was not *settler* colonialism; Israeli authority is and has been since its inception more than six decades ago. From the first days of its existence, the self-described Jewish state built on earlier, pre-state efforts to transform and claim the country for the exclusive benefit of Jewish communities in Palestine and abroad. This, as discussed throughout this book, has necessitated vast settlement campaigns to bolster the Jewish population at the expense of the indigenous Palestinian Christians and Muslims.

In exploring the racial assumptions and practices so integral to Israeli authority and the Zionist principles that undergird them, I have incurred a tremendous debt to the theorizing of Mary Douglas and her classic work, *Purity and Danger*. In it she examines the anxieties that arise when things (or people) do not fit neatly into the "cherished classifications" of dominant groups. Her notion of "matter out of place" (1966, 44) is a stellar metaphor for the tensions and fears that arise when particular people refuse to remain in their "proper" places. What Douglas refers to as "dirt" and "pollution" have compelling implications for the abiding racialization of communities and spaces in Jerusalem and throughout the entirety of Palestine/Israel.[10] I engage her discussion of such themes in each of the chapters that follow.

The social order of separation created in Jerusalem over the last several decades has been analogous in a number of respects to that of the Jim Crow U.S. South and apartheid South Africa.[11] Vincent Crapanzano (1985), writing about the geographies of racial domination in the twilight of white supremacy in South Africa, aptly notes that "difference is preserved through distance" (39). Drawing from this and other related insights from

---

use of the British Land Ordinance of 1943 to enable the expropriation of privately held Palestinian land. For an analysis of this governing strategy by Israel, see Benvenisti (1996).

10. I will be talking about the processes of racialization and the making of racial and social difference throughout this book. For trenchant discussions of the term see Omi and Winant (1994) and Balibar (1991).

11. For an analysis of some of the parallels between the Jim Crow U.S. South and contemporary Palestine/Israel, see A. Davis (2012).

the literature on racism and urban politics, this book explores how policed apartness between Palestinian Arabs and Israeli Jews, occupier and occupied, has tended to bolster beliefs among religious and national groups concerning their supposed differences.

IMAGINING THE "HOLY CITY"

Innumerable other urban centers across the globe have exhibited apartheid-like forms of separation between racial, religious, and ethnic communities. However, Jerusalem (known as *al-Quds* to Palestinians and *Yerushalim* to Israeli Jews) is distinguished from nearly every other metropolitan area in at least one or two vital respects. Not only is this site at the center of the enduring Palestinian-Israeli conflict but it also possesses a near-peerless religious and symbolic potency. The myths that envelop this realm (biblical, national, etc.) animate hundreds of millions, if not billions globally.

Detroit, Michigan or Baltimore, Maryland may be cities of intense racial segregation. But one could hardly imagine people from around the world converging on these sites of post-industrial decline to fight and die for them. Though smaller than Charlotte, North Carolina, Jerusalem has retained an almost magical intensity as mighty or mightier than places revered as "global cities" or glamorous capitals of high finance, political power, and the arts.[12]

The vast majority of those who lay claim to Jerusalem and the rest of the "holy land," as it is so often marketed, reside far beyond this sliver of the eastern Mediterranean and its approximately twelve million Palestinians and Israelis, as of 2013 roughly equal in number. Their bonds and

---

12. Western writers and artists over the last two centuries alone have underscored the magical and mythical qualities Jerusalem possesses to those who live beyond its boundaries. These include Blake's 1804 poem "Jerusalem" (later recorded by, among others, singer Billy Bragg in the 1980s) and the travelogues and personal accounts of Twain (1869), Melville (1876), and Bellow (1976). For an excellent source on some of these literary representations see Obenzinger (1999). For a superb examination of the ways in which the Western colonial gaze has sought to capture Jerusalem see Nassar (2006).

connections are routinely expressed as "sacred" or biblical ones, forged from promises and prophecies transmitted from unassailable celestial sources.[13] Relatively few who claim an intimacy with this place, however, will ever visit the land they imagine binds them to those they refer to as their gods, ancestors, and prophets.

Given Jerusalem's global importance, it is perplexing how relatively few scholarly works have sought to explore social relations and national politics in the contemporary city.[14] Even fewer ethnographies have been written about the daily, lived dimensions of intercommunal encounters and conflicts that have comprised this urban center. Lisa Taraki (2006b) and other Palestinian scholars have noted in recent years that not nearly enough research on Palestinian society has examined "the practices of everyday existence" (xxii) under Israeli military occupation. This body of scholarship has tended, she notes, to emphasize more general political and economic relations. All too often, these works have represented Palestinians as "one dimensional political subjects" (xi), as a community or communities whose struggles are regularly reduced to their nationalist dimensions. "The internal dynamics, stresses, and contradictions of the social groups and communities within which people live out their lives," she adds, "have not received much serious attention from most researchers" (ibid.).

This book takes seriously this critique and the scholarly approaches it insists upon. In the chapters that follow I examine quotidian life in Jerusalem from various perspectives. The complexities intrinsic to

13. Jerusalem is, of course, where the three monotheistic faiths were in important ways constituted. The Western Wall (*Kotel*) and the adjacent site of the Second Temple are sites Judaism claims contain the presence of God. The Via Dolorosa and the Church of the Holy Sepulcher are places where devoted Christians assert that Jesus walked to his crucifixion and was buried. The Dome of the Rock is the locale where many Muslims believe Mohammed ascended to heaven on a winged horse (what is known in Islam as the *mi'raj* and spoken of in the Qur'an 17:1).

14. Among the dozens of English readers on urban anthropology and urbanism more generally, there is rarely even a mention of Jerusalem in the modern era, let alone entire chapters devoted to the city.

manufacturing and sustaining "binarized" notions of self and other, masculinity and femininity, the divine and the secular, past and present—even Arab and Jew and Israeli and Palestinian—are countless. These are cultural divisions and distinctions that, though routinely depicted as timeless, optionless, or eternal, have forever been in flux. They have for decades helped engender forms of separation and hostility in this city but they are not, I argue, inevitable.

THE MAKING OF A COLONIAL CITY:
HISTORICAL CONSIDERATIONS

Jerusalem, like the rest of historic Palestine, was governed by the Ottoman Empire for nearly four centuries before the advent of British colonial rule in December 1917. The city in the latter years of the Ottoman period bore little resemblance to what it would become by the end of the British Mandate just three decades later. Urban environments in the region and across the globe exhibited significant growth during the same period and since. However, Jerusalem's rising population figures and territorial changes during that era (and indeed over the last century) reveal an urban environment whose expansion has been particularly pronounced.[15] Two critical transformations came in 1948 with the creation of the state of Israel and the expulsion by that new country of roughly 750,000 Palestinian Christians and Muslims (the majority of the Arab population). Upwards of 45,000 of these were exiled from Jerusalem and its neighboring villages.

These transformations of the late 1940s were crucial to the creation of a particular kind of Jerusalem. But it should be remembered that decades before British rule the Ottoman authorities had begun to usher in a range of modern alterations to the city's character. In the wake of nineteenth-century reforms to the land tenure system and the opening up of Palestine to European trade and markets, the Ottomans redrew Jerusalem's

---

15. This was due primarily to sharply rising Jewish immigration to Palestine (largely from Europe and Russia) during the first half of the twentieth century, a drop in infant mortality rates in the city and elsewhere, and economic growth within Jerusalem's expanding municipal boundaries.

boundaries in 1909, enlarging them several fold and taking in hundreds of acres beyond the former limits of the Old City walls.[16]

Budding neighborhoods, commercial zones, and religious institutions began to proliferate beyond the Old City in the decades leading up to the British conquest of Palestine. Residential areas grew even more rapidly in the thirty years of British colonial rule with at least two dozen new quarters built during that period. In the early phases of British control, officials further altered the city and transformed it administratively. However, consistent with the practices of colonial governance then and since, consultations with the native inhabitants over these changes were minor.

Jerusalem's current Israeli-drawn municipal borders encompass 125.15 square kilometers, composed of what today is referred to as West Jerusalem (55 square kilometers) and East Jerusalem (70 square kilometers). The approximately 850,000 people within these boundaries include about 325,000 Palestinian Christians and Muslims (nearly all residing on the east side of the city) and roughly 500,000 Israeli Jews (about 200,000 of whom live in East Jerusalem settlements and about 300,000 live on the west side). Since Israel's conquest and occupation of East Jerusalem in 1967, it has been in control of the entirety of this urban center. And that has meant that the Jewish state has been able to reconfigure nearly all major dimensions of this symbolic space—including its borders—with little if any participation from the Palestinian residents.

Israel redrew the borders of East Jerusalem in June 1967, expanding this side of the city ten fold (from about 6 to 70 square kilometers). Its post-1967 borders have stretched from Ramallah and al-Bireh, 12 kilometers to the north of the city center, to the outskirts of Bethlehem about 6 kilometers to the south.[17] Observing the sprawling metropolitan area today, it is easy to forget that, until the start of the twentieth century, Jerusalem was defined as little more than the one-square-kilometer of land within

16. See Kark (2001) for a discussion of the city's expansion in the early twentieth century.

17. For a fine visual representation of Jerusalem's changing spatial character, see the website of "Terrestrial Jerusalem," http://t-j.org.il/JerusalemAtlas.aspx. Access date November 27, 2013.

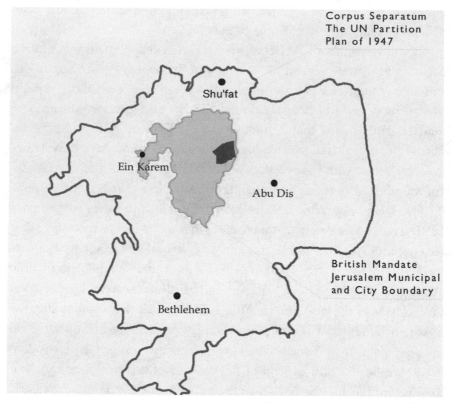

Map 1. Jerusalem in 1947 on the eve of the departure of the British colonial regime and the city's physical division. Courtesy of United Nations, Office for the Coordination of Humanitarian Affairs (OCHA), Occupied Palestinian Territory.

the 400-year-old walls of the Old City. This area contained approximately 30,000 Muslim, Christian, and Jewish inhabitants by the early 1900s, a number very close to its current population.

SOCIAL AND CULTURAL CHANGES

Running concurrently with and intersecting these vast spatial and demographic changes to Jerusalem were its shifting cultural cartographies. The rise of capitalist modernity and the rapid spread of European colonialism across the Middle East in the late 1800s and early 1900s were utterly transformational in the ways noted by Asad (1991) above. These processes

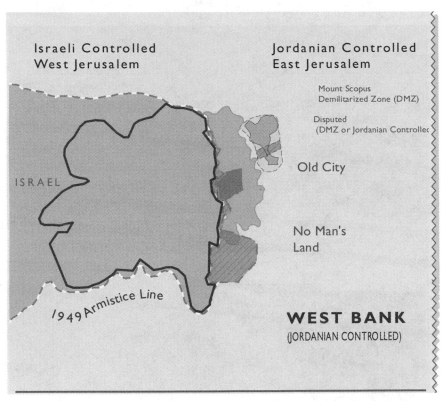

Map 2. Jerusalem divided between the Israeli-ruled west side and the Jordanian-ruled east side, 1949–1967. Courtesy of United Nations, Office for the Coordination of Humanitarian Affairs (OCHA), Occupied Palestinian Territory.

helped bring new nationalist assertions, borders, identities, and movements rapidly into existence. Zionism (or Jewish nationalism) and Palestinian nationalism were late-breaking expressions of this distinctly modern form of identity. In the Palestine of the early 1900s, these ideologies began to be wedded to colonial and anticolonial politics. More and more they were mutually understood to be sharply at odds.[18]

18. See Khalidi (1997; 2006) for a superb discussion of the rise of Palestinian nationalism in the early twentieth century. The arbitrary national boundaries that Palestinians, Israelis, and all others in the immediate region are compelled to live within (or outside

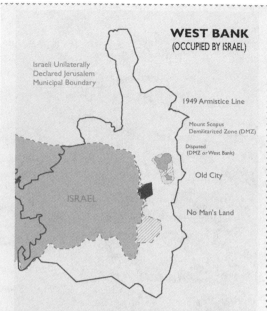

WEST BANK
(OCCUPIED BY ISRAEL)

Israeli Unilaterally
Declared Jerusalem
Municipal Boundary

1949 Armistice Line

Mount Scopus
Demilitarized Zone (DMZ)

Disputed
(DMZ or West Bank)

Old City

ISRAEL

No Man's Land

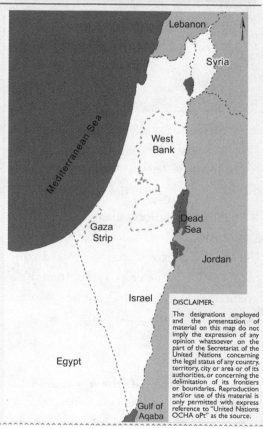

Lebanon

Syria

Mediterranean Sea

West
Bank

Gaza
Strip

Dead
Sea

Jordan

Israel

DISCLAIMER:

The designations employed
and the presentation of
material on this map do not
imply the expression of any
opinion whatsoever on the
part of the Secretariat of the
United Nations concerning
the legal status of any country,
territory, city or area or of its
authorities, or concerning the
delimitation of its frontiers
or boundaries. Reproduction
and/or use of this material is
only permitted with express
reference to "United Nations
OCHA oPt" as the source.

Egypt

Gulf of
Aqaba

Map 3. Palestine/Israel
and Israel's unilaterally
redrawn Jerusalem,
post-1967. Courtesy of
United Nations, Office
for the Coordination of
Humanitarian Affairs
(OCHA), Occupied
Palestinian Territory.

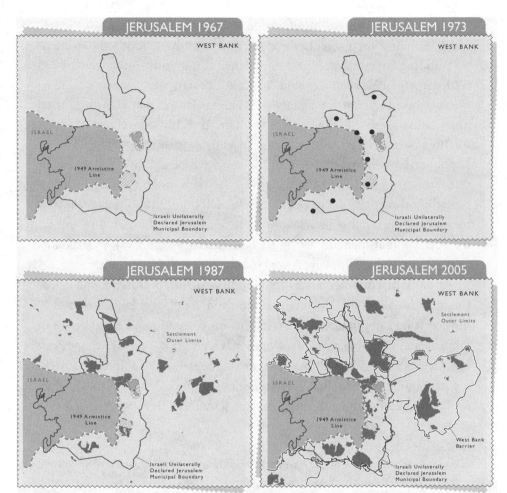

Map 4. The progression of military occupation: Jerusalem in the years 1967, 1973, 1987, and 2005. Illegal Jewish settlements are denoted by black dots in the 1973 map and by darker areas in the 1987 and 2005 maps. Courtesy of United Nations, Office for the Coordination of Humanitarian Affairs (OCHA), Occupied Palestinian Territory.

The waves of Jewish immigration to Palestine that began in the late nineteenth and early twentieth centuries typically included those intent on building a Jewish state or homeland. As already mentioned, mass settlement in Palestine was vital if such a design were to come to fruition because the land the Zionist movement had chosen was more than nine-tenths Arab Muslim and Christian in 1916.[19] Carefully examining the goals and visions of the mainstream Zionist movement reveals a strong settler-colonial dimension. Those who came to live in Palestine not uncommonly referred to themselves as "settlers."[20] To this end, Zionist officials and agencies developed dozens of neighborhoods, kibbutzim, and *moshavim* (the latter is the Hebrew word for "colonies") with discriminatory bylaws that formally excluded Palestinian Muslims and Christians from living, and at times even working, within these residential realms.[21]

It was with the emergence of this conflict between Zionism and Palestinian nationalism that the binary opposition, Arab–Jew, began to solidify in ways it had not before. As this happened, histories and experiences of more overlapping social relations, ones in which "Arab" and "Jew" were not regarded as necessarily mutually exclusive, began to be effaced by emerging nationalist visions. The rise of distinct national divisions in Palestine, as Tamari (2009) and other scholars of Jerusalem have written, created

---

of) today were only etched on the former Ottoman Empire with the advent of British and French colonial administrations in the post-World War I era.

19. See McCarthy (1990).

20. Several mainstream Zionist organizations described their activity and goals, in fact, as "colonization," including the "Jewish Colonization Association," later the "Palestine Jewish Colonization Association"; for more on their role in settling Palestine, see Kark (1991; 2001).

21. See Kimmerling (2008) for more on the motives of these pre-1948 designs. The majority of Zionist immigrants before 1948 were from Europe and Russia. By the beginning of British colonial rule, these new arrivals had outnumbered the indigenous Jews of Palestine. By "indigenous" I refer to those Jewish communities who were residing in Palestine before the rise of the modern Zionist settlement campaign in the late 1800s. Members of the latter communities, some of whom had lived in the country for several hundred years, were generally much more ambivalent about Zionism and the establishment of a Jewish state in Palestine than were the Europeans who principally led the movement.

greater separation and conflict between Arab and Jewish communities. These emerging dimensions of social life would in turn have a profound impact on the city's changing spatial dimensions, which I will address in each of the following chapters.[22]

The country's native Christians and Muslims overwhelmingly opposed the establishment of a Jewish state, perhaps primarily because they feared that as non-Jews they would eventually be marginalized in or even expelled from their own towns and villages. Jewish nationalism could offer the Palestinians little if anything because it was not premised on their inclusion but rather on their removal or absence. Unlike other colonial ventures, mainstream Zionist state-making struggles were based *not* on the conquest of land and the exploitation of native labor, but instead on the exclusion or displacement of its non-Jewish inhabitants. Arab Christians, Muslims, and others registered anxieties as early as the late nineteenth century about what a Jewish state in Palestine might mean for them. Those fears, as this book will detail, have not proven unwarranted.

DEMOGRAPHIC POLITICS

Contentious debates have arisen for decades around the population figures of Ottoman-era and British Mandate Palestine. Such disputes underline how integral demographic politics have been to the struggle over this narrow strip of territory between the Mediterranean Sea and the Jordan River. Precise figures for various religious and national groupings within particular borders have been difficult to ascertain. Among the most rigorous and perhaps the most reliable works to explore population statistics in twentieth century Palestine is that of the Ottoman historian Justin McCarthy (1990). He has addressed the flawed and at times highly ideological character of several of the supposed counts.[23] After examining all

---

22. For an excellent discussion of these Ottoman and British-era shifts in identity in Palestine, see Tamari (2009).

23. For a fascinating discussion of demographic politics in Ottoman Palestine, see Doumani (1994).

major demographic estimations from the early and mid-twentieth century, he concludes that Palestine was roughly 90 percent Palestinian Arab (Christian, Muslim, and a small indigenous Jewish community) in 1916 on the eve of British rule. This was about the time Britain's foreign secretary, Lord Alfred Balfour, declared his government's support for a "Jewish homeland" in Palestine.[24]

By the late 1940s, in the final years of British rule, there is little disagreement in the scholarly literature that the Arabs of Palestine were close to 70 percent of the total population. The Jewish communities represented approximately 30 percent. For those intent on creating a Jewish state in Palestine, the demographic "dangers" the Arab majority represented had not vanished after a half century of settlement activity. They were, however, largely mitigated in 1948 with the expulsion of the majority of the Palestinians. Israeli officials have blocked the return of even a segment of these refugees in violation of UN Resolution 194 and in opposition to the wishes of a fairly broad international consensus. The explicitly stated reason given by Israel is that their repatriation would "threaten" the Jewish "character" of the Jewish state.

I shall return to this and other racial anxieties throughout this book and to why these discourses and practices are integral to Israeli colonialism. But consistent with my interest in challenging the taken-for-granted aspects of Jerusalem's mythic landscape, I want to make a remarkably simple point that nonetheless bears repeating. It should be recalled that a city's or country's contours, its demographic makeup and those whom it includes and excludes, depend on where and how its boundaries are drawn and—just as importantly—who is empowered to draw them. The delineation of borders is rarely anything other than an effect of power. Though these dividing lines commonly assume an almost natural or fixed quality, we forget at great peril that they are human constructions that were made and can be unmade. This point is as relevant to contemporary Jerusalem under Israeli

---

24. For a superb analysis that details the budding relationship between the Zionist movement and the British Empire, see Atran (1989) and his notion of the "surrogate colonization of Palestine."

colonial rule as it was under the domination of the British Empire. As I write, the Israeli state is actively altering, once again, the de facto boundaries of the city they regard as exclusively and "eternally" theirs. These emerging borders are, since the early 2000s, becoming enclosed within high concrete walls and electrified barriers. Illegal Jewish settlements are increasingly being included within this "new Jerusalem," while burgeoning numbers of Palestinians are being left outside the expanding frontiers.[25]

These ideas about the invented character of cartographic boundaries are doubly imperative to keep in mind given that *cultural* cartographies and the borders around supposed communities, races, ethnicities, nations, and genders are invented and policed no less than territorial ones.[26] The multiple ways in which contemporary Jerusalem's social, demographic, and spatial realities have been redrawn and transformed are crucial to understanding the shifting quality of that which is referred to as "Jerusalem" at any particular historical moment. I shall take up these questions and concerns in each of the chapters that follow.

COLONIAL EPISTEMOLOGIES

This chapter opens with a pair of quotes from two keen witnesses of colonial power, Karl Marx and Albert Memmi. Both offer perspectives into what colonialism routinely entailed (and continues to entail) for rulers and the ruled alike. Precisely because their respective vantages—temporal, cultural, and ideological—are for the most part at variance, I have found their insights productive for better appreciating the diverse elements that have comprised colonial governance and the imperial imagination.

25. Throughout this book I will be referring to particular Israeli policies and actions as "illegal." By this I mean that they are universally regarded as illegal under international law and in violation of the Fourth Geneva Convention. Israel's military occupation of East Jerusalem and the other territories occupied since June 1967 are among these illegal actions.

26. Further, British records reveal that Palestinians and their institutions owned the majority of the land both within the city's aforementioned boundaries and in the Jerusalem "Subdistrict," another arbitrary creation of colonial cartographers.

Marx, ever the perceptive analyst of capitalism's development and contradictions, expressed complex feelings about the escalating project of European penetration into the Middle East, India, and elsewhere in the nineteenth century. But his writings regarding the spread of colonial conquest and the forces that "chase the bourgeoisie over the whole surface of the globe" were, I believe, held hostage by his linear view of progress and a belief in the teleological character of history (Marx and Engels 1848 [1967], 83–84).

Marx clearly understood much about the violently transformative qualities of colonialism. However, he saw these dynamic happenings as providing a revolutionary path for both a modern industrializing Europe as well as for colonized peoples that he regarded as in the throes of preindustrial "backwardness."[27] His analysis highlighted the processes of economic exploitation as well as emerging social relations and class struggles. These are vital concerns given the centrality of production and consumption to imperial designs and capitalist desires. But there have always been other dimensions of colonialism that Marx was not, perhaps, best situated to elucidate.

Enter Albert Memmi, a former subject of French colonial rule in Tunisia and one who identified as both an Arab and a Jew. He witnessed the final phase of direct European domination in the Middle East and wrote novels and theoretical works that gave an account of colonial racism as it moved through and transformed him and the multiple communities of French-ruled North Africa of which he was a part. As mentioned above, the now largely naturalized binary opposition, Arab–Jew did not possess the power that it came to in the Middle East until the ascendancy

---

27. Marx (as well as Engels) actually applauded French colonial conquest in Algeria in the 1840s. However, some of his later writings penned in the 1880s indicate that he increasingly regarded the violence of imperial ventures and the racial ideologies that arose to justify them not simply as a set of necessary and progressive energies destined to break down that which impeded the advent of capitalist development. Rather, he also came to understand them increasingly as rapacious: as a violent "bleeding process" (1881). For a close reading of Marx's complex perspectives on colonialism, capitalism, and modernity, see Ahmad (1996).

of modern Zionism. Actual, lived experiences of Memmi and other Jews of the region in the 1940s and 1950s speak to this condition. Memmi (1965) delved more deeply into the shifting, overlapping, and contradictory dimensions of identity and intercommunal relations in the colony than did Marx and others writing from the metropoles of modern Europe. He speaks of the ambivalences of social difference and the fissures and heterogeneity within the binary categories of colonizer and colonized.

What Memmi refers to as the "daily humiliations" of the colonized (e.g. quotidian dimensions of racism, cruelty, and hatred) will be among the primary subjects of this work. Everyday life for Palestinians under Israeli rule in this city and elsewhere has been fraught with persistent forms of degradation, often, though not always, at the hands of Israeli soldiers and settlers. And, in light of the ways Palestinians have watched their lands and homes being taken away from them, Marx's (1881) reference to colonialism as a "bleeding process with a vengeance" increasingly struck me as an appropriate, though blunt, metaphor for Israeli rule.

One of this book's points of departure is that it is important to understand the fears, suffering, and hardships of both dominant and subordinate national communities. In this case, that means Israeli Jews as well as Palestinian Arabs. However, any study of this ongoing struggle over land that does not point out the fundamental power differential between Israelis and Palestinians would be engaging in a discourse of parity that obscures far more than it could ever clarify. Sadly, so much of the writing and commentary on Palestine/Israel (and on Jerusalem more specifically) addresses this place and its peoples in just such a manner. Analyzing this conflict within a colonial framework helps ensure that such abiding inequalities and expressions of domination are not effaced but made sense of.

MYTHIC JERUSALEM: "TO YOUR SEED TO ETERNITY"

Jerusalem is not simply a cartographic place delineated and fixed on a map. It is, as well, a kaleidoscope of manifold myths, meanings, and contending ideologies. Therefore, I would like to mention by way of introduction two prominent mythologies about the city and those who reside there. These are notions that elements within both major national movements have deployed in efforts to enhance their claims to the land of Palestine/Israel. However, since 1948 Israeli citizens, politicians, and their supporters abroad, by virtue of their disproportionate military and political power, have asserted them more vigorously than have the Palestinians.

One of these myths declares that Jerusalem is "eternal," a place of "immutable" properties and timeless meanings. Zionists in Israel and abroad routinely refer to this contested metropolitan area as the Jewish people's "eternal and immutable capital." This connection is said to stretch back to at least the time of the biblical King David some 3,000 years ago and is rooted in supposed divine promises made solely to the Jewish people. Curiously, these claims have not simply been those of the right-wing settler movement in Israel. Rather, they are articulated by substantial segments of mainstream Israeli opinion—religious and secular, doves and hawks.[28]

Biblical stories, from which grand nationalist narratives are commonly woven, have been utilized to justify very recent human rights abuses. The alleged will of God is not only routinely announced but also has been mobilized to validate the appropriation of Palestinian homes and lands. These contentions of the colonizers have helped burnish exclusive claims to Jerusalem and the country more broadly by many (though by no means all) Israeli Jews and millions of their Zionist supporters living outside the country.

One illustration of such mythology I came upon during my research should, I believe, be seen not simply as anecdotal but emblematic. During an extended interview with Glenda, a secular Israeli progressive I came to know, she related some of the ways pervasive nationalist claims of a biblical sort function in contemporary Israel. An activist and writer whose adult life spans the entirety of the state, Glenda told me that while growing up in Israel it was routine for Jewish students, even in secular schools, to be

---

28. In 1937, David Ben-Gurion, the future prime minister of Israel, told the British Royal commission visiting Palestine that the "the Bible is our mandate" and that the biblical promises to the Jewish people were the Jewish state's "title deeds." See Masalha (2007, 16–17).

taught the Bible several times a week and to see it as an essentially historical text. Now a grandmother, she related that at her grandson's recent graduation ceremony at a largely secular, primary school, a boy was tasked with reading the following quote from Genesis 13: 14–17:

> And the Lord said to Abram after Lot had parted from him, "Please raise your eyes and see, from the place where you are, northward and southward and eastward and westward. For all the land that you see I will give to you and to your seed to eternity."

This claim, that the land of Israel is part of a celestial "real estate guide," whose "listings" can only be acquired by members of one religious group, has been deployed in innumerable ways by successive Israeli governments. Nowhere is this more forcefully done than in Jerusalem.

But this myth has been linked to a second one no less relevant to the contemporary contest over the "holy land." It declares that Israeli Jews and Palestinian Arabs must be kept apart because these two peoples' real or supposed cultural and religious differences preclude peaceful interactions and make impossible any vision antithetical to one based on separation. At root is the belief that to allow such intercommunal mixing threatens to disturb a "natural" order in which those who are different are maintained apart to preserve the interests and character of each.

Members of all religious and national communities are capable of articulating views of this kind. In the course of fieldwork, I spoke with dozens of Palestinians and Israelis, Jews and non-Jews who advanced essentialist and ahistorical understandings of themselves and others. Some were openly chauvinist and advocated quite violent solutions to maintain communal separation. Others were less so but firmly believed that "keeping the peace" meant hermetically sealing off Israeli Jews and Palestinian Christians and Muslims. This book is nothing if not a critique of these prevailing ways of depicting Jerusalem and those who reside there. I regard these representations not simply as fictitious and ideological but also as detrimental to the prospects for just and egalitarian futures for the inhabitants of Palestine/Israel.

FIELDWORK IN A COLONIAL CITY

This book is based on more than thirty-five months of fieldwork, completed during three primary research stays in the city in 1996–97, 1998–99, and 2006. I supplemented these visits with several shorter ones of two to three months in 1994, 1995, 2002, 2003, and 2012. This study relies substantially on interviews and life histories with Arab and Jewish Jerusalemites of wide-ranging backgrounds and perspectives. Because of the experiences of displacement so fundamental to this conflict, my ninety-eight interviews also, by necessity, included discussions with twelve former Jerusalemites who no longer resided in the city.

The majority of those with whom I spoke were Palestinian Muslims and Christians. However, my research also incorporates material from twenty-nine formal and lengthy discussions with Israeli-Jews, particularly human rights activists, city planners, and historians. Over the course of my nearly three years in the field, I supplemented these interviews and life histories with scores of additional informal conversations. It would be difficult, in the end, to determine which were more valuable. Unexpected exchanges and chats might arise while waiting in line for falafel along Salahdin Street in East Jerusalem, riding in a cab, or mingling with employees and visitors at one or another of Israel's national memorials or museums. These conversations routinely revealed fresh insights and knowledge concerning Jerusalem, an urban center about which I was rapidly discovering how little I knew.

I lived in Palestinian neighborhoods in East Jerusalem for the bulk of my time in the field. However, I resided off and on for about three months in West Jerusalem, comprised almost wholly of Israeli Jews since the expulsion of its Palestinian Christian and Muslim residents in 1948. The city's west side has been a place where the Israeli state, its business community, and international benefactors have incessantly constructed new and expansive things—an impressive road system, vast shopping malls, prodigious housing estates for Israeli Jews, hotels for wealthy tourists, and cultural institutions and monuments like the Wiesenthal Center's Museum of Tolerance. This segment of the city generally has the luster of first world privilege, a feel quite at variance with the Palestinian neighbor-hoods of East Jerusalem just a few kilometers away.

One discovery I made about the residents of East and West Jerusa-lem was that the most politically astute and savvy were as readily found among working-class taxi drivers and the proprietors of grocery stores as they were among privileged intellectuals, policy makers, and politicians. So few of the silk-suited *shila* (clique) around the budding Palestinian gov-ernment (the PNA), or the entrenched Israeli elites invested in military occupation and the arms industry that sustains it, ever seemed to *say* a great deal beyond the scripted "lines" they were advancing at the moment.

I found so-called "ordinary" Palestinians and Israelis generally more politically curious than their American counterparts. Their perspectives were all too often infinitely more compelling and honest than their sup-posed leaders. Conspiracy theories and misinformation would from time to time flutter through the streets of the city. But those I spoke with also regularly articulated thoughtful opinions about local, regional, and inter-national concerns. During my time in the field, these views ranged from Bill Clinton's sexual meanderings and subsequent impeachment to the successes and failures of the budding, multiracial regime in South Africa, and the assassination of Tupac Shakur. As a British colleague and friend, the late Graham Usher, who worked for a decade in Jerusalem as a jour-nalist once put it, "This place [Palestine and Israel] is a researcher's dream! *Everyone* wants to talk about politics."

In addition to interviews and conversations, I also engaged to a con-siderable extent in the ethnographic methodology of participant observa-tion. This required doing many different things in the city, but crucially it involved walking Jerusalem, something I loved to do nearly every day. As I explored this urban center more closely I grew to recognize some of the residents' everyday rituals of domination, refusal, and resistance. These were practices and activities that defined the city as much as anything possibly could.

Traversing Jerusalem by foot as consistently as I did over nearly three years helped me comprehend much more about daily life than I would have learned simply by interviewing city residents. Along the streets and at the public places I frequented dozens of times, there were nearly always details that I had not previously noticed. There were modes and patterns of encounter—both positive and negative—between and among Israelis and Palestinians that I would not have imagined occurred. Predictable happenings unfolded in utterly surprising ways.

I lived for several months during the late 1990s and early 2000s in an imposing three-story building that has housed the British School of Archaeology for more than four decades. This structure of thick stone walls, lovely tiled floors, and 16-foot-high vaulted ceilings was built in the early 1900s on a hill in the East Jerusalem neighborhood of Sheikh Jarrah.[29] From atop its flat roof, nestled among tall pine trees and other Ottoman-era stone structures, one could gaze across much of Jerusalem's rolling sprawl laid out below.

Dense, boxlike Jewish settlement towers of beige concrete and Israeli military emplacements with massive radio towers could be observed resting, invariably, on still higher ground, usually cresting Jerusalem's very highest heights. The fortress-like Hebrew University on Mount Scopus, and the neighboring Jewish settlements of French Hill and Ramot Eshkol, are about two kilometers up the road to the north. The walled Old City is an equal distance due south. The now-infamous militant Jewish settlers who have taken over several Arab homes in Sheikh Jarrah since 1998 reside directly across the street from the school. Israeli flags and round-the-clock security forces mark these sites of colonial intrusion and religious extremism.

From the vantage point of this roof, elevated and removed as one was, little in the way of human interactions could be witnessed or heard—and none could be had. Peering down on Jerusalem from this perspective was fascinating. But doing so, I came to understand, was a metaphor for too much of the writing on this city and the broader national conflict. These are representations written and observations made from safe distances, often far from actual encounters along streets, in markets, and around dinner tables.

29. The School was renamed the Kenyon Institute in 2001, in honor of British archaeologist, Kathleen Kenyon.

It was as an inhabitant of this urban environment, as a foreign researcher and writer who lived *in* but was not *of* Jerusalem, that I began to come across what the anthropologist, Malinowski refers to as the "imponderabilia of actual life" (2008 [1922], 18). As he explains in one of anthropology's seminal texts, "there is a series of phenomena of great importance which cannot possibly be recorded by questioning or computing documents, but have to be observed in their full actuality" (ibid.).

From the beginning let me emphasize that I do not claim to have observed anything or anybody in their "full actuality." The notion that a scholar possibly could has been one of social science's most embarrassing conceits. Yet Malinowski's point about the consequence of immersing oneself in the place and among the communities that a researcher writes about is a wise one. How this is done or should be done has political implications not always thought through judiciously enough by those engaged in ethnographic fieldwork. But by climbing down from sequestered heights and entering the fascinating realms of everyday existence, one can acquire perspectives about urban social relations that arguably can be grasped in no other way.

SIGNING ONE'S IDENTITY

Over the last several decades anthropologists and other scholars have increasingly come to understand that they always write from some vantage point or ideological position. Though regarded perhaps by many scholars today as a fairly banal insight, I have been struck by how rarely it seems to be taken seriously by Western researchers in other lands. Those of us who seek to represent are all located within a set of overlapping and at times conflicting interests, assumptions, and political commitments that shape our depictions of social life. I believe those positions need to be signaled in more than fleeting ways. Failing to do so threatens to draw us into a hazy self-delusion, too often—unwittingly or not—producing the voice of an "omniscient narrator."

In this book I have sought to highlight some of my assumptions and political positions. And as I do so, I follow the insights of others who have subjected the practice of anthropological writing to serious scrutiny. In an interview not long before his death, Clifford Geertz, elaborating on what he refers to as interpretive anthropology, described this approach succinctly when he noted that, in writing ethnography, "You don't get to sign just your name anymore, you have to sign your identity, and that is here to stay" (Panourgiá and Kavouras 2008, 26). To deny that scholars bring to their research sites particular affiliations is, to my mind, somewhat naïve but perhaps only slightly less naive than the suggestion that the most objective observer is the one most "disinterested."

This work moves from the premise that writers can, simultaneously, be both objective *and* partisan. This may well be difficult to pull off successfully but the two are not, as is widely assumed, a priori in conflict. In the same vein, I submit that any professed "neutrality" can, itself, be the most aggressively ideological position of all—not simply a delusional one. Therefore, in each of the chapters that follow, I have tried to be sufficiently reflexive, to turn a critical gaze back on myself and my fellow researchers who have had the luxury of picking a research site from a "menu" of scholarly privilege. To me this is part of what "signing one's identity" means and ought to mean. The importance of acknowledging that privilege and what it can *do* (including how it can damage and distort) cannot be overstated. This seems particularly true when living among vulnerable communities in the hazardous contexts of colonial governance or military occupation.

My identities, including my subject position as an *Arab* American and as an Arab American *male* researcher, came to influence my relations and encounters with both Israelis and Palestinians. As I would find over the course of fieldwork, it was not solely my affiliations that were relevant to my ethnographic pursuits but my filiation, as well. For one, it became apparent that my Arab identity tended to facilitate communication and positive interaction with Palestinians. It also seemed to contribute to a hastening of trust with the Arab Jerusalemites among whom I lived and worked.

Being of Arab background and possessing an identifiable Arab surname also meant being subjected to discriminatory profiling measures. These occurred at the Israeli airport, at the border crossings Israel controls, and at the hundreds of checkpoints the regime operates throughout the Palestinian territories illegally occupied since 1967, including East

Jerusalem. Upon arrival at Tel Aviv's Ben Gurion Airport for my first major research stay, the Israeli authorities took my laptop and camera as a "security measure," returning the latter broken two weeks later.

This and other instances of harassment that I faced are so minor in comparison to what Palestinians routinely experience as to be almost inconsequential. But there was a pattern here, an only vaguely hidden effort by Israeli authorities to discriminate against other human beings for the sole reason that they are Arab or Muslim.[30] It was in the course of witnessing everyday instances of racial profiling and cruelty in this city and in other places that I came to recognize just how central racism has been to the formation of colonial governance—in Palestine/Israel and elsewhere.

My time in Jerusalem was also mediated through a host of distinctly gendered dynamics and perceptions, ones I also discuss throughout the text. A good deal of my research relates to and was conducted in the city's public places. And because of the gendered character of these realms, my interlocutors in the commercial areas of both East and West Jerusalem (merchants, workers, the young adults who hung out on the street) were overwhelmingly males.

I had in these domains, therefore, a latitude foreign women doing similar research would not typically have had. I was able to socialize with young Palestinian men (*shebab*) or among older men for extended periods of time in public or private places without any suspicion of, say, sexual impropriety arising. I was free to accept rides with those I was only beginning to know and not run the risk of being subjected to the harassment, verbal or physical, that women and girls too often experience in Jerusalem—east and west. I could chat for hours with male merchants alone in their shops without any eyebrows being raised about possible transgressions or violations of customs and tradition (*'adaat wa taqaliid*).[31]

30. Of the scores of Arab Americans, Palestinians, and Palestinians with Israeli citizenship, I have met very few who have not experienced some degree of racism or harassment crossing through an Israeli node of control or border crossing.

31. For an excellent account of similar urban dynamics and conflicts in the Palestinian city of Bethlehem, see Lybarger (2007).

Conversely, I did not have the access a female researcher usually had to the realms principally organized and run by women. These are cultural zones that women conducting fieldwork in this and other Middle Eastern communities have described as being more available to them as women.[32] These gendered realities, limitations, and opportunities underscore the importance of acknowledging the positions from which one writes, observes, and analyzes. They underscore how *who* we are (or who we are perceived to be) can shape what we are able to understand about the cultures of others—and about our own, as well.

SYNOPSIS

The chapters that comprise this book have distinct but overlapping emphases. In chapter 2 I contextualize contemporary social and spatial relations in Jerusalem by exploring Arab-Jewish intercommunal encounters in the city during the British colonial period (1917–1948). I have chosen to write about these times and places in an effort to "denaturalize" more current, post-1967 Israeli-Palestinian interactions, ones routinely characterized by conflict, violence, suspicion, and enforced separation. The chapter examines Palestinian homes on the city's west side, appropriated and transformed by Israel in 1948 and utilized in a variety of ways in the service of colonial power.

Chapter 3 focuses on one of those commandeered Arab familial places, a home that sat on the edge of the border that divided West and East Jerusalem from 1948 to 1967. I explore this structure's at once distinctive and emblematic use in the service of Israeli national mythologies. Here I consider the role of national memorials as colonial technologies of cultural control and how sites of nationalist remembrance are as much about the present and the future as they are the past.

Chapter 4 details how Israeli officials and citizens have, since 1967, sought to advance the idea of Jerusalem as the Jewish state's "eternal"

---

32. See Abu Lughod (1986); Bishara (2012); Deeb (2006); Fadlalla (2007); Ghannam (2002); Kanaaneh (2002); Peteet (1991, 2005); Sawalha (2011); and Varzi (2007).

and "undivided" capital. I concentrate on the competing religious and national meanings that converge at the Western Wall and its environs in Jerusalem's Old City. This chapter examines how Israeli efforts at altering this locale over the last forty-seven years—including the 1967 destruction of a 1,300-year-old Arab neighborhood that lay immediately before the Wall—has been integral to Zionist claims of exclusivity over the whole of Jerusalem.

Chapter 5 focuses on the gendered politics of residential space in the city. It centers on the experiences of unmarried adult Palestinian women as they hunt for housing and seek greater degrees of independence beyond their familial realms. In doing so, I analyze some of the converging and intersecting forces of authority (e.g., patriarchy, sexual harassment, colonial racism, and class oppression) that these women routinely contend with as they seek to craft more independent lives and professional pathways in Jerusalem.

Chapter 6 explores the politics of fear and the discursive construction of "terrorism" and "security" in Jerusalem. I look principally at the years leading up to and immediately after the outbreak of the Second Intifada in 2000. I examine Israeli policies to criminalize and surveil Palestinian men in public places throughout the city. This chapter considers how fear is fundamental to the exercise of colonial power and integral to the lives of colonizers and the colonized alike.

The prospects and practices of joint Arab-Jewish activism across this fortressed landscape is the subject of chapter 7. I conclude the book by focusing on expressions of solidarity forged through activist work that began to proliferate and flourish in the late 1990s. This chapter looks with particular attention on the housing rights movement in contemporary Jerusalem. How have emerging forms of joint Palestinian-Israeli political resistance coalesced in recent years in response to Israel's policies of demolishing Palestinian homes?

CONCLUSION

Residing in contemporary Jerusalem for several years offered profound insights into colonial authority as a complex collection of daily, lived realities. Despite the character of Israeli rule and the legal and bureau-cratic strategies devised over several decades to keep Palestinians and Israeli Jews separate and unequal, I have come to the conclusion that these communities' pasts and futures are hopelessly entangled and bound up with one another—spatially, culturally, and politically. This is a critical paradox of life in this city of abiding antagonisms.

Edward Said, writing as much from a Gramscian "optimism of the will" as from a "pessimism of the intellect," describes the realities that so many of us live as the products of "overlapping territories" and "inter-twined histories" (1993, 3–13). I argue that these notions are especially pertinent in Jerusalem, a place of enormous cultural hybridity and unac-knowledged shared heritage. Though mired in the innumerable tensions, hierarchies, and fears that Palestine/Israel has become famous for the last several decades, perhaps it is these very conditions that provide for at least the prospect of more egalitarian futures.

In the course of conducting research in Jerusalem, I grew nearer to those who shared with me the complexities of their lives. These were Pal-estinians and Israelis, Arabs and Jews, men and women, the wealthy and the poor, and radicals and reactionaries. And as I did so, I was drawn into several of their hidden sorrows and unseen triumphs. Among my most poignant experiences were those in which I witnessed individuals who had been inhumanely degraded, pushed around, evicted from their homes, and knocked down defiantly pick themselves up and persevere with a resolve and a dignity that was nothing if not awe-inspiring. Equally inspiring to me were instances in which those from powerful institutions and dominant communities repudiated the role of oppressor and refused to carry the baton of military occupation. These moments have, in potent ways, clung to me and failed to let go. They have done so in ways this book will reflect—and in many it will never quite be able to.

2

Diverse Absences

Reading Colonial Landscapes Old and New

> It is striking here that the places people live in are like the presence
> of diverse absences. What can be seen designates what is no longer
> there: "you see, here there used to be . . ." but it can no longer be
> seen. Demonstratives indicate the invisible identities of the visible: it
> is the very definition of a place, in fact, that it is composed by these
> series of displacements and effects among the fragmented strata that
> form it and that it plays on these moving layers.
>
> —MICHEL DE CERTEAU, *The Practice of Everyday Life*

Salma remembers the day the Zionist underground bombed Jerusalem's King David Hotel in the summer of 1946. From the front steps of
her family's home in the then Palestinian neighborhood of Talbieh, she
and her cousin observed the explosion across British colonial Jerusalem's scarred landscape. The blast punctured the serenity of the morning,
Salma told me, as both startled girls gazed toward the hotel, their eyes
fixed on the tall, regal edifice not a kilometer away as its southern wing
crumbled.

Relating the experience to me fifty-one years later, almost to the day,
Salma stood again on those very same steps. Under the searing afternoon
sun, filtered through the long fingers of trees, she pointed in the direction
of the King David to the east. Her Jerusalem, a place she knew intimately
before 1948, had vastly changed by the late 1990s. Neither she, her kin, nor
other Palestinians still reside in Talbieh—or nearly anywhere else in West
Jerusalem, for that matter. And yet, here and throughout this part of the
city, there remain traces of a former Palestinian existence.

33

Subdivided and reconfigured, Salma's family home is one such trace. The dwelling is now the residence of three Israeli families, one on each floor of this deceptively spacious stone structure. The current occupants might well have been inside the day she and I chose to visit, but they did not appear as my guide, a thin and statuesque figure in her sixties, reclaimed her front steps for a few fleeting moments. Salma was strangely a stranger here, simultaneously an owner and a trespasser, oddly both present and absent. From the vantage point of these stairs, lush foliage and other impediments obstructed the view of the famous hotel. The passage of time also obscured somewhat the clarity of her memories.

Israel's expulsion of about 750,000 Palestinians in 1948 included roughly 45,000 from Jerusalem and its immediate environs. The "transfer" of these families, as Israeli officials and historians have euphemistically referred to these forced evictions, produced radically altered demographic and social realities in a land where both national communities wished to build a state. The area that became known after 1948 as "West Jerusalem" was, until the final months of the British Mandate, an urban environment with a modest but significant degree of mixed Arab-Jewish residential life. However, in less than one year the west side became almost devoid of Arab Christians and Muslims. The Jewish state has, since then, made West Jerusalem overwhelmingly off-limits to Palestinians, including neighborhoods like Talbieh and homes like Salma's.[1]

This chapter explores two primary concerns. In the first half, I flesh out some of the contours of Arab-Jewish intercommunal life in British colonial Jerusalem (1917–1948). I examine the extent to which these oft-ignored pre-1948 social relations included productive and even antiracist encounters in residential and commercial realms. In the second half, I turn to an analysis of specific Palestinian homes, appropriated and reconfigured by the Israeli state over the last several decades. What might their

---

1. See the *Israel Statistical Yearbook*, 2012, Table III/1—Population of Israel and Jerusalem, by Population Group, 1922–2009. This source claims that by the end of the fighting in 1948, the Palestinian population in West Jerusalem was 1,100, or roughly 1.3 percent of the population. By 1961, there were 2,400 Palestinians in West Jerusalem, or about 1.5 percent of West Jerusalem's population.

fate and the neighborhoods they comprise tell us about the designs and visions of Israeli colonial urbanism? What was made present in West Jerusalem once the indigenous Palestinian population was made absent?

This book concentrates on housing and spatial politics in this fractured metropolitan area since 1948 with a particular focus on post-1967 realities. However, early in the course of interviews with Arab and Jewish Jerusalemites, several with whom I spoke insisted that contemporary urban life could only begin to be properly understood by delving into the complex cultural cartographies that preceded the establishment of the Jewish state and the expulsion of the Palestinians. During investigations into social relations and political conflict in the city, I came to appreciate just how wise such advice was. Visits to lost Arab homes and neighborhoods like Salma's were the necessary first step in connecting Jerusalem's colonial past with its colonial present.

Israeli authorities and their supporters abroad have routinely sought to efface Palestinian attachments to Jerusalem. But by doing so, I submit, what has been negated are not simply *Palestinian* histories in the city but also chronicles of productive, more integrated, and less hostile relationships between Arabs and Jews before 1948. In writing about the ruptures and continuities of colonial power, I draw from interviews and life histories with forty-nine Israelis and Palestinians old enough to remember the last two decades of British colonial rule. Examining "the present in the past," as historians and anthropologists have referred to it, requires searching for what Michel de Certeau (1984, 108) masterfully describes as "the invisible identities of the visible."

Edward Said and his expanded kin network were among the Palestinians of Talbieh whose homes were seized by the nascent Israeli state in the late 1940s and early 1950s. In Said's writings on Palestine/Israel he has emphasized the importance of "reading" landscapes like Jerusalem and challenging what might appear to be innocent or natural about them.[2] As he noted in a lecture on colonialism and memory at Birzeit University

2. See Said (1992) for an account of his return to his family home in Talbieh in the early 1990s for the first time in nearly forty-five years.

in 1998 not long before his death in 2003, "You cannot *see* what is not there but you can *read* what is not there by looking for traces and details" of a former period (1998a). Analyzing the spatial construction of identity and difference in this multilayered and continually shifting city, I argue, requires precisely the approaches of de Certeau and Said.

THE MAKING OF TALBIEH

One of the wealthiest residential areas in all of British colonial Palestine, Talbieh had become a neighborhood of roughly 150 to 175 structures and 1,500 to 2,000 inhabitants by the late 1940s.[3] The quarter was established in the early 1920s by Palestinian Jerusalemites on a swath of land purchased from the Greek Orthodox Church. Talbieh was one of at least two dozen neighborhoods built outside the Old City walls in the first half of the twentieth century. By the end of the Mandate, upwards of 140,000 Christians, Jews, and Muslims resided in this and other quarters in what rulers and the ruled increasingly referred to as the "New City."

As this urban center grew outward and upward, it increasingly resembled a metropolitan area where the British imperial imagination intersected the desires and tastes of the colonized communities. From 1917 to 1948, within a radius of roughly 5 kilometers of the Old City, homes and businesses, convents and monasteries, military sites and municipal offices began to rise up and fan out across orchards and groves, particularly to the west of the Old City walls. Only a generation or two before, these rolling hills and verdant valleys had been principally uninhabited. Just beyond Jerusalem's British-drawn boundaries lay a string of Arab villages that fell just outside the reconfigured city limits. Places like Lifta, Sheikh Bader, Silwan, Deir Yassin, Shu'afat, Ein Karem, and Malha, though outside the official municipal border, would become by the 1930s and 1940s

---

3. See the "Population Density Map" in Kendall (1948). I have made an estimate of the number of structures in Talbieh through interviews and life histories as well as by examining several detailed British-era maps of the city.

progressively integrated into this expanding urban environment that served as the capital of Britain's colonial government.

Talbieh was a private residential initiative. As with other such ventures, a wealthy financier would typically buy a segment of land and sell off plots to those who wished to build homes on them. British authorities would then supply basic municipal services and institute the parameters and codes for building. The neighboring Jewish quarter of Rehavia, established a few years after Talbieh in the late 1920s and early 1930s, represented a noteworthy cultural and spatial foil. Like dozens of other residential areas founded by Zionist organizations, associations, and land agencies, Rehavia was centrally planned. Unlike Talbieh, it was governed by discriminatory bylaws that precluded non-Jews from living and sometimes even working there.[4]

Though hardly the norm during the era of British governance, positive intercommunal encounters in Jerusalem were distinctly more pervasive than they would become after 1948. This degree of mixed residential and commercial life is partly attributable, I submit, to the fact that relations between Arabs and Jews were less hierarchical in the age of the British. Neither national group ran the country, dictated immigration policy, or was plainly dominant over the other. At that time, both were subordinate to the colonial regime's bureaucracy, and were constrained by Britain's at times quite draconian military repression and racist assumptions. Further, these relationships were more possible before 1948 since the exclusionary principles of Zionist organizations were applicable only within the 7 to 8 percent of the country that was owned and controlled by them.

In the twenty-two months between the felling of the King David Hotel and the end of Britain's rule over Palestine in May 1948, former residents,

---

4. As mentioned in chapter 1, these prestate Zionist organizations and the residential areas they built were meant to facilitate the settlement of Palestine by Jewish immigrants intent on building an exclusivist Jewish state. Agencies such as the Jewish National Fund (JNF) were guided by what some Zionist land agencies referred to as "redeeming the land from the aliens [Arabs]" and holding it in Jewish hands "in perpetuity." See the language of the bylaws of the JNF quoted in Davis and Lehn (1983).

1. The budding Jerusalem neighborhood of Talbieh in the late 1920s and early 1930s. Courtesy of Library of Congress, Prints and Photographs Division.

newspaper accounts, and British colonial documents reported proliferating acts of intercommunal rage and revenge. The assault on the colonial offices housed in the King David Hotel represented a political watershed, for it set into motion the authorities' withdrawal from a land they had conquered only thirty years earlier from the anemic Ottoman Empire. Rather swiftly, the British regime moved to engineer Palestine's partition, a practice they were becoming quite deft at instituting throughout their vast but vanishing global holdings.[5]

Over the last six decades, Talbieh has housed several of Israel's primary governmental offices and institutions, including the president's and

5. The UN General Assembly voted to partition Palestine on November 29, 1947, clearing the way for the departure of British forces from the country and the end of the British Mandate. The UN was comprised at the time of just 57 member states and excluded much of the world's population that still lived under European colonial rule.

prime minister's residences. This picturesque, tree-lined quarter has also been the site of a range of international Zionist organizations, whose stated aims are to foster Jewish immigration (*aliyah*) and "absorption" (*klitah*) in the Jewish state. This neighborhood continues to be an upscale and fashionable place whose British- and Ottoman-era stone residences remain markers of status and prestige. But these dwellings "house," as well, specters of dispossession and phantoms of former Arab lives.

REMEMBERING AND FORGETTING
PRE-1948 ENCOUNTERS IN JERUSALEM

During my interviews with Israelis and Palestinians about life in British Jerusalem, two prevailing sets of narratives on Jewish-Arab relations began to come into relief. One collection, which I will refer to as "natural disaster narratives," characterized intercommunal encounters as essentially—even eternally—hostile and antagonistic. Another was marked by varying degrees of nostalgia, depicting these relations as nearly devoid of any conflict at all. Both types of remembrances are flawed, but both, I believe, are fundamentally about Jerusalem's colonial present, not simply its colonial past.

"Natural disaster narratives" tended to impose the present dynamic of generalized nationalist conflict and mutual distrust onto the pre-1948 period. Those who depicted British-era Jerusalem in these ways routinely asserted, implicitly or explicitly, that Arabs and Jews were and continue to be a priori unable to live together peacefully. These discordant relations were attributed variously to insurmountable religious differences or "ancient" and "eternal" hostilities. In these articulations, identities and differences distinctly cultural became almost ossified into a sort of unalterable "nature."[6]

But a second prevalent set of representations of pre-1948 Jerusalem also arose in the course of fieldwork. These were marked by varying degrees

---

6. For more on how culture and socially constructed conditions and identities can take on a "natural" appearance, see Balibar's (1991a) analysis of racism and racial politics.

of nostalgia and also call for critical engagement. Those with such views characteristically portray the British era as quite contrary to the antagonisms and inequalities that pervade contemporary Jerusalem. More than 60 percent of the Palestinians I spoke with for this chapter (and nearly one-fifth of the Israeli Jews) detailed at some length specific, harmonious relations between Arabs and Jews during the period and sometimes even represented them as the dominant mode of intercommunal encounter.

"Before Israel there were no problems," "we lived in peace," and other similar remarks arose from a slim majority of interviews I conducted with Arab Christians and Muslims old enough to remember the 1930s and 1940s.[7] This historical depiction crossed class, religious, and gender boundaries among Palestinians, though privileged urbanites were more likely to express these sentiments than workers or villagers. And as these positive relations were described, a forthright critique of British colonialism was—oddly, I thought—rarely front and center.[8] Given the threat that the stated aims of Zionism—not infrequently facilitated by British imperialism—posed to Palestinians of all classes, the downplaying of Britain's violence was somewhat surprising.

These varied ways of remembering were at times contradictory, since about one-third of my interviewees expressed elements of both nostalgia and chauvinism. Further, these remembrances were refracted through contemporary political interests, fears, and assumptions. As Trouillot

---

7. This is also recorded elsewhere, for instance, in the very first line of Sayigh's important book in which she begins with a quote from a Palestinian refugee in 1948: "We lived in paradise" (1985, 1). She continues by laying out a complex understanding of the politics of memory in this and other works. But I routinely heard some variant of that sentiment expressed during the course of my research.

8. The peasants and working classes of Palestine generally felt the hardships caused by foreign domination and Zionist settlement schemes in Palestine more substantially. It made sense, therefore, that the more privileged urbanites of the time, many thousands of whom had grown substantially wealthier during the British period, would register fewer criticisms of British governance. The 1936–39 Arab Revolt against the British was primarily a peasant uprising, born of the grievances of a colonized population primarily rural before 1948. For more on the Palestinian peasantry and the emergence of Palestinian nationalism during this period see Sayigh (1985) and Khalidi (1997).

(1995) has cogently written, following the insights of Halbwachs (1992) and others, the claims of memory need always to be interrogated since the truth of any particular historical event can rarely be as easily retrievable as pulling a document whole and unsullied from the "file cabinet" of history.[9] In other words, one must be continually cognizant of the ways in which "the past," fluid as it is, can be deployed in the interest of contemporary and future agendas.

However, what became evident to me was that natural disaster narratives have typically been articulated by those with a stake in maintaining the *current* order of enforced division and inequality between Israeli Jews and Palestinian Arabs. These accounts of earlier epochs have buttressed today's more narrow nationalist tendencies by positing the idea that, so unbridgeable are the divisions between these communities, that relations could not have been otherwise and cannot be made to be so in the future. The only "realistic" solution for Israelis and Palestinians, it is alleged, is some variant of separation (*hafrada* in Hebrew and *infisaal* in Arabic)— or, among the more chauvinist nationalist and religious elements, forced removal and ethnic cleansing.[10]

Nostalgic narratives of intercommunal life, in their portrayals of a former idyll, contradict the best of the historical work on British-era Palestine. Yet, in their articulation I consistently heard a critique of the politics that follow from the natural disaster perspectives. I interpreted these representations as a desire, at least in part, to point to the fundamental

9. See Schwenkel (2006) for a fascinating exploration of these themes in contemporary Vietnam, as well as the analysis of Swedenburg (1995) on memory and the 1936–39 Arab Revolt against British colonial rule in Palestine.

10. This has proven a convenient rationale for states and individuals intent on expelling entire populations of the "wrong" kind of people and establishing exclusivist—even "pure"—national spaces. Israeli historian Benny Morris, in a January 9, 2004 interview with Israel's *Ha'aretz* newspaper, stated that he believed that both Israelis and Palestinians would have been better off had the founders of the Jewish state finished the job and "cleansed the whole country" of its Christian and Muslim Arabs—not just the approximately 750,000 that were forced out of their homes; http://www.haaretz.com/survival-of-the-fittest-1.61345. Accessed January 5, 2014.

inequities that define *current* relations between Palestinians and Israelis in Jerusalem and throughout the country. I argue that these sentiments, however romantic, provide at least the possibility for more egalitarian futures, ones that reject segregation and apartness as guiding principles of governance.

"DISTINCT COMMUNITIES" AND "MIXED" NEIGHBORHOODS

Amid the fluctuating social and spatial relations of pre-1948 Jerusalem, British authorities produced urban planning schemes that sought to mold the city and its residents in particular ways. The boundaries were redrawn and an emerging colonial legal order, including important changes to land law, was imposed.[11] Though elements of these plans remained ink on paper, significant dimensions were translated from text to urban space in rapid fashion.

I want to briefly address the last of these documents, authored by Henry Kendall in 1948 and known as *The City Plan*. Its assertions about Arab-Jewish intercommunal life were consistent with the prevailing assumptions among colonial officials at the time concerning the need to create (or sustain) an order of spatial division between the Arabs and Jews of Palestine. Kendall's document announces some "interesting features" said to be "probably peculiar to Jerusalem" (1948, 34).

For one, he claims that "The population [of Jerusalem] tends to group itself into distinct communities." This, Kendall asserts, applied not only to the Old City, but also to the burgeoning quarters that began to flourish beyond it, such as Talbieh and Rehavia. "The only exception to this peculiarity," he continues, "is to be found in the few main commercial or shopping streets where Jewish, Moslem, and Christian shops can be found side by side" (34). The document goes on to fix these "distinct communities" on

---

11. The changes made to the land laws of Palestine during the Mandate cannot be plumbed here. Sources worth exploring that address such questions include Bunton (2007) and Atran (1989).

a cartography of scattered but bounded colors, each denoting a particular *religious* group and each represented as spatially separate and mutually exclusive. This is a mapping of urban life sketched from Olympian heights and fraught with the assumptions of those who ruled over (but kept a substantial distance from) the bulk of the colonized. I want to suggest that a more judicious exploration into Arab-Jewish encounters at the time, one that draws principally from oral sources, reveals social relations occasionally at odds with British authorities' tales of separate and distinct communities.

It is certainly true that Jerusalemites *usually* resided in quarters where others of the same religious and/or national affiliation predominated. However, Kendall's commentary ignores or is unaware of relationships and modes of contact that complicated this picture and that led Arabs and Jews to not infrequently interact with one another in residential and commercial spaces. Further, the three or four religious and/or national categories denoted in the legend of Kendall's cartography were themselves never unitary, never solely of one essential "hue."[12]

It is remarkable how few scholars of Jerusalem, with important exceptions, have examined areas of Arab-Jewish shared residential life. They are routinely written out of histories of British-ruled Jerusalem and such absences promote the idea that strict separation between communities has always defined the city.[13] A closer examination reveals that even when residents lived in separate quarters there was, typically, a range of contacts

12. I was reminded of this after reading Kark's (2001) work on Jerusalem, which talks about "mixed neighborhoods" but as a phenomenon that primarily related to intra-Jewish relations (e.g., between religious and more secular Jews in the city). She discusses what was, at times, fairly intense segregation between the ultra-Orthodox and other Jews but says relatively little about Arab-Jewish encounters.

13. Some of the prominent histories of twentieth-century Jerusalem that fail in my view to adequately address antiracist or even positive Arab-Jewish encounters include Wasserstein (2008), Armstrong (1996), Gilbert (1996), and Kark (1991, 2001). In these and other sources, there is much more space dedicated to the intrigue of competing political elites and British colonial officials than there is about the quotidian realities of Arab-Jewish relationships before 1948.

between and among Arabs and Jews that were possible and permitted. Those from different groups—especially the men—not uncommonly encountered and socialized with each other in markets, cafes, and other public spaces that were anything but severely segregated.[14]

With regard to residential space, the sources for this claim include British colonial tax and property records that indicate who owned (and thus who was paying taxes on) particular properties.[15] But the degree of Arab-Jewish intercommunal life, I contend, was even more extensive than these documents could reveal since they only record registered *owners* of homes or properties and not those who might have actually rented or lived there. For instance, a landlord might have been a Palestinian Muslim or Christian, but the renters Jews from Budapest or British officials from London.[16] In addition, these records cannot capture the fluidity of daily encounters at the time, including interactions such as visits to homes, established friendships across ethnic and religious boundaries, and a myriad of professional connections.

In the pages that follow I draw primarily from a variety of oral sources to tell some of these stories of more peaceful intercommunal relations. These sources allow for a deeper exploration into social life in the city before 1948 and reveal a higher degree of "unmapped" mixed life in Jerusalem than standard accounts. Engaging oral sources also helps to counter what Bourdieu refers to as "synoptic" representations (1990) or the problems associated with the simplification of complex relations into a unified,

14. The neighborhoods of Romema, Mamilla, Musrara, and segments of the Jaffa Street area between the New Gate and King George Street were the primary sectors of Arab-Jewish "mixed" life recognized by Mandate officials. For more on intercommunal life in Jerusalem's cafes and other sites see Tamari (2009).

15. These UN records (United Nations Conciliation Commission for Palestine [UNCCP]) are crucial for beginning to flesh out this history of intercommunal interaction in Jerusalem. Hadawi (1957, 1990) and Tamari (1999) draw from these documents in their important work on pre-1948 Palestine.

16. Though only two Palestinian families I interviewed had rented from Jewish landlords or knew those who did before 1948, four Palestinian families in Talbieh alone told me that they had Jewish tenants during the 1930s and 1940s. At least eleven Arab families here leased properties to British colonial officials and foreign consulates.

typically "frozen," frame of reference. Maps, calendars, graphs, and dia-
grams, however critical they may be to understanding urban life, are illustrative of this phenomenon.

I wish here to at least raise the question of how and in what ways
British colonial depictions of Arab-Jewish relations in Jerusalem might
have had a role in justifying and normalizing spatial orders of division
and finally the partition of the country (a particularly intense form of
institutional separation). An examination of British planning documents
toward the end of the Mandate indicates a growing momentum for formal
partition among colonial elites. These internal conversations spoke with
a fair degree of regularity of the Arabs and Jews of Palestine as not only
needing to be separated but also as constituting "two races" or "two racial
communities."[17]

BRITISH COLONIAL TALBIEH:
A NEIGHBORHOOD OF CULTURAL HYBRIDITY

Though not as integrated and diverse as the acknowledged mixed neighborhoods mentioned above, Talbieh was the site of a far greater degree
of Arab-Jewish shared residential life than colonial officials or scholars

---

17. Various British colonial documents in the late Mandate period that discussed the
prospects of partition included a general report entitled "Long Term Policy in Palestine,"
July 8, 1946, 2 CAB/129/11. Also, "Palestine: Note by the Minister Resident in the Middle
East," April 4, 1945, 9 CAB/66/64/14. These and others underscore the colonial regime's
reluctance to push for an independent binational state for Arabs and Jews, seeing it as
"impracticable" or "impossible" while also generally opposed to any political situation
in which "the majority" (i.e., the Arabs of Palestine) were permitted to rule in a single
political entity. But they also, by the end of the Mandate, realized that partitioning Palestine could not be done in a way that would satisfy both national movements. Even if the
principle of partition were accepted by Arabs and Jews, one report claimed, "either would
emphatically reject any boundary which would satisfy the other"; "Long Term Policy in
Palestine," July 8, 1946, 2 CAB/129/11. And running throughout these documents is the
fear that partition would, even more importantly, deeply undermine "our imperial interests" by alienating "the whole of the Moslem world" (3 CAB/66/64/14). It might be said
that Palestine became by the 1940s a tinderbox of Britain's own creation.

of Jerusalem have typically recognized. The point I wish to make about the extent of positive intercommunal relations in Mandate Jerusalem is strengthened, I suggest, by detailing the frequency of such interactions in quarters not usually regarded as possessing significant mixed life. Although Palestinian Christians were the majority here, Jews, Muslims, Armenians, and British colonial officials increasingly established residency in this budding quarter before 1948. Colonial maps and records along with interviews with former residents reveal that during the 1930s and 1940s, at least eight different foreign consulates rented homes or parts of homes in the neighborhood, dwellings usually owned by wealthy Palestinian Christians.

The class impediments to residing in fashionable new realms such as Talbieh were insurmountable for the vast majority of Arab and Jewish Jerusalemites. However, unlike neighboring Rehavia, in Talbieh there were not exclusionary bylaws based on ethnicity or religion. Because of these restrictions against non-Jews in neighborhoods built by Zionist organizations, areas of substantial Arab-Jewish residential life were overwhelmingly in majority Palestinian sections of town like Talbieh, Musrara, Mamilla, or Qatamon where formal covenants of this sort were rarely if ever instituted.[18]

The Jewish residents of Talbieh during the British era consisted of recent immigrants, usually from Europe and Russia, as well as prominent Mizrahim and Sephardim with roots in Palestine dating back hundreds of years.[19] I came across evidence of at least thirty-nine different Jewish households in Talbieh—owners and renters—during the last two decades

18. I do not argue that there was no discrimination against Jewish families in these neighborhoods at the hands of Christians or Muslims, only that there were far more residential options for Jews in places like Talbieh than there were for Arabs in Rehavia, Talpiot, and other places established by Zionist organizations. The very presence of Jews as owners and renters in Talbieh and other Arab majority quarters is evidence of this.

19. By Mizrahim I mean Jews historically from the Middle East. The Sephardim are Jews with roots in the Iberian Peninsula before the Inquisition. Today in Israel members of these two overlapping groups number approximately two million people.

of British rule. Among these were four cases in which Jews and Arabs shared subdivided homes. The Schockens, immigrants from Germany, came to Palestine within a few months of Hitler's rise to power. Zalman Schocken, the founder and publisher of the newspaper *Ha'aretz*, built a home that still stands on Smolenskin Street.[20]

One member of the Sephardic Eliachar family, with demonstrated roots in Palestine dating back to the sixteenth century, spoke to me about their history in Talbieh and their positive encounters with Arab neighbors. One of their familial places in the quarter lies on what today Israelis regard as Radak Street, a block from the Israeli president's residence on Jabotinsky Street. Elie Eliachar (1983, 56), the grandson of the former chief Sephardic Rabbi of Jerusalem, describes in his memoirs the Shabbat meals that his family would host for Jewish, Christian, and Muslim friends and colleagues.[21]

Munira, a Palestinian in her seventies when we spoke in the early 2000s, recalls a good deal about Arab-Jewish intercommunal life in the vicinity of Talbieh and Rehavia. These were areas she knew well as a child and young adult until her family fled West Jerusalem in the spring of 1948. She told of interactions with the city's growing Jewish population in the last ten years of the British Mandate. She remembered the Eliachar family and several other Jewish families in the vicinity and mentioned the shops some of them kept, along with Palestinian Christians, on today's Rambam Street, where Talbieh and Rehavia converged. "We spoke English, you know, because that was the [shared] language," Munira said. "A few of us knew a little Hebrew and some of them knew some Arabic. But we spoke mostly in English." The Jewish population of the city by the 1930s would have been a majority Ashkenazi, Hebrew-speaking community. However, up until the early twentieth century, according to some scholars of

20. The structure that once housed Schocken's substantial library sits just a few dozen meters away, across the street from the current Israeli prime minister's residence on Balfour Street. Today it is owned by the Jewish Theological Seminary based in New York City.

21. See also the interview with Eliachar (1976) for a fascinating and prescient perspective on Arab-Jewish relations in Palestine/Israel, old and new.

Jerusalem, the city's Jewish communities would have more likely spoken Ladino, Yiddish, and Arabic in daily life rather than Hebrew.[22]

I asked Munira if she remembered any instances of intermarriage, trying to probe the depths of these relationships. "Between Arabs and Jews? Not that *I* know of." She thought for a moment and then continued: "But you have to realize, there was not much [intermarriage] even between Christians—between Orthodox and Catholics and Anglicans. Intermarriage [among Christians] was seen as scandalous." Two other Christian women who I interviewed together, both exiled from the Talbieh area, explained that before 1948 different Christian sects used to "mourn like they were mourning death" when one of their sons or daughters married a Christian from a different denomination. "They would sometimes ring the church bells like they did when someone died. That changed after *an-Nakba* [the catastrophe in Arabic, referring to the 1948 expulsions of Palestinians by Israeli forces] because then we were *all* refugees, we were all the same. It brought us more together."

As mentioned above, in the final years of Mandate-era Jerusalem, as nationalist violence was on the rise, British authorities began to institute a creeping, formal spatial division between Arabs and Jews. Several former residents of West Jerusalem related how entire neighborhoods were fenced off and how entry into and out of these zones was regulated by British forces.[23] Yet, amid this mounting turmoil, Palestinian exiles recounted many decades later the ties that were forged with Jewish colleagues and friends as late as the spring of 1948.

A former Palestinian from Talbieh told me that though she and her family shuttled between Jerusalem and Beirut during much of her childhood in the 1940s, her parents decided to spend extended stays in Palestine in the final months of the Mandate. Her father was ill and his eyes began

22. See Eliachar (1983) and Tamari (2009) for more on pre-1948 linguistic realities in pre-1948 Jerusalem.

23. One account is from a British Jewish colonial official, Edwin Samuel (1970), who rented an apartment in Talbieh from a Christian landlord during the 1930s and 1940s. He details his family's efforts to coordinate their move to neighboring Rehavia in the final violent months of British rule.

to fail. As his condition deteriorated he wished to be near his beloved oph-thalmologist, Avraham Ticho, a Jewish immigrant to Jerusalem who had studied in Vienna.[24] I found it both heartening and ironic that, in at least a few cases, friendships and relationships of this kind actually kept Arabs from leaving Palestine as British rule waned and heightened violence washed over this city in the late 1940s.

The last months of British rule in Palestine were marked by increasingly fortified internal frontiers throughout the country. Those living in Jerusalem during the late 1940s revealed the fear and insecurity that then pervaded the city for all. But because the Jewish residents were overwhelmingly able to remain during the war while the Palestinians were forced out en masse, their accounts offer details about what exiled Christians and Muslims could not have known.

Israeli David Kroyanker, a lifetime Jerusalemite, remembers the circumstances in which Palestinians from the Talbieh area fled:

> I lived not far from here [Talbieh]. [The massacre of] Deir Yassin [on April 9, 1948] had a huge influence on the evacuation of Talbieh. The Arabs were scared to death. They left their meals on their tables and the Haganah requested people in our neighborhood to clean the houses so that Jews could move into them. There really were meals still on the tables. (quoted in Krystal 1999, 109)

The Jerusalem-area village of Deir Yassin that Kroyanker mentions above was but one site of terrorist violence waged against the Palestinians by Zionist paramilitary groups. Israeli historian and former foreign minister Shlomo Ben-Ami indicates that there was in fact "a series of massacres" (2007, 42) committed in 1948 by Zionist armies against Palestinians that were instrumental in expelling the non-Jewish population from their homes.[25] Arab and Palestinian attacks against Jewish civilians

24. Ticho's home still stands in West Jerusalem a few blocks from Kikar Tsion (Zion Square) and today houses an art gallery.

25. There were Jews in British Mandate Palestine who opposed both the expulsion of the Palestinians and the establishment of an exclusive Jewish state in Palestine. Among

during this same period were also carried out with greater frequency and ferocity. For instance, on April 13, 1948, days after the massacre at Deir Yassin, Arab forces attacked a bus carrying Jewish civilians to Mount Scopus through Sheikh Jarrah, killing seventy-nine people.[26]

In the midst of this violence and counterviolence, however, one former Israeli fighter with the Zionist fighting force, the Palmach, told me that the British colonial authorities consistently sided with armed Zionist groups associated with the mainstream Haganah and rarely cracked down on them for carrying illegal weapons in the period of the late British Mandate.[27] Among scholars of British colonialism in the Middle East, there are contesting views concerning the extent to which Britain wished to favor the Zionists over the Palestinians. But that the rulers of the country at the time helped to produce through their policies an increasingly fractured urban environment would, in my view, be difficult to contest.

PALESTINIAN HOMES AND ISRAELI COLONIALISM

In the remainder of this chapter, I want to analyze some of the ways in which the Israeli state has reconfigured Jerusalem since 1948. In what respects have these changes resembled a kind of colonial urbanism? Reconstituting the western segments of Jerusalem into a realm exclusively Israeli Jewish has involved the removal of unwanted Arab populations. But it has also required a set of interlocking spatial, discursive, and legal transformations of homes and neighborhoods consistent with settler colonialism. These changes have been crucial to Israeli visions of enforced separation between Palestinians and Israelis and have not yet come to a halt. Though the budding Jewish state destroyed thousands of Arab homes in

---

these prominent voices were thinkers such as Judah Magnes and Martin Buber. They and others were members of Ichud, an organization committed to the establishment of a binational political and cultural reality in Palestine. For more on this ideological tendency, see Magnes (1983).

26. See Segev (2001) for a detailed discussion of this rising wave of pre-1948 violence.

27. See Honig-Parnass (2011) for an illuminating encapsulation of her experience working in the Zionist movement, including the Palmach.

over 400 depopulated Palestinian villages in the first few years of its existence, familial places in urban centers such as Jerusalem, Jaffa, and Haifa were usually left standing.

During the course of research I discovered that these structures not only were utilized to house Israeli Jews but also were converted into government institutions, restaurants, centers for Jewish immigrants (*olim*), museums, artists' studios, schools, mental health institutions, and even shelters for animals. But whatever their new uses, these appropriations helped to preclude a diplomatically engineered return of displaced Palestinians, as demanded by the 1948 United Nations General Assembly Resolution 194.[28]

If one not only walks Jerusalem but also, following Said (1998a), carefully reads the landscape in places like contemporary Talbieh, it is possible to discern innumerable instances of a "layering over" of Palestinian pasts. This is true both at the sites of specific appropriated homes as well as throughout the shifting urban environments within which they are embedded. The roads and landmarks that enveloped this and other quarters were transformed in the years after 1948 as Israel began to overwrite, palimpsest-like, former names and meanings with an emerging Zionist lexicon of religio-nationalist terms.

A thoroughfare that former Arab residents knew as the "main Talbieh road," for instance, was designated "Jabotinsky Street" after 1948 in memory of the founder of right-wing revisionist Zionism. In the center of the neighborhood, Jabotinsky Street bisects Balfour Street, named for the former British foreign secretary. Consistent with Israeli officials' relations with Christian Zionists, Balfour's promise of support for a Jewish homeland in Palestine seems to have overshadowed his anti-Semitism in the eyes of the Jewish state.[29]

---

28. See Article 11 of United Nations General Assembly Resolution 194 (III), 11 December 1948.

29. The "Pro-Jerusalem Society," founded in 1918 by the British authorities and comprised of representatives of all three religious communities, was created in part to begin to formally name Jerusalem's streets. But by the end of the Mandate, there had only been partial success in this respect.

This symbolic crossroads is a locale remembered and still spoken about by former Palestinian residents as "Salameh Square," referring to the affluent Palestinian family who first developed Talbieh and who have lived for more than sixty-six years in exile. The Salameh home still stands at this intersection on the northwest segment of the roundabout. It has been occupied for decades by the Consulate of Belgium. Israelis today refer to this crossroads as "Orde Square" (*Kikar Orde*), in honor of Orde Wingate, the Christian British officer who helped train the Haganah in skills deployed to expel Arab Christians and Muslims from places like Talbieh.

When I asked Palestinian exiles in the 1990s and 2000s the streets they once lived on, or when I unfurled a contemporary Israeli map and had them indicate the whereabouts of a lost home, they would usually appear somewhat confounded. This was their city and they claimed it. However, in recent decades West Jerusalem's existing coordinates had changed so radically that, as one interviewee told me, "We feel like strangers in our own country—at least when we go over there [West Jerusalem]."

Nine former residents led me back to their lost properties on the west side. When I traveled to these sites without them, they routinely provided what Slyomovics (1998) in her superb study of the Palestinian village of Ein Hod refers to as "memory maps" (82–136). These were typically drawn in simple ways on a piece of paper ripped from my notebook or sketched on a napkin. These representations were approximations that used historical landmarks as guides, several that no longer existed. It was evident that those who spoke to me about their city could usually not remember what once was there without, in a sense, finding their bearings through Israel's imposed physical and discursive realities.

The reinscription of West Jerusalem's streets and landmarks was accompanied by a simultaneous effort to rename former Palestinian neighborhoods. In 1958, ten years after Israel's establishment and after intense internal debates among governing officials, a range of quarters emptied of their Arab residents were given Hebrew appellations.[30]

---

30. A July 29, 2011 article in *Ha'aretz* (Aderet, 2011) details somewhat the internal Israeli debate about retitling Jerusalem neighborhoods and streets in the 1950s. A great

Talbieh was renamed "Komemiyut" (independence). A contiguous quarter, known to Palestinians as "Qatamon," became "Gonen" (defense) and the former Baq'a neighborhood was renamed "Geulim" (redemption). The terms "independence," "defense," and "redemption" were neither then nor are they today inadvertent signifiers. They are, rather, components in a religio-nationalist vocabulary that has sought to portray Jerusalem as the self-evident and exclusive province of the Jewish state, as the "eternal" capital of the Jewish people.[31]

COLONIAL AMBIVALENCE?

In an urban center teeming with ironies, one of the most remarkable is that Israeli Jews (not to mention Palestinians) rarely use the official Israeli designations in their daily interactions. Names such as "Komemiyut" can be found on the official maps the Jewish state makes available. They are employed to denote institutions—such as the neighborhood community center in Talbieh, on Khovevei Tsiyon (Lovers of Zion) Street. But the older Arab names are more often than not still used in upscale real estate guides, in Israeli tourist brochures, and in common parlance among Israeli Jews. The official Israeli designations appear on West Jerusalem street signs, but in more than a dozen cases in and around Talbieh and other former Palestinian neighborhoods these signs also include the original Arab designation in parentheses. Though the Israeli state has continually negated Palestinian rights to Jerusalem—individual and collective—traces of their past still, paradoxically, linger.

What explains the persistence of the original names? Anton Shammas, in a brilliant piece on homes, memory, and Israeli colonial appropriation,

---

deal of anxiety was recorded by Israeli officials interested in effacing traces of Palestinian life in West Jerusalem. In the first few years of the state, one official cited in this article referred to the Arab designations as "foreign names," which if "not immediately changed to Hebrew names . . . will become entrenched and it will be impossible to uproot them."

31. Even Israel's official "Statistical Yearbook" (2012) puts these Arab names in their tables (though parenthetically), along with the official Israeli designation.

refers to this peculiar process as "cultural cannibalism" (1997). Shammas, a Palestinian with Israeli citizenship, resided in this transformed West Jerusalem environment for several years as a journalist and a student in the 1970s and 1980s. Drawing from Bhabha's (1994) writings on colonialism, Shammas discusses the prevalence of an at times profound "ambivalence" across Jerusalem's remade landscape.

After decades of documented attempts to layer over Palestinian pasts in West Jerusalem, the places of deep personal connection that both national communities possess might be said to, in a sense, still comprise each other in unacknowledged ways. I have always been a bit ambivalent about Bhabha's notion of colonial ambivalence. But I have come to appreciate the fact that to describe these intersecting elements of identity as he and Shammas do is not to minimize the inequities that exist between Israelis and Palestinians. Nor is it to empty the terms "colonizer" and "colonized" of their meaningful substance. It is, rather, to challenge the binarized way of seeing each group as residing in completely separate and opposed cultural, historical, and political positions.[32]

Israelis routinely regard old Palestinian neighborhoods and the distinctive stone structures that comprise them as signifiers of status. "Arab homes" here and elsewhere are highly coveted, and in quarters like Talbieh, Qatamon, and Baq'a they are usually inhabited by affluent Israelis or internationals wealthy enough to purchase or rent them.[33] These typically beautiful and spacious abodes and the subdivided apartments within them are relatively scarce and, consequently, their value has risen to levels

32. This is true not only in Jerusalem's former Arab neighborhoods but also across the former land of Palestine. In at least two dozen cases the budding Israeli state either retained the Arab word for a place or neighborhood or "Hebraized" the site. See Slyomovics (1998) on the Arab village of Ein Houd (transformed by Israel into Ein Hod).

33. A segment of the Palestinian Karmi house in the former Palestinian Qatamon neighborhood has been occupied by employees of the *New York Times* since the paper acquired the property in 1984. For more on this case, see Abunimah (2010) http://electronic intifada.net/content/ny-times-jerusalem-property-makes-it-protagonist-palestine-conflict /8705, accessed January 5, 2014. This article draws from Karmi (2002).

comparable to property in wealthy, Western capitals.[34] The signifier "Arab" in this case retains a meaning as a desirable architectural style rather than as an explicit indicator of an uprooted people. These are, to a great number of Israelis it appears, "Arab homes" but not the homes of exiled Arabs.

Bhabha's notion of colonial ambivalence can be observed in the intriguing ways in which "Arab" has served as a marker of privilege, as an object of desire across a landscape where the Jewish state consistently articulates fears of growing numbers of Palestinians under Israeli control. The fact that "Arab" has also since 1948 been regarded as a signifier of danger within Israeli society (as in "*Arab* terrorism," "*Arab* infiltration," or "*Arab* demographic time bomb") underscores unstable relationships and categories not simply produced by colonial social relations but constitutive of them. It should also be noted that despite the contradictory connotations of "Arab homes," they are only very rarely identified as "Palestinian homes" by Israelis. That association would more explicitly signal an alternate *national* claim to the home, to the city, and to the country more broadly. In the following sections of this chapter I will explore some of the specific but emblematic ways these and other traces of dispossession in Jerusalem might be read and what those readings might tell us about the making of a colonial urban space.

LAYERED DOMINANCE: THE "CONDITIONS OF REINVENTION"

The property of the Palestinian Bisharat family on the southwestern edge of Talbieh is one such Arab home. The nearly ninety-year-old structure is situated on one of the highest points in the area, at what Israelis refer to as "18 David Marcus Street." Built by Hanna Bisharat in the mid-1920s, it has housed Israeli elites from the earliest years of the Jewish state. The home is a large, stone edifice elevated from the street before it, with a verdant garden and high stone wall tightly enclosing the property.

34. Over the last decade I have seen more than a dozen advertisements in Israeli real estate guides for "Arab" homes in Talbieh listed for $3 to $4 million.

Situated as it is above a wide valley, which stretches out for several kilometers to the south and west, might well have been why the British Royal Air Force rented the home from the Bisharats for several years during the Mandate period. However, as local Palestinians and Israelis I interviewed mentioned, in May 1948 as the British were leaving the country and Jerusalem was enveloped by war, they handed the home over *not* to the Palestinian owners but to armed forces of the emerging Israeli state. And it was partly from this hilltop that Zionist armies would solidify their control over the west side of Jerusalem. Members of the Bisharat family, then already in the first days of an exile they did not know would persist for more than six decades, have been unable to reclaim their property ever since.

In conversations with the grandson of the original owners in 2004, I learned of the ways those who occupied the structure had transformed it, discursively as well as physically. The home's ironic relationship to the making of British and Israeli colonial authority is multifaceted. The ways the British authorities handed it over to the Zionist armed forces symbolized in some respects the continuities of colonial authority in twentieth-century Palestine. In the wake of Israel's conquest of Jerusalem's west side, the Bisharat abode was turned over to the nascent Jewish state's "Custodian of Absentee Property." Like tens of thousands of other Palestinian homes and properties throughout the country, it was redefined as Israeli "state land," which meant that it would be reserved for "the exclusive use and benefit of Jews only." Like other Israeli elites who gained possession of choice "absentee" properties, Golda Meir, as foreign minister, lived in this home in the 1960s. The fact that she had resided in a Palestinian home made the remark she uttered in 1968 all the more peculiar. When queried by a French paper about the fate of the Palestinians expelled twenty years previously, she famously asserted:

> There was no such thing as Palestinians . . . It was not as though there was a Palestinian people in Palestine considering itself as a people and we came and threw them out and took their country away from them. They did not exist.[35]

35. *Sunday Times*, June 15, 1969.

Both before and since Meir's declaration, the Israeli occupants have made various physical renovations to the Bisharat property. But Meir's words, negating even the existence of those whose home she once lived in, should be seen as having altered this and other structures in ways no less momentous. If it were true that "there was no such thing as Palestinians," then it would follow that this and other commandeered sites could not possibly have been stolen from them.

In the early 1990s, an Israeli developer built a third floor onto this structure. It was one of innumerable "add-on" floors that have been placed atop appropriated Palestinian homes throughout West Jerusalem since 1948.[36] In the wake of these modifications, this house appeared (and was meant to appear) at initial glance as if it were originally three stories high. When I first became aware of the home's Palestinian history and visited it in the late 1990s, there typically flew an Israeli flag on the slightly recessed third story. However, upon closer inspection, particularly as one moved along its perimeter and viewed the property from the south side, it was possible to perceive disjuncture in its architecture. Far from being merely an innocent renovation, these alterations, I suggest, reveal deeper metaphorical meanings about the character of Israeli governance and its forthright effort to assemble a seamless Israeli history of Jerusalem.

As I studied the third floor of the Bisharat dwelling, it was evident that a dubious stone somewhat different from the original edifice had been used to construct the "add-on" level. A still more careful examination revealed that the new floor had not even been comprised of rock per se but was actually a concrete wall covered by a thin, faux-stone veneer. In those places where the veneer had fallen off, the structure's purported unity is further revealed to be fabricated, its "wholeness" false, since the original two floors are comprised not of concrete but of stone.

In the quest for the illusion of wholeness and unity, the Israeli builder incorporated a string of blue tiles above the poorly rendered third-story

---

36. After studying a range of British-era maps of Jerusalem and recording oral histories with former residents, I estimate that no fewer than 27 cases of post-1948 "add-on" expansions to former Arab homes can be found in Talbieh alone.

windows. These azure squares, embedded in this wall, are meant to resemble what has been known in Jerusalem for decades as "Armenian tile." These decorative ceramic features commonly grace the facades of ornate homes built before 1948, but rarely since. This artistry and the small Armenian Christian minority who mastered it have been significant elements of Jerusalem's cultural heritage and hybridity.

An original and more decorative series of tiles line the Bisharat's second-story façade. Perhaps part of the home's status, its perceived "authenticity" might lie precisely in the fact that some of these original features have fallen off over the years. The Israeli residents' use of ersatz tiles on the side wall, along with the other dimensions of this third floor, are aesthetic attempts to interlace and unify the various segments of the structure. They are deployed to "root" the current occupants in a place and a time that belongs to another family. Here, the past is produced and the past is silenced.

These attempts to remake this and other "Arab homes" appropriated in 1948 include more explicitly ideological efforts, as well. In dozens of cases in West Jerusalem, Israeli occupants of commandeered Palestinian dwellings have inscribed Hebrew messages on these properties in a range of ways. These are not uncommonly biblical quotes or allusions that reference the sacred and divine. They are attempts, as I read them, to infuse these locales with meanings that foreground the connections of the current residents while negating those of the actual owners.

On the southern face of the Bisharat property's add-on floor is just such an ideological etching, one that gestures toward the ways the Bible and notions of the sacred have been mobilized by the Jewish state to legitimize its rule over the whole of Jerusalem. Imprinted in Hebrew on the faux Armenian tiles are words taken from I Kings 8:43. They read as follows: *Ki shmecha nikra 'alhabeit haze,* or "This house, which I have built, is called by thy name." The passage, in context, relates to God, the eternal authority, the one the Israeli resident apparently seeks to invoke as s/he asserts ownership and belonging to this specific site. "Thy" in this context refers to an unassailable source, one to be feared and loved. The laws of this authority are to be obeyed and would certainly, to not a few Israelis, trump anything that international law or United Nations resolutions might have had to say about this structure and those exiled from it. This quote also possesses a play on "house" with reference to both this specific abode and the larger home, Jerusalem, which, Israeli leaders and their supporters abroad routinely claim, God promised to the Jewish people in the Old Testament.

Like other quotes drawn from biblical texts, this one has an array of different interpretations. I cannot know, of course, what those who inscribed this message meant by it, exactly, without talking to them. Try as I might, I was unsuccessful in interviewing the current occupants of this home. But whatever its intended meaning it is the capacity to inscribe these words in the first place that underscores Israeli authority in the city. Part of colonialism's cultural dynamism is its ability to normalize spatial and social realities, to make them appear natural, innocent, and optionless. That cultural force, in this and other cases, also relies on the capacity to evaporate inconvenient histories that might belie these dominant depictions.

2. The Palestinian Bisharat family home in Talbieh, 2003. The structure was built in 1925 and appropriated by the new Israeli state in May 1948. Former Israeli Prime Minister Golda Meir occupied the home in the 1960s. Note the added-on third floor meant to look like part of an original whole.

3. "Layered dominance": a side view of the Bisharat family home, 2003. The third story's architectural differences are evident, including windows, stones, and other design features. The Israeli occupant included a biblical inscription in Hebrew above the window that reads: "This house, which I have built, is called by thy name" (I Kings 8:43).

I see in these altered Arab homes not simply individual cases of ideological artifice but also metaphors for the manner in which Jerusalem more broadly has been transformed since 1948. For one, like the city's urban landscape, only the Jewish state or those it licenses have the authority to make structural changes to these dwellings. Palestinian authorship of or claims to individual homes, like Jerusalem itself, are in important ways uninscribable and unsayable under Israeli rule. The reluctance that successive Israeli governments have shown to sharing sovereignty over Jerusalem (changing the city's "architecture" of governance) mirrors the general opposition to even acknowledging Palestinian ownership of properties like the Bisharats', let alone allowing exiled Arab families to return to them.

Secondly, under Israeli rule only Jewish connections and claims to these familial places are legally recognized. These homes have been reapportioned through a series of legal channels and categories that preclude Palestinians from reclaiming them once they have been deemed "absentee property" and their former owners deemed "absentees." This is analogous to Israel's insistence on its exclusive hold and control over the whole of Jerusalem, a realm that God is said to have given to the Jewish people and to them alone. Lands and homes classified under the Jewish state's legal category of "state" or "public" land are overwhelmingly off-limits to non-Jews.[37] The appeal of biblical promises and divine designs to a state created in 1948 largely on the land of the indigenous population is that they are said to come from the beginning of time and from an ultimate authority that cannot be challenged.

A third noteworthy parallel between the reconfiguration of these homes and the changes done to the city more broadly relates to the capacity to delineate boundaries. As with the alterations to "Arab homes" like the Bisharat's, the borders of the city have also proven to be quite malleable. They have been enlarged unilaterally over the course of several decades, added on to, and reconfigured. Perhaps most crucially, any territory encompassed by these new delineations has become, by Israeli order, "Jerusalem."

The spatial signifiers that define this urban center cartographically have shifted over the last six decades of Israeli rule and continue to do so. And yet though constantly expanding, Jerusalem is said by those who have colonized it since 1948 to be immutable and undivided. Israeli and Zionist representations of the city as the "eternal and undivided capital of the Jewish People" are incessantly encountered in post-1967 governmental statements and literature. The transformation of the Bisharat home and myriad others and the particular ways in which these locales have been represented and utilized is a metaphor for precisely these processes.

WALKING JERUSALEM'S SPECTRAL LANDSCAPE

Traversing Jerusalem with former Palestinian residents was endlessly illuminating. These journeys helped provide more tangible meaning to somewhat abstract and theoretical notions about colonial governance. As I

37. This is a fact acknowledged by former Israeli officials like Meron Benvenisti (1996) and Sarah Kaminkar (1997).

learned of the ways Israeli law has been used to preclude the return of Palestinian homeowners, I was able to more clearly understand, for instance, what Talal Asad means when he refers to colonialism's imposed spatial, legal, and discursive dimensions as being part of "an irrevocable process of transmutation" (1991, 314). In the satisfaction that life in these commandeered homes has produced for the Israeli Jews who reside in them today, I could better grasp the magnitude of Albert Memmi's assertion that "the deprivations of the colonized are the almost direct result of the advantages secured to the colonizer" (1965, xii).

Former residents of Talbieh and neighboring quarters led me through the places they once knew intimately as children and young adults. As we moved through these neighborhoods, sometimes the sight of one small architectural detail, a landmark, or a single tree could conjure up memories of life before the flight of their families. Exiles would point out what once was there but is no longer: "Over there, do you see," "here there used to be . . . ," or "this was the home of. . . ." These were traces simultaneously present and absent. They were, indeed, pointing toward what de Certeau refers to as "the invisible identities of the visible" (1984, 108).[38]

In the late 1990s I had the occasion to walk Talbieh with Salma, a Palestinian woman then in her early sixties. She and her extended kin network, composed of several Christian families, once lived in five different homes in Talbieh before fleeing the country in the last months of the British Mandate. Like every other exiled family with whom I spoke, hers believed that their departure at the time was temporary. Salma eventually came to the United States where she raised a family. As an American passport holder she was, after several decades, able to visit Jerusalem and the neighborhood she once knew as home. But to do so, she had to obtain "permission" from Israeli authorities to enter the country of her birth. Like thousands of other Palestinians in similar circumstance, the visa they granted her was for a limited stay of three months and indicated

---

38. Steven Gregory's (1998) work on memory, racial politics, and place in Queens, New York, has been hugely influential in helping me incorporate the insights of de Certeau (1984) for this urban space.

that she was a "tourist." Salma generously offered to show me the Talbieh of her youth. Her insights were immeasurably important in helping me connect the city's colonial present with its colonial past.

Traversing Jerusalem's cultural and religious divides on Saturday, or Shabbat reveals just how segregated the city has become. Traveling from the east side to the west side means leaving the commotion, car fumes, and cacophony of street noise that comprise a standard business day in Palestinian East Jerusalem, and entering the most serene hours of the week on the west side. Here, a remarkable stillness pervades from sundown on Friday until the next evening. Israeli buses do not run until nightfall on Saturday and only a smattering of cars roam the streets, bounded by nearly empty sidewalks and dark, gated storefronts.

As Salma and I made our way through West Jerusalem in her car, little stirred under the severe afternoon sun. We entered the tree-lined and unsoiled avenues of Talbieh through its southern approach, up a steady incline, from the former Arab neighborhood of Qatamon. Along the southern edge of Talbieh lay one of the dwellings where members of her extended family resided during their final decade or so in Jerusalem. Other uncles, aunts, and cousins lived not a five-minute walk down the road in four different homes. The close connection of her father's siblings, as she described, made these physically separate households function like one expanded domestic network.

My guide pointed to a small garden apartment situated below the main floor of this edifice. Her family rented it to a Jewish doctor from Romania whose name she could not remember.

> We never knew what happened to them. I think they stayed after we left
> . . . but I'm not sure. We lost track. My parents liked them and I remember good relations, even near the end [of our time here]. I always wonder what happened to them.

We alighted, approached the home's gated perimeter, and peered into the still yard for a few moments, not expecting to see the tenants of old. I wondered if the current residents might appear to inquire about our purpose, but nobody did.

Salma and I then continued a few dozen meters down the road and reached the shaded intersection of today's Alkalai and Disraeli streets. On the southeast corner, consuming a spacious lot twice the size of most others in the neighborhood, stood a stately three-story edifice built by her late uncle. This striking property at 12 Disraeli, grander than nearly every other in the vicinity, was enclosed by the same 2-meter-high stone wall that surrounded it five decades earlier. A prominent staircase led to a beautifully crafted arched doorway. The original, ornate iron gates were well preserved and still greeted the visitor, as well. Embossed on their lower half was a distinctive familial signifier. The emblem is a Jamal family design, produced in an elaborate and decorative English script, a kind of "code" inscrutable to the current Israeli occupants, I imagined.

"This was the symbol of the 'Jamal Brothers,'" she related, denoting both the family name as well as that of their successful travel agency founded during the age of the British Mandate. The Jamals were one of several prominent urban families who prospered significantly during this period, mainly due to emerging business ties with Europe and the United States.

Similar traces from the home's past could be observed at this and other Palestinian properties. These included family initials or names on gates or doors. Numbers marking the date a home was built could sometimes be seen woven into the iron lintels above doors. I found it somewhat paradoxical that these details, indicating a former Palestinian presence and signaling specific histories the Israeli state tended to deny, were typically retained by the current occupants. This was true even when significant alterations had been made to these dwellings. What, I frequently thought, did the current Israeli inhabitants *see* when they observed these elements? How was historical amnesia about these Palestinian places bound up with claims of historical Israeli connection to them?

More recent dimensions added to appropriated Arab homes not uncommonly resided in a strange discord with former ones. There was, for instance, an unattractive electric doorbell on the stone enclosure of the Jamal home at 12 Disraeli near the upper hinge of the gates. The name of the Israeli occupant at the time—"Raphaeli"—had been inscribed in English and Hebrew. The beautiful stone arches of entranceways were

4. Jamal family home on the street Israelis have renamed "Disraeli," 2002. Note both the family's initials
embossed in the original gate as well as the current Israeli occupant's name on the side of the original stone
wall.

still found intact but the original doors of iron or wood were commonly
replaced with more recent ones with less attention to aesthetic consistency.

As with the Bisharat home, the Jamals' property initially had the
appearance of being a seamless whole. But one could, after a few minutes, observe that it had actually been subdivided and served multiple
uses. As Salma and I walked along its perimeter it became evident that

the first floor of the western side had been transformed into a center for recent Jewish immigrants to Israel (*olim* in Hebrew). Israeli authorities had given the home two addresses: 9 Alkaili for the structure in its institutional uses and 12 Disraeli for that part of the house inhabited by residents. An unattractive plastic sign used to denote the "Nathan Steinberg Center" hung above the side entrance to the property, atop the original stone wall. The center's Hebrew name, *Moadon Haoleh*, means "Club of the New Immigrants."

The organization had been there for more than a decade, I learned from its staff on another visit to the property. Until the Nathan Steinberg Center left these premises around 2004 or 2005, it had the specified aim of providing assistance to recent Jewish arrivals to Israel. This Palestinian home awaited not those who built it and their descendants who wished to reclaim it. Instead, it served to actively facilitate the settlement of Jewish families from outside the country who wish to "return" and make *aliyah* (or "ascend" in Hebrew) to the Jewish state.[39]

Salma and I backtracked to the property's front entrance and walked east along its northern stone enclosure. We made our way leisurely down the narrow and serene Disraeli Street, a thoroughfare she played on as a child before it had any formal name. We passed another Palestinian home a few meters down the road, today occupied by the Israeli Institute for Psychoanalysis. An unobtrusive sign in English and Hebrew on the original front gate announced its contemporary institutional use. Just within the entrance, an eerie painting of an austere-looking Sigmund Freud in formal wear hung prominently in the empty gallery-white foyer.

We made our way down a parallel street today referred to by Israelis as "Lovers of Zion" (*Hovevei Zion*). There we came upon the house that philosopher Martin Buber lived in from the late 1940s until his death in 1965, owned by the Palestinian Sununu family. Buber had previously rented an apartment in the home of Edward Said's family a few blocks away before

---

39. One way in which the Steinberg Center facilitates the influx of Jewish immigrants is to offer instruction in Hebrew, subsidized by the Jewish Agency and known as *ulpan*.

taking up residence in this lovely and fairly modest dwelling with a splendid colorful garden that enveloped the front veranda. Dozens of other
stone homes built before 1948 grace this shaded street and several others
nearby, laid out in straight lines and right angles. They are interspersed
with more recent structures built by Israelis after 1948. Several possessed
"add-on" floors, much like the Bisharat's, with varying degrees of attention to aesthetic consistency.

Salma and I circled back to her former family dwelling on Disraeli
Street and continued a short distance down the road, where a thin, badly
paved path, scarcely the width of a car, bisected Disraeli. It snaked back a
few dozen meters to two other Jamal properties, encased in leafy lots. Just
before reaching the first of these homes, we came upon a faded yellow sign
in Hebrew and Arabic hung precariously on a rusted fence that enclosed
the land of these abodes. It was one of the very few I had ever seen in a
West Jerusalem neighborhood that actually contained an Arabic message.
The content underscored why: The sign declared that this plot was "Israeli
State Land" and that "Trespassing is prohibited!"[40]

Exhortations of this sort, however, did not deter Salma. She walked
ahead of me forthrightly through the rusted front gates, pried open and
embedded in weeds. I followed her down the short gravel driveway where
two small cars sat before a broad structure dating back to the 1920s. Only
the wind rustling through tall trees could be heard on this Shabbat afternoon. None of the current inhabitants could be seen in or around the
premises. My guide seemed without fear as she climbed the staircase that
narrowed stylishly as it led up to the front entrance. I trailed along tenta-
tively, hoping that she would not knock on the door. It looked as though
she might.

After an hour in which we had not seen even one Israeli resident of the
neighborhood, I thought for certain that these occupants would appear as

40. I came across identical notices in the 1990s and 2000s throughout Jerusalem—
east and west. They were often attached to fences and enclosures that bounded property
the Israeli state had expropriated from Palestinians over the years.

Salma held court on the front veranda. She, unlike me, betrayed not the least bit of worry. In fact, this exile told me that though she would not ring the doorbell and bother them on Shabbat, she would welcome the chance to talk to them. These were her family's steps and, for a few short moments that afternoon, she claimed them. Like other Palestinians who made similar visits back to their homes, Salma told me that each time she returns, memories of her childhood come rushing back all at once.

This property had been altered inside and out to suit the needs of at least three Israeli families. A modest third-floor apartment had been constructed atop the original home, barely perceptible from the front walkway and accessible only from a side entrance. The top flat, Salma informed me, offered scenic views of the surrounding area. And this she knew firsthand because, only a few years previously, she had been permitted to enter the home for the first time in nearly half a century.

The opportunity arose rather fortuitously, soon after Salma met the daughter of the current residents, one of Israel's best-known anti-Zionist Jewish activists. She and the Israeli woman, Orit, were introduced in Jerusalem through mutual acquaintances. Orit was intrigued by Salma's story of dispossession and had, herself, written about the events that had led to the expulsion of the Palestinians. This Israeli Jew not only expressed sympathy with the Palestinian refugees but, unlike the vast majority of her fellow citizens, she believed that they had the right to return to their homes in contemporary Palestine/Israel. The more Salma told Orit about the family's history and the location of their properties, the more curious her Israeli interlocutor grew. After a few more details were provided, Orit was shocked to learn that one of Salma's family residences was in fact the very place where her elderly Israeli parents were currently residing.

Salma was invited by the Israeli occupants to visit the apartment in the subdivided home. On her way to meet them that day, she told me that she first stopped with a friend who accompanied her and bought a bouquet of flowers for the Jewish occupants. Salma smiled broadly when she saw just how astounded I was upon hearing this.

"You can't believe it, right?" she chuckled. "Well, I did it to show that I came in peace and did not come with *any* hostility. Actually," she continued, "*they* were embarrassed. They were liberals, and they realized that they were in our house and they felt bad."

I wondered then as I do now if Salma had not experienced more sorrow and anger than she expressed while relating this odd encounter. If the current residents had appeared mortified, had she not felt humiliation at having to enter her family's property under these conditions? What had it been like to be shown from room to room and then escorted out, however humane and gracious the current residents might have been? Perhaps a more skilled researcher than I would have found a way, at that delicate moment, to probe more deeply into the sentiments that accompanied her return after so many years. Or, what the flowers she offered as a symbol of peace might have unwittingly conveyed. But confronted with the tragedy of the circumstances, I was simply at a loss.

Salma wanted to show me one more place before we concluded our visit to Talbieh. The home, a boxlike stone structure of three floors, was 20 meters or so further down the quiet path. The austere edifice was constructed in the 1920s by other members of her extended kin network. It possessed striking, twin black doors of iron and resembled less a home than a modest apartment building. As we approached the entrance, it became apparent that this site served a peculiar institutional purpose that neither Salma nor I had been aware of. The parking spaces before the front entrance drawn in yellow signaled this as did a small plaque to the right of the vault like iron door which read in Hebrew and English: "Association of Americans and Canadians in Israel (AACI)." The World Zionist Organization (WZO) ran this association, which had been housed here for several years. The sign on the door was still there as of early 2012, though the home was plainly being reconfigured once again by an Israeli developer whose business logo printed in white plastic was draped over the family's front gate.

The stated mission of the AACI then and now is "to aid North American immigrants in acclimating to Israeli society" and to assist in their "absorption" (*klitah*). A range of events, from softball games to barbeques, were organized for these North American *olim* by a staff working from this Palestinian home. These new Israelis, some possessing little Hebrew and in the country for the first time, are to be oriented to what this and similar Zionist organizations refer to as the "eternal center of the Jewish people."[41] As these immigrants enter the original black iron doors, they are celebrated for "returning home."

"Absorption" (*klitah*), or the verb to absorb, initially seemed to me an awkward way to label Israeli settlement and state-building efforts. Upon further reflection, however, I found it fitting. Absorption, after all, does not simply suggest a process of assimilating someone or something into a larger group or body. It means, as well, to engross the attention, to rivet the eyes on a specific item, image, ideology, or object of desire. And when one is absorbed, one's focus, one's thoughts are necessarily drawn away from other peoples, other histories, and other suffering. As I pondered the discursive dimensions of continued Israeli settlement activity within the space of expropriated Palestinian properties, I was reminded of Nancy Scheper-Hughes's (2004) keen insight that "all forms of violence are sustained by the passively averted gaze" (225).

Like the Nathan Steinberg Center located just a block away, the AACI has the ironic mandate of locating housing and providing emergency assistance for newly arrived Jewish immigrants. Though the AACI found it relevant to mention in their literature published in 2000 that they are located in a "75-year-old stone building with patterned tiles," nowhere do they point out that this "building" was in fact the home of an exiled Arab family who still wishes to return. In those silences and absences, the artifice of colonial domination hardens like mortar.[42]

I have been arguing that the visions of prestate Zionist organizations were those of a settler-colonial movement. Zionist bodies like the Palestine Colonization Association and the Jewish National Fund had as their principal aim to build not just a Jewish homeland but an exclusivist Jewish

41. Quotation taken from the AACI's former website (access date July 1, 2001). See the current website which announces a new Jerusalem headquarters in the neighborhood of Talpiot. http://www.aaci.org.il/. Accessed January 5, 2014.

42. Ibid.

state. Comprised of kibbutzim, *moshavim* (Hebrew for settlements), and a range of burgeoning, Jewish-only neighborhoods, this new political entity would form a "bulwark of civilization against Asiatic barbarism" (1896, 30) as the founder of modern political Zionism, Theodor Herzl, affirmed. Since the advent of this nation-building project in Palestine, there have been innumerable changes to Jerusalem and to former Palestinian quarters like Talbieh. But Israel's several-decades-old principles and practices have remained remarkably constant: Herzl's "bulwark" has become Ariel Sharon and Benjamin Netanyahu's separation wall.

As the searing afternoon heat gradually dissipated and the sun began to recede in the western sky, Shabbat was soon to end. West Jerusalem would quickly become congested as life returned to its streets and commercial zones. Salma and I retraced our steps to the car past the series of lost properties we had visited that afternoon. As we did, she described feeling what dozens of other Palestinians had told me they felt as they moved through their former neighborhoods as visitors and tourists.

"I'm sad when I leave here," Salma related solemnly. "And I guess I can't really let go because of them [her deceased parents]. They wanted to be here. They didn't want to die in exile. They wanted to end up here—and so did I."

EPILOGUE

In 2006 and 2012, I returned to West Jerusalem to observe how Talbieh and other former Palestinian neighborhoods had been reconfigured since my previous visit in 2003. The Jamals' home at 12 Disraeli Street was still there, though the Nathan Steinberg Center for *olim* had been closed. Its sign above the original gate was in disrepair and Israeli authorities plainly had other designs on this structure. A governmental notice in Hebrew, attached to the front entry, announced future alterations to the home. More floors were to be added and new residents would be housed here in upscale apartments.

Near the side entrance, still other layers of meanings had been attributed to the property by those with the authority to etch and ascribe histories and connections to particular locales in the city. On the original stone gate the Israeli municipality had hung an official blue commemorative plaque. The memorial, inscribed in Hebrew and English (but not in Arabic), was one of at least a dozen similar ones that had been attached to various West Jerusalem places in recent years. The plaque sought to remember the history of this property, but not as a former Palestinian home. Rather, passersby were told that the building once housed the headquarters of the right-wing Zionist militia, the Stern Gang (or LEHI), in the months immediately after the Jewish state was created.

Israeli officials wished onlookers to recognize this place as "Machane Dror" (or Dror's camp), named for one of the Stern Gang's leading figures, Mordechai Dror. He is said to have been killed "during the liberation of Sheik-Badder [sic]," a campaign involving the expulsion of this nearby Palestinian village's entire population in early 1948. The Israeli Knesset and Sachar Park now sit on a broad swath of the land of the demolished village just 2 kilometers to the west. Only a few traces of Sheikh Bader's ruined cemetery can still be found deep in the park, among thick foliage and next to an Israeli conservation site established to protect local bird species. And just as this moment of ethnic cleansing is ideologically transformed into one of "liberation," so, too, is the Jamal home overwritten with official tributes to those responsible for these forced evictions.

This chapter has sought to detail how dominant Israeli visions for Jerusalem have been deeply transformative ones, consistent with the practices and discourses of colonial power. These spatial and demographic designs have included not simply initiatives to conquer land and property but also closely related efforts to negate Palestinian memories and historical connections to the city. These ideologies of exclusion in a sense inhere symbolically in the structure of hundreds of commandeered Arab homes in Jerusalem alone.

But I have also emphasized that these silenced histories are not simply Palestinian pasts, but also those of shared and mixed residential environments. After several months walking these neighborhoods, I was left asking whether "mixed" Arab-Jewish residential and commercial areas, healthy forms of intercommunal life and expressions of cultural hybridity,

The plaque reads:

מחנה דרור · מפקדת לח"י בירושלים

במקום זה היתה המפקדה הראשית של לח"י, וכן היו
כאן מחסנים של חומרי נפץ ובתי מלאכה לייצור נשק.
המתחם כולו נקרא "מחנה דרור" על שם מרדכי בן
עוזיהו "דרור", שנפל בקרב לשחרור שייך-באדר.
במקום הזה נגלו חמישה מטובי לוחמי לח"י בעת מילוי
תפקידם: מרים פריד "כוכבה", לאה פריינט "אריאלה",
אסף קראווני "עוזי", בנימין שלום "מיכאל" ודוד
שנייוויס "זמיר".

"Dror", Lehi's Headqurter

"Machane Dror", acted as Lehi Headquartrs, and
housed their arms, ammunition and their expolsives
industry. This structure was named in memory of
Mordechai Ben Uziyahu "Dror", who fell during the
liberation of Sheik-Badder. Here a tragic expolsion
claimed the lives of five of the finest Lehi freedom
fighters.

5. A municipal plaque affixed to the Jamal family home by Israeli authorities, 2006. It asserts the site's significance as the former headquarters of the Zionist militia, the "Stern Gang."

have not been the threats those committed to an exclusivist Jewish state have most feared. The concurrent processes of spatial conquest and discursive domination analyzed in this chapter converge and merge in a range of ways. Israeli colonial knowledge and colonial urbanism have continued to produce and reproduce a landscape that denies in its affirmations and that speaks in its innumerable silences.

3

Myths, Memorials, and Monuments
in the Jerusalem of Israel's Imagination

But then the great wings of a memorial, like those of a panegyric, are
not expected to be clipped by tedious fact.

—GORE VIDAL, *Julian*

Jerusalem is a place where space, memory, and historical invention have
intersected in formidable ways over several centuries. Indeed, this most
symbolic of cities has, in crucial respects, come into existence through
the discourses, memories, and myths that describe it. Today, both Palestinians and Israelis insist that Jerusalem be recognized as their respective national capital. Neither would accept a settlement of the conflict
that negates their right to self-determination here. However, though
there exists a parity of desire for the city among various religious and
national communities, in the capacity to represent and reconfigure Jerusalem since 1948 there has been no parity of power.

In this chapter I continue an analysis of the spatial construction of
identity and difference in this segregated urban realm by detailing how
struggles between Israelis and Palestinians, Jews and Arabs, colonizers
and the colonized are all too often clashes over the meanings attributed
to specific places. In doing so, I explore what Edward Said (1995) aptly
refers to as Israel's "projections" of Jerusalem and how these typically
mythic and partial portrayals have been advanced through a range of
nationalist memorials. These cultural sites, I argue, do not simply represent the contours of Israeli colonial rule but aid in shaping them, as
well. As such, they are illustrations of what Bernard Cohn (1996) refers

75

to as colonialism's "forms of knowledge" and technologies of cultural control.

In the course of my research, I came upon no fewer than four dozen Israeli places of formal nationalist remembrance in the Jerusalem area alone. Frequently dedicated to military victory and valor, the sites are found in all sections of this city. These memorials are of varying size and scope, from modest plaques affixed to commandeered Palestinian properties (like the Jamal home examined in chapter 2) to the remains of damaged Israeli tanks from past wars left near busy streets and highways. They are mammoth structures with expansive exhibit halls, like Ammunition Hill (*Giv'at Hatachmoshet*) in illegally occupied East Jerusalem, and rolling green and wooded sites like Independence Park (*Gan Ha'atzmaut*) in West Jerusalem, built over the ruins of the centuries-old Ma'mam Allah Islamic Cemetery discussed in chapter 1.

These places of remembrance articulate remarkably consistent nationalist messages, usually blending the Jewish state's claim to exclusive rule over Jerusalem with assertions of the Jewish people's "eternal" spiritual connection to this urban center. They are also comprised of a host of predictable absences. Palestinian attachments to the city—their mourning, their memories—are seldom if ever mentioned. Indeed, while the term "Arab" is occasionally used in these memorials' narratives, rarely is "Palestinian." When either find their way into exhibit text or pamphlets they are almost always associated with hostility or "terrorism" directed at Israel. Memorials of this sort are where governing authorities and Zionist organizations like Taglit-Birthright Israel and Friends of the Israel Defense Forces (FIDF) squire tens of thousands of Israeli citizens and foreign tourists each year. Just how effective these cultural sites are in educating Israeli and international opinion is unclear. But that the Jewish state has invested heavily in such "meaning machines" is fairly evident.

Israel has utilized appropriated Palestinian homes in myriad ways over the last sixty-five years. Their chief purpose has been to house Israeli Jews as part of an effort to forge demographic dominance over the Palestinians in Jerusalem and throughout the country. However, in a few instances these dwellings have been converted into more explicit representational places, including Israeli memorials, monuments, and museums.[1]

This chapter will focus with particular attention on one such locale, a home appropriated from the Palestinian Baramki family in 1948 and utilized by the Jewish state in a manner at once distinctive and emblematic. Before doing so, however, I trace out some of the ways in which Palestinian exiles like the Baramkis have been made peripheral in their own city—spatially as well as historically. In other words, how the memory of Israeli sacrifice and valor so often relies on the negation of Palestinian pasts. I explore how Arabs and Jews have been shaped by the city's division and the specter of the border that once divided Jerusalem's east and west sides.

ARCHITECTURES OF LOSS, STRUCTURES OF VALOR: THE BARAMKI HOUSE

Andoni Baramki, a renowned Palestinian architect trained in Athens in the early twentieth century, designed and built several structures in the course of his forty-year career. One of them was a three-story stone home constructed in the early 1930s. The imposing edifice was bounded by its stone wall and decorative iron gate and located a few hundred meters north of Jerusalem's Old City walls. It came to assume an accidental and tragic position in 1948, lying as it did precisely on the emerging frontier that would fracture the city's west and east sides for the next nineteen years. The Baramkis owned the home and rented it out until their flight in the final months of British rule.

Within weeks of arriving in Jerusalem to conduct research, I began to hear chronicles of Palestinian exile. Among them was the story of a peculiar property owned by a prominent Arab family. One autumn morning a

---

1. One example of a Palestinian property put to ideological use is a home between Jaffa and Tel Aviv that has been transformed into the Etzel Museum, honoring the prestate Zionist paramilitary group, the Irgun, that committed the Deir Yassin massacre and other acts of terrorism against the Palestinians.

Palestinian friend pointed out this home as we sped past it in his car along the busy Route 1 that separates West and East Jerusalem.

"Look! See that house, Tom? It belonged to the Baramkis. They lost it in '48 and have been trying to get it back ever since. You need to talk to Gabi."

Gabriel Baramki (or Gabi, as he was known) was Andoni's son, the oldest of four children born in 1929 to this Arab Christian family in British-era Jerusalem. Until his death in 2012, he was a legend among Palestinian educators and intellectuals, though he would have disavowed that description with his standard modesty. I interviewed Gabi on two occasions along with four other members of his expansive kin network in Jerusalem and Ramallah. When we first spoke in the late 1990s, he was the deputy minister of higher education in the budding Palestinian government established in the wake of Yasser Arafat's return to Palestine in 1994. Previously, he had served as acting president of Birzeit University, Palestine's premier university just north of Ramallah.

Possessing the rough outlines of the Baramkis' flight and exile, I sought details about their displacement, loss, and anguish. My lengthy list of much-too-structured interview questions betrayed a desire to write a narrow narrative of suffering. That was, after all, what I felt this family had principally to offer. In retrospect I was seeking information that, however pertinent, could in a sense be "slotted" into my airtight and already formed notion of what I thought 1948 must surely have meant for Palestinians like the Baramkis. But as my interview with Gabi began, I was gently compelled to put my questions aside for a moment and to permit my interlocutor to guide me through his family's multifaceted encounters in Jerusalem.

The experiences of this and other Arab families of Jerusalem were not reducible to what military authorities had done to them. Gabi demonstrated a desire not only for recognition of his kin's hardships, of which the home I came to talk to him about was a central feature, but also of their cultural contributions to this land and its inhabitants. They were artists, architects, poets, educators, and even aerobics instructors who had contributed to Jerusalem's diverse heritage. His father Andoni's artistry was illustrative of that intellectual and cultural history. Their presence in the city, I learned, predated the establishment of Israel by more than 400 years.

"And we're *still* here," Gabi added resolutely, grinning slightly. "This will always be our city no matter what they [the Israelis] do. And we can share it with them but they can't make us disappear."

He detailed some of his father's aesthetic innovations, including his melding of local architectural traditions with the more classical ones he had studied in Greece. That cultural hybridity, that mixing of various traditions, was symbolized by Andoni's interplay of different colored pink and white stone in arches and entryways. It was also exhibited by his use of handsome Corinthian columns with features and materials of a local, Arab character. Having driven past the homes designed by his father in West Jerusalem, Gabi related with some disgust that the current Israeli residents had "mutilated" them. Former verandas that graced these properties had been enclosed with glass or sheet metal to create an additional room. Scores of these dwellings, like those described in chapter 2, had been subdivided and crowned with "add-on" floors. These renovations violated, in his view, the structure's original appearance while they sought to portray the divided property as a seamless whole, as authentically and wholly Israeli—much like Jerusalem itself.

In the face of these changes, it was understandable why Gabi and every other exile from West Jerusalem I spoke with expressed both attachment to and alienation from precisely the realms they referred to as "our home." It was routine for displaced Palestinians to register revulsion at the theft of these properties. But there was also indignation at how Israel had "renovated" the city and the country more broadly in no small part through the use of many thousands of these dwellings.

SOLIDIFYING A BORDER, NATURALIZING A NATION

The Baramkis, like nearly every other family I interviewed expelled in 1948, believed at the time that they would return after a few days or weeks. "We left with very little," related Suha, one elderly cousin of Gabi. She reminded me that it was not simply homes that were taken from them but their movable property, too. These were commonly items of immense personal significance, things that made structures of brick, stone, and mortar into intimate familial places. This looting of Palestinian property by Israeli soldiers and civilians has been, as I came to more fully appreciate, among the unacknowledged torments of exile. As Suha explained feelingly:

> All our pictures, our carpets, furniture, everything was left behind. And they took it. You know, our libraries—gone, taken, stolen. Jewelry, my mother's jewelry from her mother and her mother, all gone. When we couldn't go back there was a burning . . . I always felt about what happened to those things. I thought about that a lot over the years. I still do and I'm in my seventies! I tried to put it out of my head because it made my blood boil. Who had my mother's jewelry now?

As fighting raged in the city between Jordanian and Israeli forces in 1948, the Baramkis' home came to rest precisely on the emerging frontier separating Jerusalem's two sectors. That divide became the 1949 Armistice Line, which was negotiated between the warring parties with little if any involvement of the Palestinians. Official maps of the time reveal that this line of division was drawn in a perfunctory manner by Israeli and Jordanian generals. Drawing on maps from the time, I identified at least thirty-one structures in just the area near the Baramki home that were actually split by the width of the green wax pen used to demarcate the barrier between the west and east sides.[2]

Perhaps because of the home's imposing size and its strategic location, the nascent Israeli state appropriated it during the 1948 War and transformed it into an army post. Weapons were placed behind its thick limestone walls and aimed across the divide at Jordanian soldiers and the civilians of the east side, thousands of whom had been expelled from West Jerusalem. The Baramkis' front entrance directly faced the frontier; in fact, maps of the time reveal that the armistice line ran across the

2. In secret negotiations between the Jordanian monarchy and the Zionist leadership they had, in fact, sought to divide the territory earmarked for the Palestinian state in the 1947 UN Partition Resolution between them. See Schlaim (1988) for more on what he refers to as "collusion across the Jordan."

property's front garden and veranda. The Israeli military sealed the front door and filled in the distinctive arched windows with concrete, making most of them into turrets. Only thin apertures remained, narrow enough to accommodate the barrel of a gun and the gaze of a soldier.

Troops were stationed at this house-turned–military post in part to help stem the return of evicted Palestinians across the new borderland. I argue that this "threat," a demographic one, was the major source of concern for Israel. The mainstream Zionist goal of creating a state with a substantial Jewish majority had only been achieved through these expulsions and it could only hope to be maintained by blocking the repatriation of the refugees. Consistent with the racial policies and visions that have undergirded the Israeli nation-state, there was and remains the sturdiest resolve to preclude the return of these displaced families, of which the Baramkis were one.[3]

As I spoke to more and more exiles, I learned of a little written about but significant set of historical occurrences that never ceased to amaze me. In the first few years immediately after 1948, thousands of Palestinians were actually able to move back across what was initially a fairly porous armistice line. Dodging the militaries of Israel and Jordan, individuals and even entire families managed to make their way back to their towns or villages. Those able to do so and remain within the new Jewish state amounted to no more than 1 percent of the refugees but their stories are significant. One or two older Arab men I interviewed, refugees from the west side of the city, boasted of actually having darted across the divide and back again in one day to try to retrieve items left or hidden at their homes.

Drawing from declassified government documents, historians have noted the anxieties that Palestinian attempts to return to their homes engendered within the budding Jewish state. Those with the capacity to

3. An examination of Israel's Declaration of Independence, its subsequent documents such as the Basic Law: 1985, and even very recent debates and discourses within ruling political circles indicate the Jewish state's desire to retain what it refers to as its "Jewish character."

demarcate spatial boundaries also possessed the power to define these crossings as "infiltration."[4] This was a discourse increasingly adopted not only by Israeli officials but also by the United Nations (UN) Security Council and the Jordanian regime. Israeli authorities regarded these crossings not simply as a violation of the armistice agreement but as a breach of its "national security." And this despite the fact that from June 1949 to December 1952 75.4 percent (396 of 525) of the complaints related to Palestinian "crossings"—according to the *Israeli* authorities—fell under the category of "unarmed individuals or groups."[5]

The naming of these acts as "infiltration" was, much as "terrorism" would become in later years, an effective discursive device. It has, then and since, been used to solidify control over territory and property Israel claims ownership of but that has been expropriated from Arab exiles. Like the frontier itself, this prevailing definitional repertoire was thrown up with haste and used to police the emerging boundaries of rule. It was, therefore, not astonishing to hear Palestinians declare that their supposed "infiltrations" and "terrorism" were efforts to cross borders that had, in a sense, crossed *them*.[6]

I submit that in the continual act of reiterating these actions as dangers to their *national* security, the Jewish state began to legitimate its sole hold over segments of the city emptied of their Arab populations. West Jerusalem, by virtue of having to be protected from an "external" threat, progressively became regarded by Israeli Jews and supporters internationally as self-evidently *Israeli* national space. This cartographic imagination

4. Morris (1997) has written a book with the term "Arab infiltration" used in the title. Throughout the book he refers to the Palestinian crossings of the armistice line as "marauding," as if those who had been ethnically cleansed were engaged in pillaging property that did not belong to them. For an account that deploys some of the same language but is much more critical of Israeli policy with regard to the Palestinian refugees, see Segev (1986, 43–67).

5. See UN Security Council document S/PV. 630, 27 October 1953 Appendix II (unispal.un.org/UNISPAL.NSF/0/017EEFB458011C9D05256722005E5499).

6. "We didn't cross the border, the border crossed us," is a poignant slogan of immigrant rights activists in the United States.

could more easily be naturalized and normalized if Palestinian exiles remained absent and excluded. Such are the potent ways in which national boundaries routinely become taken for granted and fixed, from the border between the United States and Mexico to those of Palestine/Israel.[7]

During the years the city was divided between east and west, Israeli authorities reconfigured the Baramki's house discursively no less than physically. With its owners unable to return to it and the structure redefined as Israeli "state property," the locale began to acquire meanings that made sense to those who controlled it. In the parlance of Israelis on the west side, the home was not even a home but simply the "Tourjeman Army Post." This military emplacement's significance was bound up with the contiguous Mandelbaum Gate complex, which served as the one crossing point—or, at least the one licit crossing point—between West Jerusalem and East Jerusalem from 1948 to 1967.[8] The ironies that saturate the city are innumerable. Few, however, are as peculiar as the fact that an appropriated Palestinian dwelling was employed for nearly two decades to help foreclose the return of Palestinian refugees to other familial places.

MEMORIES OF WAITING

I frequently conducted interviews with those expelled from West Jerusalem in the East Jerusalem dwellings where they now resided.[9] Their current residences were rarely as spacious as those they lost and some

7. In the wake of the 1948 War, there emerged a fairly broad global consensus in support of the right of Palestinian refugees to return. However, the Israeli government has refused since its inception to accept this principle or permit significant numbers to come back. This principle was enshrined in the December, 1948 UN General Assembly Resolution 194. It is still overwhelmingly acknowledged among UN member states, whose recent votes in favor of the right of return include nearly every country in the world.

8. This point was the place from which, in accord with the 1949 Armistice Agreement, Israelis could travel to the Hebrew University campus on Mount Scopus and international travelers could move from one side of the city to the other.

9. Several of the neighborhoods of what today is known as "East Jerusalem" were not considered to be part of Jerusalem as it was defined before 1967.

even ended up in concrete hovels in Jerusalem area refugee camps. During these conversations it was not uncommon for these men and women to point to the west side, in the direction of commandeered properties that sometimes were just a kilometer or two away. Though I came to see commonalities among diverse experiences of exile, there always seemed something especially haunting about the travails of the Baramkis. Unlike nearly every other displaced family, they had the dubious privilege of being able to observe their home across the city's militarized no-man's-land from 1948 to 1967.

Gabi Baramki remembered ascending seven flights of steps to the top of the East Jerusalem YMCA, the tallest building on the east side and situated not 50 meters from the frontier. From this vantage he, his father, and occasionally other family members could gaze down and assess the condition of their war-ravaged home. But having the opportunity to reconnect visually with the structure, he said, did not assuage the uncertainty born of being separated from it.

The majority of exiles, unable to see their properties across the borderlands, relied on other sources of information about these homes' fate. Nine of the thirty-eight Palestinians I interviewed for this chapter recalled how rumors began to seep across the border concerning the state of their neighborhoods and familial sites. Such news came very sparingly and was usually carried by international travelers, typically Christian tourists and pilgrims, who were permitted to cross through the Mandelbaum Gate checkpoint. What the displaced of the east side were told suggested that their homes were not waiting still and untouched for their eventual homecoming.

Mariam, a Christian in her late seventies, fled the Qatamon quarter on the west side with her parents and brother in the first few weeks of 1948. By then already a young woman, she described the trepidation she and her kin felt amid the indiscriminate violence of the late Mandate years. Having found refuge in East Jerusalem like hundreds of other families, uncertainty gripped them as they waited to return.

We heard that more and more [Jewish immigrants to Israel] were coming and that they were being put in our homes. The Jordanians kept giving us a "morphine," telling us that we would go back and that they would make sure.[10]

Nearly every displaced individual with whom I spoke told me that in the months and even years after their flight, they were confident that they would someday return. But any optimism began to evaporate the longer they remained in exile. Questions of *when* they would go back gradually became questions of *if.* When I asked Gabi about his expectations of doing so he was silent for a few moments.

"Well, by the 60s it was clear to me that if we were ever going to get it back [the home], it would not be in his [father's] time."

Though from the top of the East Jerusalem YMCA the family could stand just meters from their property, they and their home lay on either side of a political abyss. Like other Palestinians, the Baramkis could more easily travel to Baghdad, Beirut, or Boston than return to their home, visible just a stone's throw away across Jerusalem's fractured landscape.

MAKING JERUSALEM "WHOLE"

The physical rupture Jerusalem had known for nineteen years ended suddenly in June 1967. In the early days of that month, Israeli forces conquered East Jerusalem in rapid fashion. Jerusalem, according to Israeli officialdom, had now been "liberated" and "reunified." Jordan's authoritarian rule was replaced by Israeli military occupation. The Jewish state was now in possession of the entirety of this urban center as well as the whole of historic Palestine. The victory also put them in control of an additional one million Palestinians in the West Bank and Gaza

---

10. The well-documented authoritarian character of the Jordanian regime, along with the widely held belief among Jerusalemites that the monarchy had secretly conspired with the Israelis in 1948 to split the land that was to become a Palestinian state, left few with any confidence that the Jordanian government had the interests of the Palestinian refugees at heart.

Strip, including approximately 60–65,000 Palestinian residents of East Jerusalem.[11]

Within a few weeks of the war's end, and after some internal debate, the new occupiers brought down the physical barrier between east and west. Tens of thousands hastily traveled to the sector of the city foreclosed to them for nearly two decades. Palestinians who had waited to return made their way back to their former neighborhoods, villages, and homes. Israeli Jews streamed to the Western Wall and the Jewish Quarter of the Old City. However, the emerging spatial realities and the extension of Israeli governance over all of Jerusalem would mean very different things for each national community.

The new occupiers began to restore areas of East Jerusalem from which about 1,500 to 2,000 Jews had fled or been evicted during the fighting of 1948. But the roughly 750,000 Palestinians who lost homes in West Jerusalem and elsewhere throughout the country encountered Israeli legal barriers that would preclude them from reclaiming their properties. More than 70 percent of the Arab exiles and refugees I interviewed (26 of 38) related that, in the wake of the war, they felt a rekindled hope that they might now repossess their homes. None of them had, after all, repudiated their rights to them. However, they usually discovered that though their dwellings were still there, they had been altered in discernible ways.

Nearly every interviewee recounted how their former neighborhoods were at once familiar and foreign. As exiles moved through parts of the city they had not seen since the late 1940s, they found that Arabic was all but absent from the daily life of the west side. Hebrew enveloped public space and conversations; it was inscribed on street signs, awnings above businesses, and most everywhere else. The language had acquired a nation-state and by the late 1960s had been melded to an emerging colonial urbanism that I began to detail in Chapter 2.

---

11. Tens of thousands more Palestinians from the West Bank and Syrian Druze from the illegally occupied Golan Heights were expelled from their respective lands during the 1967 War. See the Arab Centre for Human Rights in the Golan Heights (2007).

The June 1967 War had eventuated in Jerusalem's spatial unification in some respects, but the city remained deeply fractured in other ways. Sustaining an order of division and segregation in a "reunified" city has been among Israel's chief dilemmas in Jerusalem. Doing so has necessitated imposing onto the newly occupied territories particular legal strictures already in existence within Israel's internationally recognized borders. These laws and policies made large areas of East Jerusalem off limits to Arab Christians and Muslims just as the majority of West Jerusalem had become since 1948. As I have argued in previous chapters, these dictates have proven to be distinctly colonial in character rather than simply illiberal because the properties designated as Israeli "state land" (and thus reserved for the exclusive use and benefit of Israeli Jews only) had been overwhelmingly appropriated from those now excluded from them.

I began to reside in the city about three decades into Israel's military occupation of the east side. Within the first few weeks of my arrival it was evident that there were not simply stark walls of concrete and barbed wire that separated Arabs and Jews but also more subtle, sometimes imperceptible bureaucratic and legal divides. Palestinians classified as "absentee" might well be able to travel back to their homes and neighborhoods in the "reunified" city as visitors, but Israeli authorities barred them from reclaiming these properties. Their ownership was and continues to be unrecognized by Israel. Old keys have been of no value in opening present-day doors and gates. British Mandate or Ottoman-era deeds have been ineffectual in pushing forward claims to lost homes and lands.

The Baramkis, too, crossed over the former frontier with their keys and deeds soon after the end of the fighting to repossess their badly damaged property. But when they arrived and tried to access the home, having waded through the ruins of war that littered the front yard, Israeli military personnel precluded them from entering. According to Gabi and other family members, officials refused to relinquish the home that day and in later attempts, declaring alternately that it was still required for purposes of (Israeli) "security," that it was in need of repair and thus a physical hazard, and finally that the family members were not the rightful owners but rather "absentees" and "foreigners."

Andoni Baramki hired an Israeli lawyer to fight his claim, but some among his kin described the skepticism they felt about the prospects of recovering the home through these or any other means. Gabi related to me the impact on his father of being defined in a sense out of legal existence:

> You know, this question of being defined "absent" [by the Israeli Government] is unbelievable. Imagine, my father at the time [1967 and 1968], a seventy-year-old person going to the Israelis and telling them, "here I am now and I want my property," and them telling him that, "no, you are an 'absentee.'" And he said, "How am I absent?" He could not understand how he was absent and present at the same time.

Israel never did permit Andoni Baramki to set foot in his home again, and he died an exile in September 1972.

THE DISCURSIVE CONSTRUCTION OF A REGIME OF POWER

Within weeks of conquering East Jerusalem, the new occupiers began to radically alter boundaries, laws, currencies, and political hierarchies. Palestinian Jerusalemites who came under Israeli colonial control in 1967 were transformed almost overnight from citizens of the Jordanian state into what the new rulers referred to as "permanent residents" of the "reunified" city.[12] I will say more about these changes in later chapters. For now, it is worth noting one key alteration, namely, the manner in which Israeli authorities unilaterally redrew Jerusalem's borders in the weeks after the Six-Day War. This spatial reconfiguration inflated the area of East Jerusalem by a factor of more than ten, from 6 square kilometers under the Jordanian regime to about 70 square kilometers. Thousands of acres of Palestinian land that had never been regarded by Israelis or Palestinians as "Jerusalem" were incorporated within a newly comprised urban space,

---

12. Palestinian East Jerusalemites recognized as "permanent residents" of the city were given a different (and slightly higher) status than those living in the rest of the West Bank and the Gaza Strip. But their status is different still from Palestinians with Israeli citizenship. They possess a kind of "in-betweenness" of rights.

which was then claimed exclusively by the Jewish state.[13] Old borders and dividing lines were eliminated and new ones arose in their place.

These arbitrarily imposed municipal lines have paradoxically contained within them what Israel projected as the Jewish people's "eternal" and "immutable" capital. Jerusalem has, in fact, become for significant numbers of Israeli Jews and Zionists abroad anything the Israelis government ment declares that it is—historically, culturally, and cartographically. In the next few sections of this chapter, I detail some of the multiple ways these representations have been advanced at memorial sites. I contend that the investment in creating so many places where nationalist ideology is ceaselessly projected is attributable in part to the fact that more than half of the "Jerusalem" that Israel claims exclusive right to (70 of its 125 square kilometers) is regarded by the United Nations to be held in violation of international law.

DOMINATION ON DISPLAY

"Reunifying" Jerusalem meant sweeping away concrete walls, barbed wire fences, mines, and military emplacements along the former frontier in the months after the 1967 War. But it has also entailed a perpetual ideological struggle, a "cleaning up" of history. Israeli authorities have projected particular portrayals of Jerusalem through a range of cultural technologies. Not least among these are nationalist memorials and I turn now to a close reading of one such site.

As the Jewish state moved to eliminate the physical partition between east and west, the Baramki home/Tourjeman Post, alone among the nineteen former Israeli military border posts, was kept intact. The Israeli deputy mayor of Jerusalem in the 1970s, Meron Benvenisti, has recounted how officials retained this locale, as he curiously put it, "for posterity" (1976, 125). Just what meanings this edifice was meant to convey for future generations was not entirely evident at the time. However, by the 1980s it became

---

13. See Badil (2005), Dumper (1997), and Kaminkar (1997) for more on the spatial reconfiguration of the city in the wake of the 1967 War.

clear that the property was to function in the service of legitimating Israeli rule over all parts of the city and, indeed, throughout the country.

Benvenisti has been a prominent critic of his government's human rights abuses against the Palestinians for years. However, as I also detail in chapter 4, his description of Israel's transformation of Jerusalem has at times been remarkably akin to more conventional Zionist accounts. For example, the former deputy mayor has been silent in his major writings about what a historian as knowledgeable as he must surely know: namely, that the site he refers to as "the former Tourjeman Army Post" was constituted within the Baramkis' confiscated home. I submit that this omission is representative of the Israeli state's efforts to efface in various ways the claims of exiled Palestinian families in the telling of the Jewish state's "reunification" narrative.

Precluded from entering their property since 1948, Andoni's descendants were finally permitted to do so in the early 1980s. However, the circumstances were for them as odd as they were agonizing. In 1983 Israeli authorities unilaterally changed the home's status once again. Without notice or the owner's permission, they transformed the former "Tourjeman Post" into what they termed the "Tourjeman Post *Museum.*" I will return to the Baramkis' encounters with this cultural site later in the chapter. First, however, I want to analyze the ideological and mythic potency this locale has held and the ways it has served as a metaphor for Israeli colonial power.[14]

14. This chapter focuses on the first representational space housed in the Baramki home, the Tourjeman Post Museum (1983–1999). I discuss very little this institution's successor, the Museum on the Seam, whose doors were opened around 2000, but I will do so in an upcoming publication. Because I am focusing in this chapter on a former cultural space, I refer to the Tourjeman Post Museum in the past tense even though the property itself is still there. For now let me indicate the discursive continuity of the two institutions by citing a prominent message from the current one's literature: "Museum on the Seam is . . . located in *an historical building that served as a military outpost between the wars*, bordering Jerusalem's old city. A tour of the museum is a unique experience that provides the visitors with *a new outlook on reality*" (2013; http://shop.mots.org.il/about-the-museum). Emphasis mine. Accessed January 10, 2014.

THE SPECTER OF THE BORDER: YEARNING AND DENIAL

The creators of the Tourjeman Post Museum utilized the former home's interior and exterior in the service of projecting Jerusalem as the exclusive province of the Jewish people. But as is generally true of memorial sites, it was also this structure's whereabouts that provided a commanding ideological function. These various dimensions—the interior, the exterior, and the location—are mutually informing and have interacted dialectically in helping to project Israel's assertions of "reunification" and "liberation."

As suggested above, the importance the Baramki home came to acquire in the battle for Jerusalem was accidental. Those lines of separation have since given way to different borders and spatial divisions. Yet, decades after the home-turned–military post ceased to guard any physical frontier, Israeli officials have deployed it as a sort of sentinel of "truth," protecting a specific representation of the city's history. The structure continually evokes not simply the former divide but a highly selective reading of it.

For Israeli opinion as well as that of its powerful backers abroad, dominant notions about Jerusalem have had to be, in a sense, "educated." It is not a meager task to overcome the very broad international consensus that recognizes Israeli rule over East Jerusalem to be illegal. I witnessed the campaign to counter this consensus in visits to more than a dozen of Israel's primary memorial sites over several years in the late 1990s and 2000s.[15] One crucial way in which this is done is by representing the age of the fractured city as one of (Israeli) national distress and denial. This was a period when Israeli Jews were precluded from visiting religious sites on the east side, particularly the Western Wall. The frontier certainly produced yearning among Israelis for such realms. But remembering the former divide solely in this way, infusing the Baramkis' home and the location it marks with only these understandings, is ideological as much for what is not acknowledged as what is.

15. They include Ammunition Hill, the Tourjeman Post Museum, the Museum on the Seam, Museum of the Underground, Memorial to the Defenders of the Jewish Quarter, and the Tower of David Museum.

EXTERIORS AND FACADES

Bound up inextricably with the significance of the Baramki home's location along the former divide have been the layered meanings attributed to the changes its exterior underwent between 1948 and 1967. These alterations are more easily observable than the spectral border, for they remain. However, they are no less the product of the colonial and nationalist imagination. The capacity of the Baramki home to advance messages convenient to Israel's dominant ways of remembering the border is the product of two sets of changes the property underwent in its use as a military outpost.

The first of these were implemented by the Israelis for purposes of "national defense" and "security." The alterations to the structure in its transition from familial place to military post included the elimination of precisely those dimensions most *familial*, starting, of course, with the Palestinians who once resided there. Structurally these changes involved the filling in of the home's arched windows to create turrets, the sealing of entranceways and doors, and the elimination of other components of a standard domestic realm.

The second were the hits and damage the structure sustained by Jordanian fire, resulting in its pockmarked and bullet-ridden façade. Those who sought to transform this former home from a military emplacement into a site for colonial knowledge production wished to mobilize these physical scars of battle and make them, in a sense, "speak" in ways that have legitimated the Jewish state's control over the entirety of Jerusalem. The home's mangled form became in many ways its content. The damage it sustained as an outpost guarding the budding state was also substantial enough to have eroded its appearance as a family home.

As one reads the structure's façade and confronts the discursive and contextual "setup" that passersby and visitors to the museum are provided, it is productive to consider some of the varied meanings of "façade." The term relates both to architecture (the primary, exterior face of a building) and to ideology (a form of concealment, false appearance, or mystification). I argue that Israeli authorities have used the former home's varied exterior wounds of war like colors on an ideological palette. These alterations and the meanings given to them have been mobilized to help assemble a standard, post-1967 tale convenient to Israeli control over Jerusalem. This account asserts that the defenders of the new state were, in those turbulent years, endlessly under mortal threat from "the Arabs," ceaselessly in a defensive posture. Those scars of war and the beleaguered state they are meant to point to are utilized to advance the idea that these conditions represented an existential threat to the Jewish state and, thus, had to be ended. This could only be done by conquering the city's east side.

The façade also serves to conceal, since its appearance cannot readily reveal the violence the Israeli state used against those on the other side of the divide. Traces of *that* violence remain in the form of bullet holes on East Jerusalem homes and buildings near the border. They can be observed in the remains of structures partly or wholly destroyed by Israeli forces before and after 1967. They include the human losses among Palestinian families little mentioned in this and other similar memorials. The face of the Baramki home diverts attention away from that aggression and the military occupation established in the wake of 1967, as well.

6. The Adoni Baramki home in 1999 in its closing days as the Israeli Tourjeman Post Museum.

INTERIORS: THE PRODUCTION OF VALOR

The convergence of meanings associated with the Baramki home's damaged exterior and its location along the former dividing line were melded with more explicit textual assertions advanced within. The Tourjeman Post Museum's interior representational spaces included the primary exhibit hall on the second floor and other smaller exhibits throughout the structure. The production value of this museum/memorial was, I always thought, generally quite mediocre. Yet, I came to see how its images and texts fairly effectively communicated an overarching story about Jerusalem. That narrative was encapsulated by the words inscribed on a plaque next to the front entrance, which read in English and Hebrew: "JERUSALEM—A DIVIDED CITY REUNITED."

To enter this museum was to move into a realm where a teleological tale was unfurled, a story with a beginning and an end. The chronicle concludes not simply with the Jewish state's liberation of the city in 1967 but with a kind of "end of history" restoration of Jerusalem to its natural, divinely designed equilibrium. One might expect, therefore, that the beginning of the story told here would be God's seminal bequest of Jerusalem to the Jewish people. But in fact, while exhibits referenced divine authority and the sacred from time to time, the historical portrayal began with the "divided city" in 1948.

The injustice of spatial division was communicated in the primary exhibit, which displayed a range of pictures of the former physical frontier. But it was not that Palestinians and Israelis were divided during those years that this and other memorials portray as objectionable. There is next to no mention of Palestinians throughout the museum. At issue was the Jewish people's distance from that said to belong to them eternally. Throughout the exhibit there were several black-and-white photos of concrete walls and hazardous minefields. Images of Israelis navigating walls and barbed wire were displayed along with those that depicted West Jerusalem's population under siege, sometimes living along that dangerous border. However, beginnings and origins are tricky things, constructed as they frequently are in the cauldron of dominance. Given the imperatives of Israeli rule in Jerusalem, it might well come as little surprise that the museum's description of this site did not begin with the appropriation of the Baramkis' home. Nowhere in this memorial is Palestinian ownership acknowledged. Further, the manner in which its familial past was effaced reveals much about Israeli colonial knowledge production and its capacity to obfuscate as much as simply erase and negate.

In consistently scripted brochures provided to visitors and exhibit text, a standard story of the site's beginnings is provided. It typically begins thusly: "The Tourjeman House was built in 1932 by the Arab architect Antony [sic] Baramki."[16] Though the family's name is occasionally mentioned (as it is here), nowhere does it acknowledge that the "house" was actually *owned* by the Baramkis and not, as is suggested, by an individual or family named "Tourjeman." The "Tourjeman house" is used to denote what the museum asserted was "the former owner of the land, Hasan Bek Tourjeman [sic]." Gabi Baramki told me that his father had purchased the plot on which this dwelling was built from a Palestinian man named "Tourjman" but that the latter neither owned nor lived in the home.[17] The Baramkis' specific familial connections are further negated by descriptions of the property as a "fort." In presenting the origins of the structure in this manner its creators muddy both its Palestinian and familial past. Families, after all, do not typically reside in "forts."

In contextualizing this edifice within the city's war-scarred landscape, nothing is said about the primary reason for these hostilities then or since: namely, the fact that, like the Baramkis, hundreds of thousands of other Palestinians were driven from their homes and precluded from returning. They and their descendants now number over 5 million people but do not rate a sentence at this cultural site or any other major Israeli memorial in the city that I was able to find.

Just as the damage done to the home's exterior is deployed to emphasize the violence visited on Israelis, the museum's exhibits portray the

16. These quotes are taken from a brochure I was given during my first visit to the Tourjeman Post Museum in the mid-1990s.

17. I was not able to learn why or when exactly Israeli officials began to use the appellation "Tourjeman" to refer to the location. The fact that there are also Israeli Jewish families with a similar name is the source of further confusion.

Jewish state as the victim of "terrorism" and aggression, never as the initiator of violence. Obscuring the ways the home was occupied in the first place provide a kind of ideological scaffolding. It is through these representations of the former city and the frontier that ran through it that the trope of Israeli valor and victimhood are emboldened. If, however, this locale of supposed defense were to be revealed to have been stolen, and if the Baramkis' dispossession and suffering were to be understood to be emblematic rather than as simply anecdotal, the Zionist nation-building project might begin to look rather less heroic to those who visit memorials such as this one.

EXHIBITING ISRAEL'S "PURITY OF ARMS"

The part of the home that had served as bedrooms on the Baramkis' second floor was transformed into one dimly lit gallery. This the museum termed "the main exhibition hall," and it resembled nothing like a familial space. Spartan, dark, and austere—the area announced itself as the inside of a former military post. The absence of windows here and throughout the structure, I always felt, was among the most powerful ways this atmosphere was produced. Those who moved through the interior of the edifice had only the narrow apertures of the turrets to glimpse outward. Looking for traces of the Arab residents of this home on the second floor was, I found, all but impossible.

Consuming the exposed brick walls was a collection of images and artifacts displayed with accompanying text. But as with the museum brochures and literature, the exhibit's narrative was only in English and Hebrew and not in Arabic, the primary language of nearly 40 percent of the city's inhabitants. In light of just this one seemingly simple omission (reproduced at most other Israeli memorials), it was possible to understand for whom these nationalist assertions were meant, to whom they spoke.

Throughout this locale there were pervasive representations of militarism and military triumph. Israeli prowess was melded to an innocence and righteousness that was found at a range of memorials and museums in the city and beyond. This professed convergence has been described

7. The scarred façade of the former Baramki home, 1999. Note the original window filled in with concrete after the Israeli government turned the structure into the Tourjeman Army Post in 1948.

in official Israeli documents (military and civilian) as a "purity of arms" (*tohar haneshek*). This, the state has declared, is part of its army's code of ethics, which it claims draws from "the tradition of the Jewish People throughout their history." Here again one can see Israeli officials' efforts to merge and blend the Jewish state with "the Jewish people." This is done in a way that is typical of myth making and mythologies, meant to "evaporate history," in the words of Barthes (1957). But the idea that the Israeli Defense Force (IDF) only deploy violence as a last resort or in strictly defensive postures has been critiqued by innumerable Israeli scholars and human rights organizations.[18] The content of the Tourjeman Post Museum's exhibits and the more implicit messages attributed to the partially wrecked exterior bolster this projection of a "purity of arms," of victimhood, and of valor.

The exhibit area with its exposed brick walls and filled-in windows brought together several exemplary items of military culture. A range of guns, mortars, and other weapons used during the 1948 and 1967 wars were displayed. These purported ornaments of defense were interspersed with sprays of Israeli flags, plaques with the insignia of IDF brigades, and pictures and names of Israeli soldiers fallen in battle. All of these elements converged to help constitute a broader narrative of sacrifice of these young men. These soldiers' deaths were acknowledged at this memorial and at others, too. Their actions in battle were dealt with uncritically and their humanity recognized and captured. This is done even more substantially at the more expansive memorial in East Jerusalem that Israeli officials have named Ammunition Hill. Here every one of the Israeli soldiers fallen in battle is identified and accounted for—names, faces, and personal details were provided. Personal letters of soldiers killed during the 1967 War were exhibited, along with their poems and art work.

But there was no specific mention of Jordanians and Palestinians— civilians or soldiers—lost in the course of hostilities. There were a few

---

18. See Ben-Ami's (2007) description of the series of massacres Zionist forces committed against Palestinian civilians in 1948. See as well Stanley Cohen's (2001) critique of Israel's "purity of arms" discourse.

photographs from several meters away of dead Jordanian soldiers along the streets of East Jerusalem. But these bodies were distant textually as well as visually: unnamed, obscure, and anonymous. They were the corpses of those who menaced the Israeli people, who threatened to destroy the Jewish state. Indeed, they were little more than "terrorist" bodies. Though more than 600 of the 850 people killed during the 1967 War for Jerusalem were Palestinians and Jordanians, those losses are negated at nearly every one of the major Israeli memorial sites in the city.[19]

The Tourjeman Post Museum invited visitors to use the actual physical structure of this former outpost to more fully grasp its principal assertions. All were invited to gaze out from the thin openings that once served as turrets, supplanting the windows of a family home. Here, during the months and years of the divided city, Israeli soldiers peered out at a threatening enemy across the no-man's-land. Looking out across this spectral landscape, it was possible to imagine the terrain of the divided city but as Jerusalem's "liberators" once did.

From this vantage, Israeli nationalist myths that inform this narrative were meant to ossify into a kind of self-evident "historical truth," one unencumbered by the voices of the vanquished. Here, one looked out not only through this narrowed aperture but also through a limited and circumscribed discursive and historical purview. From this location—spatial and ideological—one could understand Jerusalem's history, in a sense, through the sights of an Israeli gun—not looking down its barrel.

A vital point about the production of the past revealed at the Tourjeman Post Museum was that, in exploring the dimensions of a national landscape, one never simply "sees" or observes outside of a particularly crafted context, one that all too often presents a set of axiomatic givens. In an analysis of the vibrancy of ideological work, Slavoj Zizek (1994) notes:

One of the fundamental strategies of ideology is the reference to some self-evidence—"Look, you can see for yourself how things are!" "Let the

---

19. This number is drawn from a former Israeli deputy mayor's estimate of the war victims. See Benvenisti (1976, 328–329).

facts speak for themselves" is perhaps the arch statement of ideology—
the point being, precisely, that facts *never* "speak for themselves" but are
always *made to speak* by a network of discursive devices. (11)

These "devices," these "networks" have been critical to Israeli colonial knowledge production, most powerfully I submit in Jerusalem. What
successive Israeli governments have not wished visitors to come to terms
with, either at this site or in the city more generally, is the reality that when
we look at this former house, its crumbling exterior, and the representations articulated through its physical characteristics, we "see" these things
against the background of a "discursively pre-constructed space" (ibid.).

THE BARAMKIS RETURN
(DURING NORMAL BUSINESS HOURS)

The descendants of Andoni Baramki described feeling stunned when
word reached them that Israel had changed their property into a museum.
They had had no sense that this was in the works and consequently were
unable to contest this transformation. Gabi and other family members
related how these reconfigurations not only undermined their effort to
retrieve it but also underscored the Jewish state's refusal to recognize their
connections and rights to this property.

"How did you hear about the museum?" I asked Gabi.

"There was an article in the Israeli press right," he said, looking around
on his desk for the clipping he had saved to show me.

And they wrote that I refused to come to "the opening." Well, I wasn't
even *told* that it would become this museum—not that I would have *considered* attending their "opening." But, you know, they did not even have
the *decency* to inform us that they were making this museum.

It was only after the conversion of the property into a Zionist memorial that the Baramkis were able to access it for the first time since 1948.
Family members, including Gabi, went back on various occasions, not all
at once. Some expressed feeling true ambivalence about returning at all,

and one member shared that he even considered getting out of line as he neared the entrance of the museum. There was curiosity and a real desire to return to their property, but there was also a great sadness and disgust that accompanied this journey back.

A younger member of the Baramki kin, a man in his twenties, related his experience visiting the former home. He told me how he had intended to ignore any Israeli worker at this site and refuse to recognize their authority. The young man walked up the front steps, through the entrance, and moved forthrightly past the place where visitors were required to purchase tickets. Invariably, a staff member came from behind the ticket table after calling to the Palestinian several times. The employee instructed him that he needed to buy a ticket to enter the museum. But the young Baramki became even more steadfast and asserted angrily, his voice rising, that this was his family's home and that he refused to buy entry into it. The employee, at first unfazed by the irony of the circumstances or perhaps incredulous that the building had ever been a home, insisted that he— "like all other visitors"—had to buy a ticket. A short standoff ensued after which the fee was finally waived and the descendent of the home's builder and owner entered.

This encounter in the foyer represented for the Baramkis and their friends a moment of proud refusal. Several family members told me a version of the story on a range of occasions and it was usually recounted with levity and a degree of discernible pride. It seemed to embolden them and I could understand why. But the confrontation ultimately symbolized the limits of Palestinian resistance as well as the enduring strength of Israeli colonialism. Across Jerusalem and elsewhere, in an age of layer upon layer of checkpoints and prodigious concrete walls that envelop this urban center, Palestinians may sometimes enter the city they refer to as their "home." They have, at times, been able to assert that Jerusalem is their national capital and have built a broad international consensus for this claim among governments the world over. Occasionally they have won modest victories by subverting the rules and regulations of military occupation. Ultimately, however, they have been compelled to do so within a political and spatial arrangement organized to facilitate Israeli dominance in the city.

When the young Baramki man demanded access to his family's home, he was still compelled to pass through Israeli gatekeepers during prescribed business hours. Had the museum employees wished to, they could have called the army or police and had him removed by force. In other words, whether with regard to space or memory, those who have had the greatest capacity to project Jerusalem since 1948 have overwhelmingly determined who is permitted access and, indeed, what the price of entry shall be.

Gabi spoke to me about his first visit to the home after thirty-five years. When I asked him what it was like, he replied, almost inaudibly, "It was awful." He reclined into silence for a moment in his enormous leather armchair and then continued, "It was just a shell of what I remember, just a shell." Relating his walk through the home for the first time in nearly four decades, the son of the architect recounted feeling curiosity, powerlessness, and anger all at once.

His dismay at the state of the property, he explained, was intensified with each discovery of how those who had built the museum had stripped it of its domestic dimensions and the aesthetics his father had created. Gabi searched for traces of his family's past using the coordinates of memory. But he described how those attempts were, in a sense, "jammed" by alterations to the home's original design, by the new meanings etched, palimpsest-like, on and over the property.

Patterned tile floors he had remembered had been damaged, covered over, or sometimes ripped up and taken away. He spoke repeatedly about the arched windows, now filled in with concrete, eliminating all but a thin sliver of natural light. The foyer was where museum officials placed a ticket booth and sold postcards and literature about the history of this locale as an Israeli military emplacement. The former dining room was converted into what looked to be a conference room, illuminated by long, uncovered fluorescent lights hanging incongruously from the high vaulted ceilings.

"They destroyed the inside like the outside," he lamented.

A "CACOPHONY" OF IMAGES

While living in Jerusalem, I often had occasion to pass the Baramki home. It became for me a complex and intricate semiotic locale. I knew of the structure's varied historical uses as a home, a military emplacement, and now a memorial. I tried to reconcile and disentangle the contradictory meanings that converged here along the former border, to see and recognize the original familial place, and its layered meanings. The site was reminiscent of an image I had come across at about that time, Salvador Dali's *Slave Market with the Disappearing Bust of Voltaire*. This painting depicts the revolutionary Voltaire's head as composed of two slave merchants in a market. In this single, shifting image contradictory notions and images are almost parasitically bound up together: some opposed to slavery and others as one of its organizing institutions. These divergent elements merge in the same representation, in a sense battling it out for visual superiority.

Gazing at the Tourjeman Post Museum produced a similar tension. If images were sounds, the structure would have produced a noisy cacophony of meaning. But as is true of so many other contexts in innumerable other cities, without knowledge of the Baramkis' histories of loss, this locale would have represented a much less confusing visual reality. It might well have appeared a perfectly innocent, even noble project of remembrance, drawing as it did on the discourse of "unity" as against "division," liberation as against the denial of rights. With a measure of awareness about its Palestinian pasts, though, its supposed harmony of meaning is fractured. One can discern the edifice as being—or having been—a home, a former army emplacement, and a monument to Israeli valor, but never all at once.

I visited the Tourjeman Post Museum on six or seven occasions over three years and by doing so was able to observe Israeli nationalism continually in production. On one outing in 1998, I observed a rotund middle-aged man dashing nervously around the building's first floor. He had a lengthy beard, carried what looked to be a pistol in a holster, and wore a knitted skullcap common among right-wing religious Zionists. A group of four or five adults soon joined him and he began to show them around, almost as though it were his private residence. The man spoke in English, pointing out features of the edifice that had nothing to do with its history as a home. Drawing from elements of the former "fort," he provided a narrative one might find reiterated in official Israeli government pronouncements.

This visitor wove into his presentation events in Jerusalem said to have taken place in biblical times, and then he would dart back to the city's present period. He compared, for instance, the building record of Herod the Great two thousand years ago with that of then mayor of Jerusalem Ehud Olmert. King David and the Second Temple were cited and then it was back to Arafat, King Hussein, and "the Arabs." I wondered if this man had even heard that this structure had been appropriated from a Palestinian family. I shadowed the group a bit, listening and gradually drawing closer. Eventually, I began to politely ask questions. The guide welcomed my queries. I believe he read me as an American neophyte discovering my own roots in "the land of Israel." We began a friendly conversation about our respective stays in Jerusalem during the era of the withering Oslo Accords, as his colleagues drifted off to explore other parts of the museum.

My new acquaintance, a doctor from Miami who spent half of the year on a Jewish settlement and half the year in Florida, described the fear he and his wife felt that "Judea and Samaria" (biblical expressions for the West Bank) would be given back to "the Arabs." Then, as if sharing a crucial secret that would elevate my consciousness to a new level, he remarked: "You know, the Jews are not returning to this land. This is what the Arabs don't understand. We're not *returning* here—we never left! We never left!"

The transhistorical "we," "the Arabs," and "the Jewish people" were not simply the expressions of one American-born settler. They aid in forming fairly mainstream Israeli tropes vital to successive governments' assertions to the Jewish people's "eternal capital." The claim that Jews (or any people) represent an eternal or immutable community, any member of which could claim land or property where any other allegedly lived thousands of years ago, is as mythical as it is prevalent among Zionists in Israel and elsewhere.[20] During the course of my stay in Palestine/Israel, it was important

20. For a very mainstream assertion that draws on similarly essentialist and mythic notions, see Elie Wiesel's (2010) "Open Letter to Barack Obama" that appeared as a paid advertisement in the *Washington Post*. In it he states: "When a Jew visits Jerusalem for the first time, it is not the first time; it is a homecoming."

to remind myself that Israelis do not, alone, manufacture notions of time-less, communal essences and divine promises. However, what was and con-tinues to be distinctive about assertions of this sort are their use in the service of an ongoing military occupation over another population who does not wish to be ruled by them. Armed with these notions about divine directives and under military protection, wealthy U.S. citizens from Miami not only can relocate to Jewish settlements in East Jerusalem denied to Pal-estinians but also may even move unencumbered into and through the very homes of Arab exiles such as the Baramkis.

The declarations of the settler from Florida were mirrored in museum literature made available to visitors. One brochure produced and distrib-uted near the ticket counter as late as 1998 asserts:

> In weighing ostensibly competing claims to the city, it must be recalled that the Jewish people bases its claims to Jerusalem on a link which dates *back millennia* and to King David, and that there is no legal basis for the "historical" Palestinian claim that Jerusalem was their capital. Moreover, though the Palestinians may have a strong *emotional* attach-ment to Jerusalem, it does not necessarily follow that Jerusalem should become the capital of any Palestinian political entity.

A LANDSCAPE OF MEMORIALS

While traversing Jerusalem it was difficult to avoid Israeli memorials established since 1967. One of the first I ever took close notice of happened to sit outside the gates of my residence in the middle of the Palestinian neighborhood of Sheikh Jarrah in East Jerusalem. Incised on its six-by-four-foot marble face are the names in Hebrew of the seventy-nine Jews killed by Arab militants in April 1948 as their convoy passed through this neighborhood on their way to Mount Scopus. This place of remembrance, established by Israel in the years after it conquered East Jerusalem, partly obstructs the Palestinian home before which it was erected.

This is a memorial quite different than the Tourjeman Post Museum or Ammunition Hill, both less than 2 kilometers away. It does not posit an explicit narrative justifying Israeli military rule or conquest. It commemorates civilians killed in the course of war. But what I argue here is that there are broader realities that permeated Jerusalem that can make something as seemingly innocent as remembering victims of indefensible violence an implement in the service of colonial rule, as well. One of these realities is the wider context and conditions of military occupation under which this and similar memory-markers have been produced and positioned. In the process of creating such a memorial site in the location in which it is erected, the occupying power's presence in East Jerusalem might be said to be strengthened and legitimated—at least in the eyes of Israeli Jews.

A second dimension complicating the assignment of meaning at this and other locales relates to the question of silences that arose at the Tourjeman Post Museum. In a city in which civilians of all national and religious groups have been targeted and killed, whose suffering is regarded by dominant powers as worthy of acknowledgment and whose is unworthy?[21] How do deeply selective portrayals (even if what is mentioned in these representations is entirely factual) impact broader notions about who Jerusalem belongs to?

One day in 2003 as my Palestinian colleague, Najwa, and I walked by the black marble memorial on our way to the Old City, I stopped to make sense of it hoping that she might help me read the Hebrew inscription.

"Yalla! come on, keep moving!" she quipped, a bit irritated that I would have paid this memorial any notice. We had been talking earlier in the day about two teenage Palestinian boys shot by Israeli forces outside of Jerusalem, two of hundreds of Palestinian children and young adults killed by Israel during the Second Intifada. That broader context compelled her, it seemed, not to exhibit a shred of interest in the names etched on the marble monument. Najwa was as capable of empathy toward innocent victims of violence as anyone I have ever met, but her reluctance to engage this site and to help tell the story it sought to provide was not about the capacity for empathy. As Najwa explained:

---

21. For a splendid analysis of this subject in times of war, see Butler (2009).

Can you imagine how cluttered Jerusalem would be if we [Palestinians] were allowed to put up memorials for every massacre they [Israelis] do against us? You wouldn't be able to move three steps without tripping!

Palestinian efforts to construct memorials to those killed by Israel over the last several decades have been met unfailingly with opposition from those who rule the city. Even attempts to publicly remember those killed by Israeli soldiers and settlers not with permanent markers but at funeral processions have at times been violently suppressed. As the streets arose as theaters of remembrance, particularly during the two principal uprisings against military occupation (from around 1988–1994 and 2000–2005), funerals occasionally became sites where another Palestinian was killed as the forces of military authority fired on mourners.

In the last decade, there have been attempts by Palestinians, Israelis, and internationals to build a memorial to the Arab victims of the Deir Yassin massacre in 1948. Elements of the Zionist movement (primarily members of Menachem Begin's Irgun Tsvai Leumi) perpetrated this killing of more than 100 Palestinian civilians just a week before the Jewish civilians memorialized at the site in Sheikh Jarrah were gunned down. But Israeli officials have actively obstructed this and other efforts for years.

Long before the current struggles to secure a memorial for Deir Yassin, another battle arose over the politics of public remembrance. With the end of the 1967 War, Palestinians demanded to build a memorial to the hundreds killed during the conquest of the West Bank and the Gaza Strip. The storm not only unfolded between occupier and occupied but also, according to those involved, within Israeli ruling circles. This struggle over how suffering was to be acknowledged, if at all, underscored precisely the mechanisms of spatial and ideological regulation that I have been discussing throughout this chapter. But it also highlighted the fact that colonial power is never fully coherent internally and at times is riven with divisions from within.[22] Even when diverse factions in Israel hold to

22. See Cooper and Stoler (1997) and Comaroff (1997) for discussions of these dimensions of colonial authority.

fundamental principles like "unifying" Jerusalem, they are routinely split on how and through what means that should be accomplished.

In an interview in the 1980s with a reporter for the *New York Times*, former deputy mayor Meron Benvenisti describes the controversy. He asserts that in the face of enormous Israeli opposition to any Palestinian initiative to remember their dead, he was finally able to prevail upon his fellow officials to "allow" them to establish one unobtrusive memorial. As Benvenisti notes, he sold the idea by presenting it as in the best interests of continued Israeli control over East Jerusalem:

> I used the pacification terminology: you need to give these people [the Palestinians of Jerusalem] an outlet, a safety valve. If they want to demonstrate, this is where they will demonstrate. It is a good place because not many people can gather there. They cannot bring thousands there because it is a very steep slope, it was on a steep slope where hundreds could not gather. (quoted in Shipler 1986, 54)

The municipality eventually "permitted" the monument to be built, provided that it was in a "good place" where any oppositional content could be sufficiently contained. Acts of Palestinian public remembrance would be subject to the constraints of the regime that has sought to dissolve their national presence in the city with predictable outcomes. I visited this monument, which lies about 50 meters outside the northeast corner of the Old City, in the early 2000s. Three and a half decades after it was built, this thin, two-meter-high pylon of dubious stone had become dilapidated and rundown. The memorial rests, as the former deputy mayor states, in a seldom-traversed place under the shade of a small cluster of trees. No signage can be found in the vicinity that announces it, though there are directions pointing visitors to several other places in the city. The script on the pylon is faded and its surface area is not even substantial enough to inscribe the names of the hundreds of Palestinians killed during Israel's invasion in 1967. There is only a general reference to these victims and little else.

Palestinian residents I spoke with about this out of the way place normally gave me blank looks when I inquired about it. Few had even heard of it. And why, I thought, would they have visited or paid any attention to a memorial subject to the stipulations of the regime that daily violates their human rights? What, I thought, would Israeli Jews in Tel Aviv make of a memorial to their civilian dead created under conditions laid down by those who had conquered them?

CONCLUSION

In this chapter, I have examined a few of the critical ways in which memory and history are made usable for contemporary colonial governance in Jerusalem. Policing the past has allowed Israeli authorities to substantially dictate the present and, indeed, with hopes of molding the city's future. Just as the occupying power has regulated movement into and through the Baramki house, so too have the Tourjeman Post Museum and myriad other Israeli memorials served as gatekeepers of a different kind, repelling "infiltrations" of a narrative sort—what Foucault describes as "insurrections of subjugated knowledge" (1980, 81).

The Baramki home, designed by a deceased Arab architect of brilliance, has served since 1948 as a different architecture of knowledge production, a scaffolding of truth making, a foundation for ensuring that particular histories are present, while others remain invisible. The edifice continues to rest on the frontier of competing national imaginations, anchored in place but simultaneously on the moving edge of Israeli colonial power.

4

Arabs Out of Place

Colonizing the Old City

We particularly ask you—
When a thing continually occurs—
Not on that account to find it natural
Let nothing be called natural
In an age of bloody confusion
Ordered disorder, planned caprice,
And dehumanized humanity, lest all things
Be held unalterable!

—BERTOLT BRECHT,
The Exception and the Rule

Every year in Jerusalem since the advent of Israel's military occupation of East Jerusalem in 1967, the Jewish state has organized festive national rituals that celebrate the city's "liberation" and "reunification." When the occasion takes the form of a parade, as it does each spring on Jerusalem Day (*Yom Yerushalim*), the human thread of merriment winds through the segregated metropolitan area, provocatively entering Palestinian neighborhoods along the way. During these dramatic moments of national devotion, thousands of flag-waving marchers, consisting disproportionately of Israeli-Jewish men affiliated with right-wing religious parties and militant settler groups, lay claim to their "eternal capital." Through chants, songs, and aggressive gestures they express their commitment to protect a land bestowed upon them—and, them alone, they believe—by God. During this and other annual events, the processions usually conclude at the Western Wall (*HaKotel HaMa'aravi*) within the Old City, where Jewish clerical authorities (and not a few secular politicians) proclaim the "presence of God" has forever been found.

However, on these ritual occasions it is also possible to witness the no less ritualized forms of regulation and repression that Palestinians are subjected to throughout the city. Even more than on most other days, military authorities keep the Arab communities they rule behind cordons and checkpoints. Palestinian Christians and Muslims are precluded from moving through their own neighborhoods and to their shops and places of worship for several hours, lest they compromise even minimally the "security" of the Zionist revelers.[1]

This chapter explores myth, racism, and the production of urban space under Israeli colonial governance in Jerusalem. I examine these concerns with a special emphasis on the Western Wall area and the former Palestinian Moroccan Quarter, which lay before the Kotel for hundreds of years before Israel destroyed it in June 1967. Given its central role in the national rituals mentioned above, the Western Wall and its environs within the weathered Old City walls should not, I argue, be understood merely as a religious realm. Rather, it is one where biblical assertions, nationalist imaginations, and forms of colonial domination converge and merge.

I traversed the city on Jerusalem Day and other Israeli holidays on numerous occasions over the last fifteen years. And unlike Palestinians who have resided here their entire lives, as a U.S. citizen my freedom of movement was only vaguely constrained. I and other internationals could even have marched with the militant settlers if we had chosen (not a few of whom also hailed from the United States). During days like these it was not difficult to observe a phenomenon that has persistently haunted the construction of modern identities and the modern nation-state itself. Namely, the reality that peoples, territories, and conflicts that appear to possess—or are said to possess—the most "eternal" and "age-old" qualities are all too often of relatively recent invention.[2]

1. Israeli authorities apply even harsher travel restrictions on Palestinians each year on Yom Kippur. On this holiday the Jewish state has even turned off the traffic signals in Palestinian neighborhoods to adhere to Jewish religious rulings and traditions.

2. For more on this set of modern phenomena see Asad (1991, 1993), Hobsbawm and Ranger (1992), and Schama (1996).

Since the rise of the Zionist movement in the late 1800s, supporters of a Jewish state in Palestine have sought to establish an exclusive claim on this land based on a range of justifications. But what they have cited as the Jewish people's unique spiritual connection to *eretz yisrael* (the land of Israel) has been perhaps the most potent. The Israeli government frequently declares that this divine link stretches back without interruption at least 3,000 years to the age of King David, when this figure of biblical lore is said to have presided over a city of a few hundred acres in the shadow of the Mount of Olives.[3]

Making Jerusalem a metonym for Israel, much as "Washington" is for the U.S. federal government, has helped solidify the Jewish state's control over the entirety of the city. But doing so would be a rather more challenging task if Palestinian national claims to this urban center were permitted expression—which is why, as discussed in chapter 3, they usually are not. The checkpoints erected each year on Jerusalem Day that keep Palestinians at a distance are metaphors for the manner in which this occupying power has sought to keep alternate assertions to the city peripheral. This is no more evident than in Jerusalem's Old City, the symbolic, one-square-kilometer core that envelops the cornerstones of monotheism.

THE MOROCCAN QUARTER/WESTERN WALL PLAZA

The Western Wall, once the western enclosure of the Herodian Temple (or the Second Temple), has been a locale of Jewish worship for several hundred years.[4] Yet, like Jerusalem itself, this realm can hardly be said to

3. The supposed location of "the City of David," as it is referred to within the Israeli settler movement and particular currents of biblical archaeology, has for hundreds of years been the site of the Arab village of Silwan. Today the settler organization, Elad, with the aid of successive Israeli governments, has gradually taken over at least six acres of Silwan in the name of building a national park honoring the legacy of King David. For more on Israeli uses and inventions of a biblical past for contemporary political purposes, see Whitlam (1997) and Abu El-Haj (2001).

4. The Herodian-era Wall was used as a regular site of Jewish prayer from at least the time of the Ottoman sultan Suleiman (1520–1566). However, before the era of Sulieman,

constitute an "eternal" or "immutable" site. Of which city, neighborhood, or nation, after all, could such a claim be made? And yet, Zionists—religious and secular—have commonly deployed rhetoric of this kind about the Kotel. The open space before the Western Wall, what today dominant cartographies refer to as the "Western Wall Plaza," was established only in the last four-and-a-half decades and is not even as old as the Jewish state's forty-seven-year-long military occupation of East Jerusalem.

Further, contrary to prevailing Israeli accounts and little known beyond communities of devout Muslims, the space around the Kotel—indeed, the Kotel itself—has been a vital component of Islam's formation and its adherents' religious and national cosmologies. The Wall and areas contiguous to it were deemed *waqf* (religious endowment property) by local Muslim authorities several hundred years prior to the establishment of the Jewish state in 1948. To Muslims its importance lies in the fact that it serves as the western enclosure of the *Al-Haram al-Sharif*, the site from which Muslims believe the Prophet Muhammed ascended to heaven in the seventh century, after having first tethered his horse near the Western Wall.[5]

Perhaps as surprising to Israeli Jews, international tourists, and not a few Palestinians is the fact that the current space of the Western Wall Plaza had for nearly 700 years before June 1967 been the precise location of the Arab Moroccan Quarter (*Harat al-Magharibah*). First constructed in the twelfth century, this neighborhood had become home to

---

evidence of prayer at the Wall is somewhat uncertain. According to Peters (1990), the accounts of Jewish visitors to Jerusalem during the Islamic Middle Ages suggest that "most Jewish prayer was conducted within synagogues in the Jewish Quarter and, on public occasion, most often on the Mount of Olives overlooking the Temple site from the east" (242–243).

5. The famed wall, itself, physically embodies these converging meanings and traditions. It is widely believed that the visible lower courses (or layers) of mammoth stones were the original western face of the Second Temple. However, the upper layers composed of smaller stones of a distinctly different character were added by Muslims in the Umayyad period (661–750). Like the city and the country more generally, this locale is neither unitary in composition, nor eternal in meaning. In addition, several courses of the wall are unseen, lying below that which is visible today.

8. The former Moroccan Quarter and the Western Wall as viewed from a neighboring area near the historic Jewish Quarter in the 1920s. Courtesy of Library of Congress, Prints and Photographs Division.

approximately 600 to 1,000 inhabitants by the 1960s.[6] The Jewish state evicted these mostly Muslim residents and demolished their dwellings, mosques, and other institutions in the days immediately following the June 1967 War.

The stone and brick structures of the Moroccan Quarter, made up of modest one- and two-story buildings, enveloped a network of narrow

6. Historians of Jerusalem claim that the Moroccan Quarter dates to the time of the Ayyubids. See Abu El-Haj (2001); Hiyari (1989, 168); Ricca (2007); and Khalidi (1999). Tibawi (1978, 12), citing a fourteenth-century account by Mujir al-Din al-Hanbali, relates that Afdal al-Din (son of Salahdin) "endowed as waqf the entire quarter of the Maghribis in favor of the Maghribi community, without distinction of origin" and that the "donation took place at the time when the prince ruled over Damascus (AD 1186–1196), to which Jerusalem was joined."

9. The Western Wall and the Western Wall Plaza from the contemporary Jewish Quarter, 2006. Note the gender-segregated place of prayer before the Wall, with the men's section on the left and the smaller women's section on the right.

paths and alleyways that snaked through this generally poor neighborhood. Some routes led to mosques and schools, others to the Western Wall and the roughly five-by-twenty-five-meter space that lay then before it.[7] Interviews with former Moroccan Quarter residents and local Palestinians familiar with this segment of the Old City revealed that at least ten families resident here in 1967 traced their genealogies back to Morocco

7. Cartographic, photographic, and textual representations of the densely populated quarter can be found in maps dating back hundreds of years, as well as in texts as diverse as twentieth-century British colonial reports and the travelogues of eighteenth-century religious pilgrims. There have even appeared in the Israeli press in recent years aerial photographs from the pre-1948 era showing the quarter in relation to the Kotel, including a 700-year-old mosque built in the time of Salah al-Din and destroyed by Israel in 1967. See Hasson (2012).

10. The Western Wall and the former space of prayer before it in the 1920s. Courtesy of Library of Congress, Prints and Photographs Division.

(*al-maghrib*). Several claimed historical connections to this segment of Jerusalem dating back hundreds of years, while others, driven from Arab villages west of Jerusalem during the 1948 War, found a haven here as recently as the early 1950s.

LIBERATING JERUSALEM

Chapter 3 documented Israel's practice of turning former military emplacements and battle sites into national memorials. The ritual parades mentioned in the opening of this chapter frequently pass by or make stops at such places along their way to the Western Wall. Yet, none of these memorials, no matter how grand, have possessed even remotely the nationalist utility for the Jewish state that the Western Wall has since 1967. Israeli authorities have viewed this segment of the Old City and the meanings and identities produced here as essential to winning the battle for control over Jerusalem. The arrival of Israeli soldiers, politicians, and the chief rabbi, General Shlomo Goren, at the Western Wall at the end of the 1967 War has been recorded in innumerable pictures, news reports, and memoirs.[8] The convergence of these various sources of authority spoke to the ways in which they all would play a part in refashioning Jerusalem in the years to come. As several Israeli memorials discussed in chapter 3 record, soldiers declared euphorically at the end of the war that the Western Wall was "in our hands"; the city had finally been "liberated" after nearly two millennium.

Palestinian Christians and Muslims subjected to Israeli military rule have not, generally, regarded themselves as "liberated." Of the scores of Arab Jerusalemites with whom I spoke, not one described their condition thusly. Nor have they, whether privileged or poor, male or female, tended to see the continual appropriation of their land as part of any divinely guided design. Rather, Palestinians old enough to recall the advent of

8. There is no dearth of historical accounts that describe this moment. See Rabin (1979, 111–112) for a particularly fond recounting of Israel's conquest of East Jerusalem.

military occupation detailed wide-ranging expressions of racism and violence directed against them in the decades since 1967.

From the very first days of Israeli control over East Jerusalem and
for the next twenty-six years, the administration of Mayor Teddy Kollek
would oversee a vast reordering of this urban landscape. These changes
included the imposition of the Israeli mayor and municipal apparatus of
West Jerusalem over the Palestinians of the east side, the unilateral expansion of the city's boundaries by a factor of ten, Israel's appropriation of
thousands of acres of privately and communally owned Arab land, and
the rapid construction of sprawling hilltop Jewish settlements.[9]

But before initiating any of these alterations, the new rulers first
appropriated and refashioned the Western Wall and its environs. Seizing
the symbolic currency of the Kotel, I argue, provided the ideological foundation upon which Israeli governance would project itself as legitimate
and natural, both to its citizens and supporters abroad. Doing so facilitated a wider campaign to possess territories illegally occupied in 1967
while negating competing Palestinian claims to their city.

Kollek (1978), his former deputy Meron Benvenisti (1976, 1996), and
two former Israeli city planners I interviewed suggested that there were
three widely held assumptions that guided the Jewish state in its efforts to
appropriate East Jerusalem. The first was that the Western Wall area must
be remade by demolishing the Arab neighborhood before it; second, that
Israel had an unquestionable right to do so despite the international community's belief that this was in violation of international law; and third,
that the Palestinians of the city's east side (who in 1967 comprised all
60–65,000 of its residents) must have no say in any major decisions related
to Jerusalem's "reunification." Israel did not then or since propose a for-
mula of shared national sovereignty in the city. In fact, all major expressions of Palestinian nationalism (including the flag and the movement's
institutions) were banned.

9. The Palestinian mayor of Jerusalem, Ruhi al-Khatib, was dismissed by Israel
within weeks of the conclusion of the war. He would later be sent into exile.

Israeli governing officials understood as well as any semiotician the paramount role that signs and symbols play in naturalizing and normalizing spatial and racial orders of dominance. If the Jewish state were to successfully remain in a section of the city universally regarded as illegally occupied territory, an ideological campaign, not simply a military one, would have to be waged to justify their presence. Possessing the Western Wall and drawing on its connections to a biblical and sacred past—real or imagined—were wisely seen as imperative to realizing this aim.

"CLEANING UP HISTORY"

Kollek, Benvenisti, and other Israeli officials were all too aware of the Moroccan Quarter residents. However, consistent with the way colonial regimes generally tend to "see" native communities, these Arab inhabitants were regarded as an obstruction to the designs of the new occupiers. In Kollek's and Benvenisti's respective accounts, they speak for the most part of the neighborhood in its *in*animate dimensions, as a physical impediment, even as a zone of filth.

When the families of the Moroccan Quarter are referred to at all, they tend to be discursively merged into their maligned, built environment. Those who eliminated the quarter routinely spoke of the inhabitants as what Mary Douglas (1966) refers to as "matter out of place" (44). As mentioned in previous chapters, I have found Douglas's theorizing of social difference to be invaluable in examining the spatial and racial assumptions of regimes committed to orders of forced communal "apartness." These beliefs undergirded Israeli policies vis-à-vis unwanted Arabs in areas of the country like West Jerusalem in 1948. After 1967, these racial notions and civilizational discourses continued to be mobilized as the Jewish state extended its rule over 1 million additional Palestinians in East Jerusalem, the rest of the West Bank, and the Gaza Strip.

Douglas highlights the centrality of one's location to the production of identity and alterity, order and disorder. What she refers to as "dirt," "pollution," and other elements deemed "impure" are compelling metaphors for subordinate racial and racialized communities.[10] As I have been arguing, the Jewish state's abiding principle of *hafrada*, or the desire for separation between Arabs and Jews, reflects the racial anxieties that Douglas's work illuminates. As she perceptively notes:

> As we know it dirt is essentially disorder. . . . Dirt offends against order. Eliminating it is not a negative movement, but a positive effort to organize the environment. (1966, 2)

Kollek and other officials' reaction to the "disorder" the Moroccan Quarter families were thought to represent reveals a good deal about the designs of Israeli authority. The elimination of this and other zones deemed dirty, it was asserted, could be advanced as a progressive, even humane effort, as indeed it was in this specific case. The practices and discourses that enable and justify often violent acts of cleansing and classifying Douglas refers to as "pollution behavior" or "the reaction which condemns any object or idea likely to confuse or contradict cherished classifications" (ibid., 36). These classifications under Israeli rule have been both spatial and racial and remain integral to the kind of city officials like Kollek have been intent on creating.

The Jewish state's discourses about and designs for the Kotel resembled in microcosm the visions the new occupiers had for the city and country more broadly. These included the consistent diminishing of the Moroccan Quarter residents' attachments to their homes, both at the time of the destruction of the quarter and since. This Palestinian community's historical connections to Jerusalem and, indeed, to one another have been quite absent in the accounts of those responsible for evicting these and other Arab populations. Faced with the impediment that the Moroccan Quarter community represented, the new rulers devised a very specific "pollution behavior" summed up in the Israeli mayor's declaration that "The only answer was to do away with the slum hovels of the Moghrabi

---

10. These racial policies and discourses of "pollution" within Israel have also been directed at Mizrahi and other non-Ashkenazi Jews, particularly in the early decades of the state. For more see Shohat (1988), Behar and Ben-Dor Benite (2013), and Segev (1986).

Quarter. . . . My overpowering feeling was to do it now [immediately after the 1967 War]; it may be impossible to do it later, and it *must* be done" (Kollek 1978, 197). The mayor, continuing to speak of this place as if it were empty of human beings, adds that this segment of the city "that should have been spacious and bright was cramped and dark" (ibid.).

When the Arabs living in this targeted quarter are mentioned at all by Kollek, Benvenisti, or others, they are frequently spoken *for* by those with an interest in displacing them. For example, in his memoir the former mayor justifies both the destruction of the Moroccan Quarter as well as the removal of neighboring areas' Palestinians in the 1970s by stating simply that these communities were just as happy to live in another part of the city and that they, in fact, "had no special feeling for the place" (Kollek 1978, 228). In properly historicizing Israeli settler colonialism in Jerusalem, it is worth pointing out that the families of what Kollek refers to as these "primitive" and "cramped" quarters (ibid.), those allegedly devoid of meaningful attachments to this urban landscape, had typically resided in these neighborhoods for generations before Kollek's own family arrived in British Mandate Palestine from Austria in the 1930s. And yet, the connections of the dominant populations are projected as transhistorical and eternal, while the bonds and feelings of the native population are said to be only loosely held, ephemeral, and "unspecial."

These discursive moves, I argue, have been part of a process of dehumanization or reification consistent with other colonizing projects. A multifaceted idea, possessing a deep genealogy in Marxist thought, reification has a crucial relevance for analyzing colonial (and, indeed, postcolonial) racisms. Michael Taussig (1991, 1992) and Aime Cesaire (1972) speak of it as a method of "thingifying" human beings deemed dangerously located. As Cesaire succinctly put it, "colonization='thingification'" (1972, 21). Policies of removing those deemed wrongly situated, as in the case of the Moroccan Quarter, relied on the reduction of human beings largely to physical impediments, to dirty and camped hovels. The ideologies that justified these efforts at removal then and since have had far-reaching consequences for those subjected to Israeli military occupation. But I want to suggest that they have impinged on the colonizers, too. For one, they might help to explain how it is that otherwise good people are compelled to engage in acts of ethnic cleansing and the cruelties associated with these policies discussed throughout this book.[11]

Under international law and the Fourth Geneva Convention, the Israeli state had no right to destroy this neighborhood. Further, they would have had no basis for negotiating with the Moroccan Quarter residents over *how* their homes and religious sites were to be done away with. But in trying to make sense of the violence meted out against these civilians, I wondered if the refusal to even consult with these inhabitants before evicting them was about Israeli officials insulating themselves from any kind of human interaction. Might such encounters have compelled some among the new occupiers to see the Arab families of this densely populated quarter as more than an obstruction or a collection of filthy shanties?

REORDERING THE ETERNAL

The demolition of the 700-year-old Moroccan Quarter took place swiftly and unexpectedly. Israeli and Palestinian eyewitnesses describe that on the evening of Saturday, June 10, 1967, after Shabbat had ended, Israeli officials ordered those living in the neighborhood to vacate their homes. Bulldozers and tall floodlights had been brought to the edge of the neighborhood soon after sundown, and armed men were positioned alongside the demolition crews who would soon deploy these instruments of destruction.

Former residents described the chaos that washed over the targeted community that night. The hour chosen was a time when many inhabitants and certainly most of the children would have been asleep. This I was told contributed to panic, terror, and confusion. These Palestinians, in their first encounters with Israeli authority, witnessed what Brecht (1965) might have referred to as "ordered disorder." Homes were searched by Israeli soldiers screaming at residents in Hebrew and Arabic as they threw them out into the night. Entire families were evicted with little warning

11. For an analysis of these dynamics in other highly racialized contexts, see Arendt (1969), Levi (1988), and Malkki (1995).

and no recourse. Several were compelled to flee with only the belongings they could carry, and more than a few were carrying children. All was done on a strict timetable as the remains of razed homes were bulldozed into piles and as Israeli officials tried to load some of those evicted onto busses to take them elsewhere. The imagery harkened back to the experiences of Palestinian refugees in 1948, not uncommonly forced to flee under similar circumstances.

One interviewee expelled that night, Sufyan, was a boy in his early teens at the time. He recalled how his uncle, a big and powerful figure, had sought to resist the soldiers' directives by refusing to leave his home. The man was even able to fend off the Israelis at first, who then went to remove other families. Eventually his uncle sent his distraught wife and children out of the targeted dwelling but defiantly remained inside for some time.

Sufyan remembered the pervasive anguish among those holding screaming children and the loud raucous noise of the bulldozers as they leveled the stone and brick structures. He also told me that he can still picture his uncle standing his ground but then, as properties adjacent to his began to be crushed, how he was compelled to flee his home and join his family on the periphery of the mounting ruins. Even decades later, his nephew related that he could still see the grief-stricken expression on the face of this hulking man as he was reduced to a most humiliating state.

Israeli journalist Uzi Benziman, one of the few eyewitnesses of these evictions, would later corroborate some of the accounts of those made homeless that evening. In his work he details several instances of expulsion, including the story of a Palestinian woman who lived in one of the first homes leveled. She apparently did not hear the command to vacate her home and was stuck beneath the rubble.[12] As Benziman writes:

> One demolished wall of a room revealed an unconscious middle-aged Arab woman in the throes of death. She was placed on her bed in the open amid the debris and clouds of dust stirred by the bulldozers . . .

12. Benziman's book originally written in 1973 was published in Arabic in 1976 as *al-Quds: Madinah bila Aswar*.

an engineer who supervised the demolition, tried to revive her. But by
midnight Rasmiyyah 'Ali Taba'ki was dead before medical assistance . . .
reached the spot. (1976, 110)

Former residents of the Moroccan Quarter revealed other quotidian
dimensions of these expulsions. Munther, a man in his late forties by the
early 2000s, was evicted from the Moroccan Quarter as a child. He spoke
to me about living in Jerusalem since that time as a kind of "internal exile."
We met in a small Arab-owned restaurant near his current home in the
Old City, tucked away amid a row of shops along the Street of the Chain.
This quarter of mostly Muslim families lies just a few hundred meters
away from the site of his former neighborhood.

The traumatic experiences associated with that evening have stayed
with him ever since. Hearing his and others' accounts of that night reinforced an important but often ignored point: One can measure and record
the number of buildings destroyed, the number of people displaced, and
the size of the territory seized that evening. But it is rather more difficult
to document adequately the emotional and psychic damage done to those
removed. When Munther thought back on these events from a distance of
more than thirty-three years, there were times when anger still bubbled
up in him. "We were nothing to them," he related gravely. "They looked
through us to see what *they* wanted there [at the Moroccan Quarter]. They
saw us as trash [*zabaale*], and they were going to clear us like you do with
the trash," motioning as if emptying a garbage can.

Thirty-two years later after the destruction of the Moroccan Quarter,
one of the Israelis involved in eliminating the quarter, Etan Ben Moshe,
was interviewed in a Hebrew publication about this act. Consistent with
the ways senior Israeli officials spoke of the disorder and filth of the Arab
neighborhood, he mentions little about the actual people made refugees
that night. At one point the bulldozer operator recalls with a certain non-
chalance the fact that he did not spare the Muslim religious sites:

There was a mosque in the area called the *Masjid al-Buraq* built on the
site where the horse of Prophet Muhammad ascended to heaven. I said

if the horse ascended to the sky, why shouldn't the mosque ascend, too! I crushed it well, leaving no remains. (Cited in Abowd 2000, 10–11)

Nearly all of the neighborhood's 135 structures were flattened that night and over the next two days.[13]

Israeli leaders would write in the years after the creation of the Western Wall Plaza about the supposed emancipatory quality of this act for the Jewish people. Kollek betrays a distinct pride in having swiftly reordered the space before the Kotel. The assumptions that he and others worked from, their "pollution behavior" vis-à-vis the Palestinians, were years later expressed, in part, in the idiom of sanitation. Relating in a celebratory way the emergence of this expansive place of prayer and nationalist ritual, Kollek asserts: "In two days it was done—finished, clean" (1978, 197).

Mainstream Israeli desires to keep Palestinians peripheral have been actualized in diverse ways. Indeed, the visions of Labor Party leaders, such as Kollek and Benvenisti, have been at variance with those of, say, militant religious settlers, armed with a literal reading of the Book of Joshua as their guide. However, undergirding a very broad Israeli and Zionist consensus on these matters has been the principle of appropriating the maximum amount of Palestinian land with the minimum number of Palestinians.[14] These are notions that rely on a racialization of space typical of colonial regimes. They draw on religious and national myths that speak of essential

13. Though the residents of this quarter were removed that evening, certain buildings on the neighborhood's periphery were initially retained, most notably a mosque near the Bab Maghribeh and the Zawiyya Fakhriyya. However, the Israeli authorities eventually razed both structures in 1969.

14. These Israeli policies of mass eviction have increasingly been referred to as "ethnic cleansing," even by Israeli writers and analysts who once were involved in such practices. For a particularly powerful critique of some of these efforts to negate Palestinians and their pasts, see Benvenisti (2002) in a chapter entitled "Ethnic Cleansing" (144–192); and Ilan Pappe's (2007) more recent work. See also Israel's Koenig Report from 1976, a document of the Israeli Ministry of Interior that deploys the language of "Judaization" to describe the intentions of the Israeli state vis-à-vis the Palestinian citizens of Israel. The report was leaked to the Israeli newspaper *Al-Hamishmar* and published on September 7, 1976.

differences between Arabs and Jews, and the dangers associated with subordinate communities "mixing" with or being "too close" to the dominant.

THE PRESENCE OF THE "HOLY"

The motivations for removing the Moroccan Quarter community were similar to those Israeli governing officials had expressed when altering other locales in Jerusalem before June 1967. They revolved around two related and perceived needs, one spatial and one temporal. Nearly thirty years after these expulsions Meron Benvenisti explained the logic at the time as he saw it:

> The former space in front of the Wall could not have accommodated the 400,000 people [i.e., Israeli Jews] who swarmed to the site; the maximum number able to pray there during the Mandate [before 1948] were 12,000 per day. *Practical considerations* were the determining factor in the demolition of the *buildings* of the Arab [Moroccan] Quarter. (1996, 82; emphasis mine)

The occupying force's imperative to expand an already existing space of prayer to accommodate Israeli visitors and Jewish pilgrims was deemed sufficient cause to remove a several-hundred-year-old Arab neighborhood, including its religious sites, and to make those who resided there homeless.

In an interview with a Palestinian filmmaker, the former deputy mayor, Benvenisti, was challenged on the ethics of destroying the quarter. Almost forty years after the removal of this community he was little more capable of condemning it:

> When I think about it today . . . there were many excuses I can bring out. You see there had to be a price to be paid for the fact that Jews were not allowed to go to the Western Wall [between 1948 and 1967]. (Alatar 2007)

These two quotes are significant not simply because of the indifference, even disdain, expressed for this and other Palestinian communities under Israeli military rule. Nor are they noteworthy simply in their refusal to acknowledge the hardship caused by these evictions. These statements are also remarkable in their essentialist depictions of both Arabs and Jews. These views underscore many of the ways in which the Israeli state has governed since 1948. These perspectives, I submit, held by a prominent member of the Israeli left, are ensnared in precisely the racial and spatial assumptions that I have been discussing throughout this book.

For one, assuming in Benvenisti's second statement that he means Israeli Jews when he says "Jews," the responsibility for the arrangement that led to their inability to travel across the divided city and access the Kotel between 1948 and 1967 was hardly that of the Palestinians of the Moroccan Quarter. They, like the other Palestinian residents of Jerusalem, lived during those years under a semiauthoritarian Jordanian government not of their choosing. It was this regime along with Israel that had signed the Armistice Agreement of 1949 and who regulated movement across that line.[15] Further, even had members of the Moroccan Quarter somehow been responsible for this spatial arrangement or been involved in harming Israelis, those who illegally occupied East Jerusalem would still not have been justified in razing an entire community's homes.

Secondly, it was the Palestinians more than any other party to this conflict who were opposed to the 1948–1949 division of the city in the first place. The armistice line, after all, prevented hundreds of thousands of them from returning to their homes in West Jerusalem and throughout the country. But if those on the other side of the frontier were "all just Arabs, after all" (a typical essentialist framing used in the service of racist violence in innumerable political contexts), then the Moroccan Quarter residents—the "they" Benvenisiti refers to—could be forced to "pay the price."

By this logic, because of real or fictive grievances with the Egyptian or Jordanian governments, the Jewish state could invade Palestinian East Jerusalem in the name of "retaliating" against "the Arabs." If an Israeli Jewish soldier or settler killed a Palestinian in Bethlehem, then a Jewish

15. The Jordanian regime was sufficiently hostile to the Palestinians; they had even conspired with Zionist leaders in the late 1940s to divide segments of the land earmarked for a Palestinian state under the 1947 UN Partition Plan. For more on this documented history, see Israeli historian Schlaim's account of the period of the late 1940s (1988).

civilian in Tel Aviv or Paris could be made to "pay the price." Colonial racism has relied on precisely this mode of thinking in Palestine/Israel. The fallacious character of these broad brush portrayals of an undifferentiated "them," frequently so appealing to dominant communities, can often only be seen for their ethical shortcomings once the roles are reversed.

In addition to the spatial imperative justifying the removal of the Moroccan Quarter there was, as well, a related temporal one. When one of the Israeli soldiers who oversaw the demolition of the Moroccan Quarter was asked years later why it was that its residents were not permitted even to remove their belongings before their homes were bulldozed, he replied:

> *There was no time.* That day was Saturday and the next Tuesday observed the feast of Passover [*sic*]. At that time, many people were expected to arrive at the Wailing Wall, and we had two days only to prepare the yard. (Cited in Abowd 2000, 11)[16]

The holiday to which the soldier refers was actually *Shavuot*, not Passover. I argue that the justifications he advances for razing the Moroccan Quarter are emblematic of broader colonial assumptions about places, identities, and claims to land. Indeed, since 1948 Israeli officials have periodically invoked religious myths, moments, and traditions in similar ways, fusing them with policies of conquest, violence, and racist exclusion. Simon Schama (1996), for example, writes how the Jewish holiday *Tu B'shevat* became increasingly wedded to Israeli nationalism. He explains that throughout Jewish history *Tu B'shevat* had always been a moment that celebrated the end of a period of tithing, but in the hands of the Israeli government it has been "wholly reinvented" as a "Zionist Arbor Day" (1996, 5–6).

Each year on this holiday, the Jewish state has promoted the planting of trees across territory it asserts has been given to the Jewish people by God. These pine saplings and the forests they eventually become are meant to signify a national vitality and an unbreakable connection between the Jewish people and what is projected as the biblical land of Zion. That the

16. Emphasis mine.

sites chosen for these sprawling forests have at times been the remains of destroyed Arab villages figures not at all in these narratives. Typically sponsored by Zionist organizations like the Jewish National Fund (JNF), these trees have had the simultaneous effect—and, it would seem, the intention—of concealing traces of a former Palestinian presence.[17]

In the wake of the destruction of the Moroccan Quarter, it was not trees that were to provide "cover" for acts of expulsion but assertions of "sacred space," "eternal" spiritual connections, and the "presence of the holy." Here, a demolished residential environment has been supplanted not by serene foliage but by beige pavement, tourists with cameras, and ritual moments of national devotion. Used and mobilized in these ways, the locale has since 1967 taken on a goes-without-saying quality: What could be more natural than the Jewish state in full control of "the Jewish Quarter" and Judaism's most important religious site? As with other Israeli locales of monumental importance, that which is *not* mentioned, seen, heard, or asserted at the Kotel is every bit as significant as that which is.

VISITING THE MUKHTAR

What became of the families of the former Moroccan Quarter? I had heard about the neighborhood's physical fate before I arrived to conduct fieldwork but had never met any of the survivors. During the first months of my research I was able to find few people in the tight-knit communities of East Jerusalem who even knew where any of the survivors could be found. A surprising number of Palestinians in their twenties and younger had not even heard about the demolition of the quarter. I was finally put in touch with one former inhabitant, Salim, the mukhtar (community leader) of the exiled families. I was surprised to learn that the position of mukhtar continued to exist, decades after the neighborhood had been effaced. But among the survivors there was still a measure of commitment to retaining a collective identity and refusing to disappear.

17. For a discussion of the use of trees and Israeli spatial politics see Bardenstein (1999).

Salim, in his role as mukhtar, was not simply the person who had, for several years, handled disputes within the community. He had also been a political activist, imprisoned and beaten by Israeli officials for protesting military occupation. He continued to resist the occupation in ways an ailing man in his sixties was able, including a dedication to keeping alive the histories of the neighborhood. To that end he maintained a remarkable archive of materials documenting the quarter's existence and its demise. He generously shared a range of documents with me, including old property deeds from the British Mandate era, photographs of the neighborhood at various moments, and the actual Israeli expropriation orders.

I twice had the opportunity to interview Salim in his present home, a modest apartment in the Muslim Quarter of the Old City. The second-story flat was located on one of the narrow lanes that run off of the noisy, covered *suq khan zeit*, a primary, commercial artery. His street is tranquil, a strip of pavement roughly the width of two cars and mostly open to the sky. Two to three stories of densely packed buildings, some centuries old, rise up on either side. Armed Jewish settlers had taken over a Palestinian residence across from Salim's abode a few years before our interview. These recent arrivals displayed an Israeli flag behind reinforced, grated windows and came and went with semiautomatic weapons slung over their shoulders.

We sat in the mukhtar's dark sitting room, a picture of the Dome of the Rock affixed high on the wall behind him. Salim detailed some of the conditions of displacement that he and those he grew up with had undergone. He related the events around the Moroccan Quarter's destruction and how a host of social ties, domestic networks, and close relationships were dissolved that night, not simply dwellings of brick and stone. The mukhtar described how those were uncertain times, but days of rage, too, as dozens of men and women who had the responsibility of protecting their children were unable to do so.

In the course of our first conversation, Salim related a story that underlined the gendered dimensions of humiliation that dozens of men and women I met in Jerusalem had experienced. In the days after losing their home and most of their belongings in June 1967, his wife and child returned to the site of their demolished neighborhood to try to salvage property that they had left behind. The Israeli authorities did not permit Salim and other Arab men to enter what became a closed zone, so he saw them off and waited for their return. On two successive mornings they stood on the periphery for long stretches of time, the mukhtar told me, as near as possible to the demolition crews working furiously to clear away the mounds of debris in time for the impending Jewish holiday. There they stood under a harsh summer sun for several hours, hoping that the bulldozers might, unwittingly, unearth their belongings in the course of "cleaning up" the Kotel area. However, on each day his wife and child returned with nothing—their dejected and sad faces, hair, and clothes covered with dirt and dust.

Sharing these happenings was for this elder plainly painful, even from this temporal distance. Evident sorrow appeared across Salim's face and he rubbed his eyes with his hand as he leaned over and stared at the floor. It was at moments like these that I witnessed the ways in which acts of cruelty could affect victims of military occupation for decades. These hidden injuries have been little written about in the literature on contemporary Jerusalem. But I came to gradually understand that they comprise as much as anything Palestinian existence under Israeli rule. Here, I thought, in this lengthy and awkward silence, was the time to thank him and end our first interview.

In future conversations, Salim and another exile from the Moroccan Quarter, a man a little younger than he, pointed out some of the ways in which Israeli legal practices had been deployed after 1967 in the remaking of Jerusalem. And in doing so, they alerted me to a stark example of what the Palestinian writer and legal scholar, Raja Shehadeh (1988), has referred to as the "occupier's law." Curiously, it was not until ten months *after* the actual demolition of the homes of the Moroccan Quarter that the Israeli Treasury Ministry presented former residents with eviction notices.

In April 1968, officials provided written documents to community leaders stating that they had expropriated 116 dunums (29 acres) contiguous to the Kotel—including the targeted neighborhood. This earmarked territory included the Palestinian Sharif and Medain quarters, segments of the Muslim Quarter contiguous to the former Moroccan Quarter. It included, as well, a slice of the Armenian Quarter, including St. Mark's Church. These segments of the Old City were taken for what occupation authorities defined as "public use." The land was owned for the most part by Christian and Muslim Palestinians who had resided in the Old City before Israel was established. It was now earmarked for what the new rulers referred to as the "reconstructed" Jewish Quarter.

The mukhtar provided me with a copy of these a posteriori eviction notices of April 1968, served as part of a purported legal process. However, the manner in which this was done, giving legal notice to an already expelled community whose homes were no longer standing, foreclosed any attempt to successfully contest these appropriations through the channels available to Jewish citizens of the Israeli state.[18] Policies and practices of this sort, I contend, speak to the regime's colonial character. Israeli law has created two distinct levels of rights to land and housing based on whether one is Jewish or non-Jewish.[19] Democracy and the protection of property rights have, for the most part, been afforded the Israeli Jewish citizenry in Jerusalem (including the approximately 200,000 Jewish settlers living in East Jerusalem settlements). At the same time, these legal mechanisms have been deployed to marginalize and discriminate against Palestinian residents living in the city, for the simple reason that they are not Jewish.

INVENTING AND REINVENTING TRADITION

The enormous crowds the Israeli government predicted did in fact arrive at the Kotel in early June 1967. The elimination of the Moroccan Quarter

18. With the belated arrival of written orders of expropriation came an Israeli offer of "compensation" to those whose homes were demolished. The mukhtar related that some of the residents of the Moroccan Quarter community took the compensation. But most, including his family, have refused the money in principle to this day. The official Israeli notification estimated that the mukhtar's property was worth 200 Jordanian dinars, a sum not even remotely approaching the value of his home. Salim made available to me and a fellow researcher who interviewed him a photocopy of the original document that he maintains in his private archive.

19. This has been true whether the non-Jewish Palestinians are citizens of the state, "permanent residents," or classified as an even lower status assigned to the majority of Palestinians resident in other parts of the West Bank and the Gaza Strip.

made possible the accommodation of hundreds of thousands of Jewish visitors who traveled here in just the first few days after the Kotel was opened up. But those who journeyed to the Western Wall were also greeted by an emerging spatial order said not only to be "clean" but also sacred and divinely inspired.

As this new religio-nationalist realm was being constituted, the chief rabbi of the Israel Defense Forces (IDF) at the time, Shlomo Goren, and other clerical authorities declared that one section of the plaza, a roughly 35-by-25-meter strip directly before the Western Wall, possessed the "presence of God." Here, the Israeli Ministry of Religious Affairs established an open-air synagogue that exists to this day and that has been established in part over the ruins of the Moroccan Quarter. A metal divider, roughly a meter high, bounds the synagogue's west side, marking it off from the larger portion of the plaza. In the tradition of Orthodox Judaism, the place of worship was (and remains) partitioned between men's and women's sections. The latter, separate and smaller than the former, consumes the southern section of the visible Wall.[20] The floor of the synagogue would eventually be paved with a light, polished stone different from the rest of the environs.

Who had the authority to determine the dimensions of the "holy"? What did it mean that Israeli officials could engage in the making of such "eternal" cartographies? Despite continual Israeli and Zionist assertions concerning the "immutable" quality of this area, little in the vicinity of the Kotel was left unchanged in the wake of the June 1967 War. Even the Western Wall itself was altered by those who illegally occupied the city. The elimination of the Arab quarter, by some Israeli and Palestinian accounts, reduced the prominence of the Wall relative to the expansive plaza. Before the destruction of the Moroccan Quarter, to actually experience the site, visitors and worshippers were required to stand relatively close to its base,

20. It should be noted that, as with the reinvention of the Western Wall as the "eternal" site of Jewish prayer, the division of the Kotel between men's and women's sections is only a product of the last one hundred years of Zionist settlement in Palestine/Israel. Historically, as photographs from the nineteenth century indicate, the space was not segregated on the basis of gender.

never more than a few meters from its layers of mammoth stones. That narrow space between the Moroccan Quarter and the Kotel, that necessary proximity to the Wall, gave it the appearance of being taller and more imposing than it became after the Moroccan Quarter was done away with.

Israel attempted to remedy this by excavating the base of the Western Wall by roughly two meters in the first weeks of its occupation.[21] These changes accentuated the Kotel's size relative to the emerging plaza before it. These and other revisions were efforts to nationalize the sacred, all within the context of a colonial project that sought to mark the city with an exclusive stamp of ownership.

But in reading this segment of this shifting urban landscape, I could not help but think that the Kotel's former grandeur was produced in part by the *presence* of the largely Muslim Quarter that lay contiguous to it for hundreds of years. Those living here in this shared space, the different peoples who converged on this very site, did not diminish the Kotel. The cultural hybridity of this locale where hybrid monotheisms were constituted, not only resisted exclusivity but also served to bolster in at least a few ways the prominence of the wall. In reading this site further it should not be forgotten, as mentioned above, that the height of the wall, itself, was partially attributable to the stones added to it by Muslims and others over several centuries. Here, perhaps, it is possible to see another historical parallel with this city of multiple and shared meanings more generally.

NATURALIZING THE "JEWISH QUARTER"

Israel's expropriation of the land of the former Moroccan Quarter was not simply about opening up the space of worship before the Western Wall and creating a site of nationalist devotion. It was also an attempt to help bring an expanded and exclusive Jewish Quarter into being, one that would in turn help legitimate and secure the Jewish state's hold over the

21. A slight watermark can be seen to this day on the Wall, indicating the segment excavated in 1967.

entirety of the city.[22] Though an identifiable "Jewish Quarter" has existed in Jerusalem for hundreds of years, its spatial coordinates and composition have shifted over the centuries. Further, the proprietorship of the land of the quarter has historically been mixed and in the centuries leading up to 1967 owned mostly by Muslims and Christians. Jewish residents and religious institutions owned only about one-third of the territory of the neighborhood on the eve of the 1948 War, a segment of the quarter that included its four primary synagogues.[23]

In the mid- to late 1970s, the plans first initiated in the wake of the 1967 War to make this part of the Old City an exclusively Israeli Jewish province were put more fully into force. The twin processes of expansion and exclusion, so fundamental to colonial governance, were again in motion. The 29 acres of Old City land formally expropriated from Palestinian inhabitants of the city in 1968 (including the roughly two to three acres of the Moroccan Quarter) were earmarked for this expanded Jewish Quarter.

A semiotics of domination was at work as Israeli myths about this space and the city more generally were produced and, as Said (1995) asserts, "projected." Signs were constructed by linking radically shifting signifiers (e.g. new, expanded cartographic boundaries) with an "eternal" signified (the "Jewish Quarter"). In this post-1967 mythic rendering, the "ancient Jewish Quarter" would be anything the contemporary Israeli state defined it as. And the association between this specific signified and signifier has, I argue, assumed a taken-for-granted, goes-without-saying quality similar to other myths and mythologies.[24] These articulations of spatial dominance and exclusion in this part of the Old City were analogous to the ways the borders of Jerusalem more broadly were remade at the same time: The Jerusalem of Israel's imagination, the "eternal" and "immutable" capital

22. The organization that Israel established to create an expanded Jewish Quarter is the Company for the Reconstruction and Development of the Jewish Quarter (CRDJQ).

23. For fascinating discussions on this particular subject see Abu El-Haj (2001) and Dumper (1997).

24. This and other segments of this book draw from perhaps the most perceptive analysis of semiotics, myth, and ideology by Barthes (1957).

of the Jewish people, would include large swaths of West Bank land whose populations never regarded them as part of the city.

By the mid-1970s, as many as four or five thousand Palestinian Christians and Muslims lived within the expanded earmarked space of the reconstructed "Jewish Quarter."[25] These appropriations and redelineations allowed for the expansion of the pre-1948 Jewish Quarter by a factor of five into neighboring Palestinian residential areas. This meant that the vast majority of this larger territory had never been known as the Jewish Quarter—either by Jews or non-Jews, Israelis or Palestinians. More than 60 percent of the area brought within the Israeli-drawn boundaries of the quarter was, in fact, appropriated from private Arab owners and the Islamic *waqf* (religious endowments).[26] It was through this spatial reordering that Israel would create continuity between the Kotel and the pre-1967 Jewish Quarter. Actualizing the expropriation orders of April 1968, Israel began to drive out the non-Jews of this zone in the mid-1970s.

Among those evicted was a small but significant number of Palestinian families, including the former mukhtar's, who had found refuge in these contiguous neighborhoods after the Moroccan Quarter had been demolished. As I spoke at greater length with Salim, I learned that he and his kin had actually been expelled from their homes three times since the establishment of Israel. In 1948 the forces of the nascent Jewish state drove them out of an Arab village west of Jerusalem. Then a teenager, Salim and his family fled to Jordanian-controlled East Jerusalem, where they found refuge in the Moroccan Quarter. When their dwelling here was razed in 1967, they moved to a neighboring area, only to be displaced again in the 1970s to make way for the expanded Jewish Quarter.

Scores of properties in this "reconstructed" neighborhood were seized for "public" purposes. Israeli authorities eventually auctioned them off

25. Ricca (2007) estimates that several thousand Arabs were living here in the 1970s. The Israeli state has made use of previously devised British colonial legislation in its efforts to seize segments of Palestinian land. One such regulation is the British Land Ordinance of 1943. For more on this colonial continuity, See Adalah (2010) and Benvenisti (1996).

26. For more on the specifics of these efforts, see Khalidi (1999), Dumper (1997), and Abu El-Haj (2001).

to bidders who, under the terms the Jewish state established, precluded Palestinians from purchasing them. Discriminatory provisions that have barred non-Jews from owning or leasing land in the Jewish Quarter were upheld by a decision of the Israeli Supreme Court, *Burqan v. Minister of Finance* (1978). The case involved the contest between Palestinian homeowner, Muhammed Burqan, and the Israeli state over the former's home, which after 1968 lay within the boundaries of the expanded "Jewish Quarter." The rationale in the decision was consistent with Israeli and Zionist priorities historically, whether expressed in Israeli law or articulated in less formal, more quotidian expressions.[27] In it the Supreme Court recognized that the property did in fact belong to Burqan, but they refused to allow him the right to it because the area had "special historical significance" to Jews. This unique and eternal connection was said to supersede all other claims by non-Jews, including that of the actual Muslim owner.[28]

A COLONIAL "PUBLIC"

Since the late 1970s, Israeli authorities have been able to keep the "redeemed" Jewish Quarter largely free of Palestinian Muslims and Christians. This has been done through a range of discriminatory discourses and practices, aided by the assumptions expressed in the *Burqan* decision and Kollek's memoir, too. Crucial among these is the need to maintain different national communities apart—separate and unequal. Integral to realizing this vision of *hafrada* (separation) has been Israel's creation of a peculiar kind of "public" sphere.[29]

27. In several cases, these properties were subsequently put up for "public" auction in Israel but could only be bid on by those who, in the words of the bylaws of the CRDJQ, "had served in the [Israeli] army or were new immigrants (i.e. [Israeli] Jews who came to Israel under Israel's [1950] Law of Return)" (Kretzmer 1990, 80).

28. See Abowd (2000) and Ricca (2007) for more on the character of this segment of the Old City.

29. Leading Israeli civil libertarians and human rights activists have referred to Israel not as a democracy but as an "ethnocracy." For specific critiques see the work of

Under Israeli authority land defined as "public" or "state" has had an irregular meaning, one different than in countries with broader and more consistent democratic freedoms. Under Israeli rule public land has historically been reserved for the exclusive use of the *Jewish* public. Even Palestinians who possess Israeli citizenship (sometimes referred to as "1948" Palestinians) are formally precluded from accessing, leasing long term, or owning public or state land only for the reason that they are not Jewish. This central legal and spatial dimension of the Jewish state is, I believe, vital to acknowledge because it points precisely to the colonial character of Israeli rule. While international observers may condemn Israel's military occupation of territories conquered in 1967 many believe nonetheless that "within Israel" there exists a more or less democratic and egalitarian system. I have been arguing that Israeli practices of exclusion are expressed in ways that overlap and intertwine the entirety of Palestine/Israel on both sides of the so-called 1967 borders. This is most evident in Jerusalem, a city that straddles these various zones of governance.

PAVING OVER HISTORY: PERFORMING THE ETERNAL

Today, the Western Wall Plaza and the contiguous Jewish Quarter appear to form a seamless spatial and historical unity. Few traces of the former Moroccan Quarter remain. But as I walked this part of the Old City over the last twenty years, aware of some of the transformations that had taken place there since 1967, I searched for elements of an erased existence. Could fragments of lost communities and homes be observed? What remained among the ruins of history?

Like the thousands of others who visit the Kotel area each week, I would typically enter it by heading down a narrow alleyway that bisects Tariq as-Silsilah (The Street of the Chain) at the site of the Khalidi Library (Maktabe Khalidiyya). A sign at this juncture, erected by the occupying

Israeli Jewish scholars Yiftachal (2006), Halper (2010), and Honig-Parnass (2011). This, it is argued, is true not simply in East Jerusalem and other territories occupied in 1967 but within Israel's internationally recognized borders, too.

force after June 1967 as part of a vast renaming effort, announces in Hebrew *LiKotel* ("to the Western Wall"). The alley, about 10 feet wide and open to the sky, descends gradually toward the western edge of the spacious plaza. Stone structures of varying ages (some hundreds of years old, others but a few decades) envelop this path. Security cameras, mini panopticons, can be seen peering down at those who move into the Israeli-defined Jewish Quarter. The former Arabic designation *'Aqabat Abu Medain* has been renamed "Western Wall Street."[30]

Twenty meters or so down this thin lane lay an unobtrusive and barely noticeable entryway on the right. The door's diagonal wooden panels were painted green. The arched entrance was diminutive, not two meters high, and set within centuries-old stone. Inscribed delicately in black Arabic lettering were the words: *Zaawiya al-Mughariba*. Below the inscription was a hand-drawn Moroccan flag, its red background and black star barely discernible to passersby. Just inside the entry, insulated only slightly from the pedestrian traffic of those who typically stream to the Western Wall, was a shaded, serene courtyard. Further in, locals informed me, lies the tomb of Abu Medain, an Andalusian Sufi mystic who traveled to Jerusalem several centuries ago from North Africa. The ritual visits to this spot by Muslims have continued through the years of diverse rulers, occupations, and conquests dating back hundreds of years.[31]

The name of the saint has been taken as the signifier of this tiny subquarter, the last remaining Arab residential space within the region now delineated as the Jewish Quarter. Its roughly twenty Palestinian families refused to leave when the neighboring Moroccan Quarter was demolished in the late 1960s. Perhaps it was because this tiny area was somewhat peripheral to the center of the expanded Jewish Quarter that residents were able to win the right to remain when the rest of the area's Arab population was removed in the 1970s.

---

30. *'Aqabat* is Arabic for "gradual descent."

31. A *zaawiya* is a locale that usually hosts a saint's tomb and often a *nadi* (club) or *madafa* (guesthouse). Communities and neighborhoods in the Old City often grew up around such sites.

A few meters past the *Zaawiya al-Mughariba,* a permanent Israeli checkpoint with metal detectors and armed soldiers regulates movement into the Western Wall Plaza. If permitted to enter, hardly a guarantee for Palestinian young men, one can access the Kotel by descending a broad stone staircase. However, before doing so, it is possible to peer across the spacious plaza from this elevated position. From here one can observe the entirety of this reconfigured place, including where the Moroccan Quarter and its hundreds of residents once lived. From this vantage before 1967, one would have seen the rooftops of the former neighborhood and the top layers of the Kotel. Today, one sees much more and much less.

As I have been arguing throughout this book, it is not through sheer coercion alone that Israeli colonial authority is produced and sustained. The conscious ideological use of naming and renaming, the act of ascribing particular meanings to locales and overwriting others, the mobilization of particular legal discourses like "public" and "absentee," and a range of national rituals performed in the supposed shadow of the "presence of God" have all been crucial elements in the colonization of Jerusalem.[32]

What Benjamin (1973a) refers to as the "aestheticization of politics" relates quite centrally to the Israeli nationalist rituals and mass spectacles performed before the Western Wall since 1967. They routinely merge alleged divine directives with the IDF's supposed "purity of arms," discussed in chapter 3. This "holy site" is not only where graduation ceremonies for Israeli army officer corps are held but also where their weapons are consecrated. I spoke with a handful of Israeli men who took part in these ceremonies (among them "refuseniks," or Israelis who refuse to serve in the Israeli army in protest of its policies toward Palestinians). They shared with me that it was during these moments in the shadow of the Kotel that they were given a gun and a Bible upon the completion of

32. Across the plaza and contiguous to the Western Wall, a former Islamic school of religious instruction (the Mamluke-era *Madrasa Tankiziyya*) is situated near another Israeli security post, this one a police station. The forces of occupation have displaced the religious purposes of this building and set up the machinery of observation and spatial regulation. A slightly beat-up Hebrew sign on the Islamic school's ornate thirteenth-century northern portal announces its current uses.

their training.[33] The plaza hosts memorial services for fallen Israeli soldiers on Yom Hazikaron,[34] huge celebrations on Yom Ha'atzmaut (Israel Independence Day), and other gatherings of tens of thousands on Jewish religious holidays.

Not least, it is a vital site for the remembrance of the Holocaust, including on Holocaust Remembrance Day (Yom HaShoah). A series of flagpoles, each the height of a two-story structure, line the western fringe of the plaza. During special occasions, each flies an enormous Israeli flag. Here, the Jewish state is "unfurled" in the "presence of God." It is done so through the reiteration of particular notions of identity and alterity, the sacred and the profane. Within this area Israelis—religious and secular— claim that the Jewish people have been "redeemed" and made whole as they and others stride atop the site of the disappeared Moroccan Quarter.

REMEMBERING AND FORGETTING

The dialectical relationship between remembering and forgetting in Jerusalem and across the entirety of Palestine/Israel is quite noteworthy. It is not simply land, after all, that is fractured, cleansed, and circumscribed, but also the past. One curious locale where this can be observed is about 100 meters from the Kotel on the northwestern corner of the former Moroccan Quarter. Here, in the 1980s, a private Israeli interest built a memorial to the Nazi Holocaust.[35] It was established swiftly and without a government-issued building permit. Though constituting an illegal act under Israeli law and one that not uncommonly leads to demolition orders being served and properties razed if committed by Palestinians, this memorial has not been touched.

Its entrance is located halfway up a broad stone staircase, only meters away from the western entrance to the plaza, further up the stairs. The

---

33. Benvenisti (1996, 83) also mentions these military rituals and swearing-in ceremonies.

34. The formal name of this day is "Yom Hazikaron: Israel's National Remembrance Day for the Fallen and the Victims of Terror."

35. See Rubinstein (2001).

building possesses unimpeded views of the Kotel and from its windows one can observe for miles the rolling hills beyond the Old City walls to the south. This two-story edifice is made of smooth beige stones, which vaguely blend with the much older neighboring structures, some dating from at least the thirteenth century.

In 2003, I came upon the memorial and spoke with an employee, an animated man who I shall refer to as Sy. He was old enough to have been both a survivor of the genocide this site remembers and to have fought in the war that led to Israel's conquest of East Jerusalem. My interlocutor detailed the significance of the building's design in the dark main chamber of the memorial. Below this air-conditioned space, scores of camera-toting tourists milled about the plaza under the intense summer heat. They were grouped together by matching colored shirts and led by local guides approved by the Israeli government.

I wanted to learn a bit more about the genealogy of this memorial, knowing what had existed in this vicinity before 1967. Sy began to fill me in about Jerusalem's recent history as he saw it but somehow got sidetracked and began to tarry a bit in the "holy land's" biblical lore. He evoked the rule of King David, who, he claimed, was buried a short distance away and whose former "village" right wing Jewish settlers are working furiously to appropriate from the Palestinian villagers of Silwan just outside the Old City walls.

My interlocutor traced the significance that Jerusalem has possessed for Jews "since the beginning." I regret not asking him since the beginning of what? Or how we know, precisely, where King David was buried? He moved rapidly through history and covered great ground in our short conversation. But in the course of his grand narrative, not one word was uttered about the Palestinians—neither those uprooted from the area where the Holocaust memorial now stands nor in the city more generally. When I raised the issue of the destroyed Moroccan Quarter, he dismissed it out of hand, referring to it as "Arab propaganda."

We returned to a discussion of the memorial and I learned that its very design was intended to remember the roughly six million Jews killed by the Nazi regime. The site possesses six square windows that look out onto the Western Wall. The centerpiece of the memorial, which resembles a bulky chandelier made of metal and glass, is six-sided. Consistent with the overall theme, six prominent, encased torches are lit on the structure's roof with six Star-of-David-shaped containers enclosing these lamps. Israeli flags are also placed atop this and neighboring buildings, a subtle merging of Israeli nationalism and Jewish history under the aegis of the call to never forget.

Situated atop this commemorative edifice, amid the six lamps and Israeli flags, was an additional feature that spoke to the ways in which the past is continually under construction in Jerusalem. High above the plaza in large Hebrew letters was the word *yeskor* ("remember"). The message is meant to be seen by those traversing this part of the Old City. It exhorts all of the necessity of this task, while the land on which it rests has been wrested from those the Israeli state has wished to excise from history.

11. The word "remember" in Hebrew (*yeskor*) atop the Israeli Holocaust memorial, 2012. The structure sits on the fringes of the former Moroccan Quarter and the current Western Wall Plaza.

One need not question the importance of remembering genocide—any people's genocide—to challenge the manner in which a particular expression of tribute is mobilized here for colonial ends. As I came to meet more and more Israelis, some survivors of the Holocaust, I was inspired by those who invoked the annihilation of millions of European Jews, Roma, and others in the service of creating more justice and equality between Palestinians and Israelis today. That mode of remembering, done in the spirit of Auschwitz survivor Primo Levi (2002) and the Israeli civil libertarian, Israel Shahak (who survived Bergen-Belsen camp), can inspire and promote antiracism and contribute to more egalitarian futures in Palestine/Israel. Alternately, the exhortation to "never forget" can be mobilized in ways that overwrite the suffering of others, that etch the memory of certain victims over the homes, lands, and legacies of another people.

CONCLUSION

In *Mythologies*, Roland Barthes (1957) penned what I regard as a veritable poem about contemporary Jerusalem:

> Myth deprives the object of which it speaks of all History. In it, history evaporates. It is a kind of ideal servant: it prepares all things, brings them, lays them out, the master arrives, it silently disappears: all that is left for one to do is to enjoy this beautiful object without wondering where it comes from. Or even better: it can only come from eternity: since the beginning of time. (151)

Jerusalem the "beautiful object," as Zionists in Israel and elsewhere routinely contend, arrives divinely crafted, God's exclusive bequest to one people. This urban center of symbols and myths comes to us from the "beginning of time" but is also meant to exist under Israeli rule into the future and "in perpetuity." It has been my aim in this chapter to demonstrate how spatial and racial practices integral to Israeli colonial rule are processes always in motion, forever in flux, continually being made and remade but in a city all too often said to be "eternal" and "immutable." The Moroccan Quarter and its exiles, its destroyers and deniers underscore how orders of exclusion are envisioned in Jerusalem, how they are assembled, and, crucially, how they are resisted.

5

National Boundaries, Colonized Spaces

The Gendered Politics of Residential Life

> Between patriarchy and imperialism, subject-constitution and
> object-formation, the figure of the woman disappears, not into a
> pristine nothingness, but into a violent shuttling.
>
> —GAYATRI SPIVAK, "Can the Subaltern Speak?"

In the early hours of May 4, 1998, the night marking the fiftieth anniversary of Israel's establishment, a bomb was detonated in Musrara, a West Jerusalem neighborhood comprised overwhelmingly of Israeli Jews. Homemade explosives in a shopping bag were stealthily placed outside the entrance of a fourth-story apartment by a figure who then disappeared into the still evening. The blast jarred the residents of the building from their sleep and set the door of the targeted dwelling on fire. However, though the attack took place in a quarter where Israeli Jews predominate, the victims were not Jewish. The intended targets were three Palestinian women, tenants in the flat for nearly ten months. The only Palestinians living in this recently constructed apartment complex and three of only a handful of Arab residents in this neighborhood of a few thousand Israelis, these unmarried women in their twenties had been studying and working in Jerusalem for several years.

Awakened by the explosion that shook their living space with immense force, they sought refuge on their tiny balcony. From there, four floors up, they screamed for help. One of the women, Mona, told me how the bombing on this night of Israeli national ritual and remembrance was deeply distressing—but hardly astonishing. This had not, after all, been the first

145

time but the *third* time in seven months that an explosive device had been placed at their doorstep under the cover of nightfall.

"After the first two [bombings] we waited for the next one," Mona explained a few weeks after the third attack. "We *knew* they would bomb us again. But we refused to leave. I told Randa [one of her roommates] that day, before we went to sleep, that they would bomb us that night. I *knew* they would."

The "they" in question became a matter of intense controversy after the first assault on these women's home back on October 15, 1997. While nothing at the crime scene provided any evidence as to the perpetrator's identity, the residents (along with every other Palestinian I spoke with about these attacks) were never in doubt about who the bombers were. Keenly aware of the history of Jerusalem's geographies of racism, Palestinians and the Israeli Jews who supported these women expressed an unwavering certainty that the bombers were Israeli men, probably from the neighboring ultra-Orthodox (or Haredi) community of Mea Sharem. Mona and her roommates' suspicion was not unfounded. Nor, in the end, did their accusations turn out to be false. For weeks, beginning soon after they had signed a rental contract the previous July with the Israeli landlord, they had been subjected to acts of racial hatred and intimidation from Israeli men in the vicinity.

"They cursed us," related Mona's roommate Samia, describing the harassment. "They would yell, 'Go to Jordan!' 'Go to Gaza, bitches!' or 'This is not your country!'" All three roommates recalled how, when walking through the quarter, men—at times standing in groups—would stare at them or insult them as they passed. Boys from the Talmud Torah School, just up the street in Mea Sharem, occasionally threw stones at them as they walked by. Their Jewish neighbors in the same building, with one or two noteworthy exceptions, generally ignored them or treated them rudely—especially after the bombings began. All of these encounters contributed to a milieu in which they felt scrutinized and self-conscious. But as their time in the apartment progressed, they began to feel quite vulnerable, too—both before and for months after the initial attack in October.

Usually quite nimble when bombs explode in Jerusalem, the Israeli security services were somewhat sluggish in reacting to the initial act of terrorism directed against these Palestinian citizens of Israel. In the wake of the first bombing, the police stated that the regular harassment the residents had described—the stone throwing, the insults, and the intimidation—was irrelevant or incidental. Even if this had occurred, authorities informed them, it did not prove that the attackers were Israelis. And as these officials downplayed the victims' accusations, they posited their own theory: The assault, they asserted, was likely the work of Palestinian men threatened by these Arab women's "independent lifestyles."

That Palestinian men have frequently sought to regulate the boundaries of social and sexual propriety in their own communities is undeniable. As several writers have noted in other contexts, colonial and national conflicts have never failed to produce the simultaneous reality and fiction of girls and women as the "boundary markers" of the nation.[1] Palestinian men—and women, at times—have not uncommonly expressed anxieties about young, unmarried women living alone, particularly in places beyond the watchful eye of their families or communities. Although nearly every Arab Jerusalemite I spoke with about these bombings expressed support and sympathy for Mona and her roommates, a few questioned what these women had been doing in a residential area in West Jerusalem, populated by Israeli Jews and in what some regarded as the "Jewish side" of town.

But while only circumstantial evidence was found to suggest that the attackers might be Israeli Jews, absolutely none pointed to any Palestinian men. To what extent the police or other Israelis who advanced the "Arab honor" thesis believed its veracity is difficult to know. Given the context and character of the harassment and the pervasive (though not universal) conviction among Israeli Jews that Palestinians should live apart and in separate neighborhoods, I suspect that not all of the officials who attributed the violence to Palestinian men actually believed this to be true.[2] Had

1. See Joseph (1999), Kanaaneh (2002), McClintock (1995), Moallem (2005), Peteet (1991), and Stoler (2002).

2. Three of the Israeli Jews who supported the victims of these bombings and who spoke to the police about getting these women greater security told me that, in more than one instance during the period between the first and second bombings, the police handling the case admitted that the perpetrators were probably not Palestinian men.

they assumed an "Arab terrorist" was at large, one who had placed dangerous explosives in the middle of an Israeli neighborhood, a more substantial investigation would certainly have been opened after the initial bombing. As Israelis and Palestinians familiar with this case mentioned to me repeatedly, had there been evidence that the assailant was Palestinian, the women's demands for extra protection would not have been disregarded, as they initially were.

In a country like Israel, where residents incessantly declare how precarious is their "security" (and demand instant remedies in the face of "Arab terrorism"), why were Israeli officials so slow to address the needs of *these* victims of terrorism? The answer, I argue, strikes at precisely the dynamics of spatial exclusion in Jerusalem that this chapter explores. The three roommates believed they knew from whence this inaction came and they regarded it as simple racism (*'unsiriyya*). As Mona explained to me during the course of her year in the targeted apartment:

> If we were Jewish, Jewish women whose lives had been threatened, and the police even *thought* the attackers were Arab, they would have gone out into East Jerusalem and caught some Arab guy. Even if the attacker was not Arab they still would have caught the Arabs who "did it"! Israel would never have tolerated any Palestinian man threatening a Jewish woman like this. But when we are attacked by Jews, they do nothing.

Hostility toward girls and women regarded as "immodestly dressed" in this part of Jerusalem has become legendary. However, the men most likely to use physical violence to police behavior and dress (as innumerable Israeli women have attested) are from the ultra-Orthodox Jewish communities that reside in Mea Sharem. Signs erected at the entrance to this quarter—in Hebrew and English—warn that "Women in Immodest Dress Are Strictly Forbidden to Enter Our Neighborhood." Jewish men from this residential area have verbally and physically attacked female pedestrians on scores of occasions since the early 1990s for violating "local norms" of dress and behavior. To be a woman in this area—Palestinian, Israeli, or foreign—dressed in a sleeveless top or short skirt, for instance, is to be vulnerable to verbal harassment and physical abuse at the hands of these religious communities.

This chapter explores the gendered politics of residential space in contemporary Jerusalem. I concentrate on the lives of unmarried, adult Palestinian women and examine their experiences as they move away from familial environments in their towns and villages and seek to craft futures of their own choosing in Palestine's most diverse and vibrant city. By examining the gendered dimensions of nationalist politics in Jerusalem, I detail some of the everyday expressions of racism and sexism at the center of the Palestine-Israel conflict. What particular forms of authority do Palestinian women encounter under colonial rule and what spatial practices have they engaged in to resist or accommodate these strictures?

This chapter is based on interviews and conversations with forty-three Palestinian women from the mid-1990s to 2012. Those I spoke with explained the multiple challenges they confronted as they sought to work, study, and engage in political activism in a city under sole Israeli political control. More than eight in ten of my interviewees come from the roughly 1.7 million Palestinians residing within the Jewish state and holding Israeli citizenship. They are the children and grandchildren of the first Arabs to fall under Israeli rule in 1948. Fluent in Hebrew as well as Arabic, they generally know Israeli society quite well. Indeed, in certain ways they are fundamentally *of* Israeli culture, not simply a minority population living *in* the Jewish state. But in important respects, as nearly every woman I spoke with articulated, these Muslim and Christian citizens are all too often treated by the Jewish majority as outsiders, as unwanted, or as a sort of social pollution. They have even been referred to by more chauvinist elements in Israel as a foreign presence that should be expelled.[3]

3. An examination of the burgeoning, post-2000 Israeli laws and prohibitions that impinge on Palestinian citizens of the state points to a growing chauvinism against non-Jews in the Jewish state. For more see Mada al-Carmel (2012) and other recent reports produced by this Palestinian human rights organization.

By virtue of holding Israeli passports, these "Arab Israelis" (as the state has sought to classify them) have resided in a decidedly "in-between" status of rights and responsibilities. Denied the same economic opportunities and civil liberties as the Jewish citizens of Israel, they nonetheless have privileges that Palestinians living under military occupation in the West Bank and Gaza Strip do not. But if the roughly four million Arabs in the territories occupied by Israel in 1967 have been deprived of their right to national self-determination, those who possess Israeli citizenship remain citizens of a state that is not the state of its citizens but instead of the Jewish people wherever they may live.

The movement of these women away from their familial realms, and their concomitant efforts at forging more substantial personal autonomy, have been part of broader trends over the last few decades of rising levels of Palestinian female labor participation and matriculation in institutions of higher education. A number of important scholarly works that examine these trends, in Palestine/Israel and elsewhere, have argued that, though fraught with dangers to women, these emerging opportunities have generally enabled them to more effectively confront patriarchal authority and familial forms of control.[4]

Those I interviewed spoke of the promise their journeys to Jerusalem held out. But as they detailed these moves away from the spheres of family and kin, it became evident that their travels to and travails in the "big city" rarely represented a linear path toward liberation. Such struggles at achieving economic and social independence, though often advantageous, in a majority of cases exposed unmarried adult Palestinian women to other dynamics of domination and forms of chauvinism. Consequently, their experiences in this deeply segregated urban center were typically characterized by movement into, through, and out of a range of residential realms, a sort of zigzagging through neighborhoods of East and West Jerusalem.

4. Among the important studies that discuss the impact of Palestinian female participation in the labor market are Muhammad et al. (2012), Kuttab (2005), and Vitullo, Araj, and Said (1998). For more general studies on the politics of gender and labor participation see Rofel (1992), Salzinger (2003), and Sassen (1999).

I argue, therefore, that these women's treks to Jerusalem have been matched in significance by the circuits they have been compelled to travel within the city. As they crossed Jerusalem's internal frontiers—contending with economic hardship, racism, and sexism as a matter of course—they almost always pressed ahead with their quests for personal, professional, and political advancement. Those I spoke with defined these goals differently and though they have not always met these goals, they have, in virtually all cases, fought hard to achieve them.

INSCRIBING HATRED: THE GENDERED RACIALIZATION OF PALESTINIAN WOMEN

Racism, national chauvinism, class oppression, and gender discrimination all impinge on the lives of the Palestinian women with whom I spoke. But as I have been arguing throughout this book, so too does the persistence of colonial power. Therefore, I pursue an intersectional approach to the varied forms of domination that affect those I interviewed and observed. Following the work of others who have written in this vein,[5] I detail how specific oppressions intersect in contemporary Jerusalem and how they inform and constitute one another as they converge, merge, and diverge. How, for instance, do both Palestinians and Israelis seek to keep Palestinian women in their "proper places"—spatially, culturally, and morally?

One illustration of these attempts to constrain and control these women were the multiple expressions of abuse directed at the residents of the bombed apartment. If the messages intended by the bombings were at all ambiguous, a steady stream of accompanying graffiti, scrawled on the walls outside the targeted women's flat throughout their stay, clarified a great deal. These inscriptions were emblematic of the various forms of authority that Mona and her flatmates had contended with during their fourteen collective years residing, working, and going to school in Jerusalem. But these missives, always written in Hebrew, were particularly

---

5. For particularly good studies on these topics see Anzaldua (1999), Brodkin (1999), Crenshaw (1996), Naber (2012), and Smith (2005).

intense. They helped indicate who the attackers might have been and underscored how these residents were regarded, both as Arabs and as women.

Among the written and verbal insults leveled against them, one could see a convergence of misogyny and anti-Arab racism. In one instance *nevella*—an arcane biblical Hebrew term for a rotting female carcass—was inscribed on the stairwell outside their front entrance and greeted them as they left for work in the morning. Others referred to the Arab residents as "wild animals" and "Nazis." The Hebrew message *manyakim hakhutsa* (Fuckers Get Out) was scrawled above their mailbox early on in the course of their stay in the targeted apartment. Samia remembers coming home to find these words one night, shortly before making her way up the three flights of dimly lit stairs that led to her apartment.

On another occasion a swastika was drawn near their front door. Harassment of this sort—deploying this specific symbol—was leveled at four other Palestinian women I interviewed who resided in Israeli neighborhoods in Jerusalem. The use of Nazi symbols not only signaled that these Arabs were unwelcome but that they constituted a presence as antithetical and offensive to Jews as could be imagined. Etching such a message on the site of the targeted apartment seemed to indicate a desire to continually clarify where the national (and racial) boundaries were in this city and who belonged where.

The written texts, therefore, mirrored the jeers these women faced in Jerusalem's public spaces throughout their years here. These were exhortations that demanded, among other things, "Whores get out," and "Go to Gaza, bitches!" The gendered racialization of these Palestinians, this process of solidifying notions of who belonged where, illuminated the complexities of domination under Israeli colonial rule. I shall take up these concerns and their effects at greater length in the sections that follow.

A SECOND BOMBING: "MATTER OUT OF PLACE?"

The first bombing in October 1997 was followed by a second one six weeks later, on the night of November 30. Then mayor of Jerusalem Ehud Olmert and other Israeli governmental authorities reacted to this potentially deadly attack in a peculiar manner. After dismissing the first assault as the work of Arab men, their general response to the subsequent bombing indicated a shift in the direction of their accusations—though never explicitly.

Violent and audacious, the second bombing precipitated media coverage from Bethlehem to San Francisco. *Tikkun* magazine, Israeli newspapers, and National Public Radio covered the story. The series of attacks against these women even eventuated in the intervention of a U.S. Senator on behalf of these women after a progressive, Vermont-based rabbi took the cause of these Palestinians to his elected official. But it was also followed by ever more intense calls from Israelis for the women to leave the building. State authorities and, in fact, most of the Jewish residents of the apartment complex chose to blame the Arab residents for the attacks.[6]

How, one might ask, did three, unarmed college students provoke the planting of potentially lethal, explosive devices outside their front door? Responses came in different forms from various corners. But the prevailing answer was some variant of the following: By moving into a Jewish neighborhood, these Palestinian women unleashed the predictable sorts of sentiments and reactions that transgressing such moral and physical boundaries were sure to set off. "What did they expect?" or "They knew what they were doing" were frequent responses to these bombings, ones both the victims and I heard from Israeli Jews in the course of the year.

When these women resisted by remaining steadfast (*samud*) in the wake of the first attack and refusing to leave, Israelis they knew not infrequently disparaged their practices of antiracism as being themselves responsible for subsequent violence. This is not an exceptional reaction in circumstances such as these, whether in Palestine/Israel or elsewhere. As Etienne Balibar notes with regard to national chauvinism in Europe, dominant racial, religious, or ethnic communities frequently assert that "it is anti-racism which creates racism by its agitation and its manner of 'provoking' the mass of the citizenry's national sentiments" (1991a, 23).

6. This rationale, of course, finds its parallel in the discourses that blame victims of rape (e.g., "she asked for it" or typified by questions about "what she was wearing"). The Palestinian women attacked in the Musrara apartment were said by a number of Israelis to have "provoked" the bombing. Their persistence in resisting attempts to remove them, their refusal to move away, many Israelis remarked, was further provocation.

As I interviewed other Palestinian Jerusalemites similarly situated to these women, it became clear that Israeli Jews in Jerusalem frequently regarded attempts at subverting this arrangement of apartness as themselves inflammatory. These acts of resistance were controversial to many because they were seen as threats to a supposed natural spatial order. This sentiment has, at times, been expressed quite publicly in Jerusalem. A few months before the second bomb was placed before these women's door, Mayor Olmert made a statement that encapsulated these sentiments:

> I can't tell you that my dream is to find more Arabs living in Jerusalem. I hope there will not be more Arabs living in Jerusalem, because national differences have an impact on the way of life. (1997, 67)

By crossing Jerusalem's "internal frontiers," these targeted residents came to be seen as what Mary Douglas refers to as "matter out of place" (1966, 44–50). Like the residents of the destroyed Arab Moroccan Quarter discussed in chapter 4, these women by their very presence violated the "cherished classifications" created by the city's rulers to ensure separation between Palestinians and Israeli Jews.

Israeli responses to these bombings were, in fact, varied. Most comments that I heard were unsympathetic or indifferent to the victims of this attack. But other Israeli Jews articulated declarations of support and even acts of explicit solidarity with the targeted Palestinians. These attempts to embolden the women were at times quite moving, including efforts by a Jewish American college student who slept on a worn couch near the front door of the beleaguered apartment for several weeks as part of an unarmed "civilian guard" organized by a Palestinian feminist organization.[7] This kind of courage and solidarity, however, was more the exception than the rule.

---

7. The civil guard was comprised of Israeli Jewish, American, and Palestinian volunteers. According to a leader in the Palestinian feminist group al-Fanar, who I interviewed at the time, the purpose of the guard was "to ensure the security of these women who are persecuted by racists with religious and national motivations."

Curiously, the residents related that, even among the Israeli leftists who visited them in solidarity, there were a small number who saw them as somehow wrongly situated. A few tried, politely, to persuade them to leave and find housing elsewhere in a neighborhood where their presence would not cause such heightened controversy. In the wake of the first two attacks, then, it was Palestinians who stood accused: After the first, they were blamed for being the probable perpetrators. After the second, they were blamed—in varying ways—for being the victims.

During a visit to the apartment following the second bombing, Mayor Olmert expressed as much. In a meeting with the women, he asserted that the bombings had taken place because these women had chosen to live in a Jewish residential area. His solution was that they move back to an Arab neighborhood of East Jerusalem. He would even help them. Never, according to the Palestinian residents, did the mayor refer to the assaults as "terrorism" or affirm that he would offer better protection. Mona and Samia spoke with me about the encounter with Olmert several months after they moved out. They still exhibited evident fury about the entire affair.

"He [Olmert] spoke to us as if he were interrogating us," Mona recounted. "He said, 'Why don't you go live in an Arab neighborhood? Why do you insist on living here?' as if *we* were the problem." When the women excoriated him for not providing them with better security (an issue that Olmert spoke routinely about when discussing the scourge of "Arab terrorism" in the city), he replied that the bombings were regrettable but that "Arabs bomb us [Israeli Jews], too."[8]

It would be difficult, I believe, to make the case that the mayor's remarks were anything other than deeply insensitive, particularly given how potentially lethal were these explosions. Further, and consistent with prevailing Israeli racial discourses, was the use of the all-encompassing term "Arabs bomb us." The linkage between these Arab women and those who had used violence against Israeli civilians spoke to precisely the

8. An account of this meeting was reported in *Ha'aretz*, December 1, 1997. Information about this encounter also comes from interviews with the Palestinian residents of the targeted apartment.

essentialist, they-are-all-just-Arabs-after-all assertions that I critique in this book.

Yet, in the process of attempting to obfuscate the meanings of these attacks, Olmert implicitly acknowledged that he believed the bombers were Israeli Jews. And from then on, the façade of the "Arab honor" explanations for these bombings would fade away in Israeli officialdom. This did not, however, compel Olmert to stand on the principle of equal protection nor to declare publicly that such hostility would not be tolerated. Instead, he tried to pressure these women to move to an "Arab" part of town in East Jerusalem. This would, in a sense, reclarify national and racial boundaries in the city, something the Israeli state has assiduously sought to do since 1948.

Mona and Samia expressed finding solace in the fact that they did not allow Olmert, a skilled political actor, to make of this meeting a photo opportunity favorable to him. Pictures of this encounter that appeared in the Hebrew press showed an interaction in which the bombing victims and the mayor are standing in the women's living room and observably at odds. The body language alone revealed the degree of tension in the meeting. The tenants cleverly allowed the press into their home but acted in ways that embarrassed Olmert. During the short visit, they lambasted him for his policies of exclusion in the city, which, they claimed, resulted in anti-Arab violence. They did not ask the mayor to sit down when he arrived and refused, as Palestinian custom dictates, to serve him anything to drink. "I'm sure he probably thought he could storm in and manipulate us because we were three little Palestinian girls," Samia asserted ironically. "Instead, he left very angry and nervous, especially since we told him we were not leaving."

THE ILLS OF INTERCOMMUNAL "MIXING"

The set of specific circumstances I have detailed above is significant not least because the women in question had, in this instance, found housing in one of the few Israeli-controlled quarters of Jerusalem where Palestinians were not at the time formally excluded from living. Unlike other areas of Israeli-occupied Jerusalem defined as Israeli "state land," this was a locale where Arabs were able to reside if they could persuade an Israeli landlord to rent to them. However, other methods were deployed to try to remove them, and those acts were not checked by the government in any fundamental way. In fact, those who sought to intimidate these Palestinians, I suggest, were encouraged by the state's inaction—by what officials did *not* say, what rights they did not affirm, and what they did not do.

Fear is an enduring feature of life in Jerusalem. At particular moments of heightened conflict, violence that targets civilians is something that concerns Israelis, Palestinians, and other residents of the city. But for all the talk of terrorism, the anxieties that have informed the policies of Israeli planners and politicians most forcefully over the last six decades seem to grow out of an abiding anxiety about the presence of "swelling" Arab populations and the Palestinian "demographic time bomb" within areas the Israeli state wishes to retain as exclusively Israeli Jewish. In no place does the presence of "too many" Palestinians or Arab-Jewish "mixing" create more fretfulness and agitation among Israelis than in Jerusalem, a city dominant Israeli discourses have projected as the "eternal capital of the Jewish people."

What became apparent to me after speaking with dozens of Israelis and Palestinians about demographic politics and cultural "mixing" in Jerusalem was that the vigorously held notion that different communities should live apart was not always premised on the view that one group was inferior or superior to another. Rather, as Balibar perceptively notes, an interest in "apartness" can be driven by a belief in the "insurmountability of (cultural) differences" (1991a, 21). This, he asserts, is a racism "which at first sight, does not postulate the superiority of certain groups or peoples in relation to others but 'only' the harmfulness of abolishing frontiers, the incompatibility of life-styles and traditions" (ibid.). In the following sections, I detail a bit more the impact that this and other racial and spatial logics have had on the lives of other Arab women in Jerusalem.

JERUSALEM AS AMBIVALENT HAVEN

For hundreds of unmarried Palestinian women who have moved away from their families and have come to reside in Jerusalem, the city has indeed been an ambivalent place. Nearly all of the women I interviewed for this chapter had found this fractured urban center, at least in part, a site of greater self-fulfillment, newfound freedom, and independence from family-based forms of control. Palestinians who travel to Jerusalem from villages and towns, both women and men, regularly obtain the benefits that cities of this size tend to offer. However, those advantages have rarely been realized without continual struggle, sometimes simply to feel safe within one's own home.

Roughly 75 percent of the Palestinian women I interviewed for this chapter noted that upon arrival in Jerusalem they possessed, at least initially, a desire to find living arrangements with other Palestinians. They felt safer in such places, which included one or another of the Arab neighborhoods of East Jerusalem or, for students at Hebrew University, with other Palestinians in the dorms. This was also frequently expressed as a need to locate themselves within a culturally familiar space. Because those with whom I spoke were mostly Arab citizens of Israel, the majority had the option of looking for housing in other Israeli cities such as Haifa or Tel Aviv. In response to my question "What brought you to Jerusalem?" nearly all mentioned that a major attraction was its large and vibrant Arab community.[9]

"It was not easy leaving my family," Rosa explained as we sat one evening in her apartment, a modest flat located in one of the more fashionable Israeli quarters of West Jerusalem. She shared the two-bedroom flat along a sedate, tree-lined street with two other Palestinian female students. These renters, all of whom worked and went to school, seemed to possess much of what they came to the city to find. This included a private residential space where they and their boyfriends could come and go as they wished and close proximity to several bus lines and shopping. However, in most cases they could only establish these conditions by actively creating distance from their families and by moving to a city several hours away from the villages and towns of their youth.

9. Jerusalem has, in fact, the largest Palestinian population of any urban center that Israel rules over—roughly 325,000 strong. Furthermore, in East Jerusalem there are at least a dozen neighborhoods where Palestinians predominate.

"In the U.S.," Rosa once reminded me, "you can move a million miles away from your family if you want. For us who grew up in the Galilee, Jerusalem [two to three hours away by car] is about as far away as we can go. When you run away," she smiled, "you come to Jerusalem."

Rosa literally did run away from her family. Born and raised in a small village south of Nazareth, she described progressively rejecting the at times restrictive gendered dictates of kin as a teenager. She left for Jerusalem at seventeen in the late 1980s in search of a life independent of fathers, mothers, brothers, and uncles. She arrived as a precocious but penniless young woman who had substantially severed ties back home. In Jerusalem Rosa created new bonds of solidarity, political relationships, and notions of commitment and community. The city became for her not just a place of exile but also a land of promise and possibility.

Like the vast majority of Palestinian Arabs who grew up in Israel and who are fluent in Hebrew, Rosa appeared to straddle various political and national communities. However, she related feeling completely at home in none of them. She spoke about the vast complexities of possessing various identities all at once, being a myriad of things at the same time, and having to negotiate these various notions of self in different contexts. For her, that meant discussing what it meant to be an Israeli citizen, a Palestinian nationalist, an orthodox Marxist, a radical feminist, a woman, daughter, and sibling all at the same time. These identities meant diverse things depending on where she happened to be located at any particular moment or in relation to whom she was encountering.

With the precision of a highly trained social scientist and the passion of an activist, Rosa detailed the specificities of gender relations in the Palestinian society in which she grew up. She drew distinctions between words like "tradition(al)" (*turath*) and "backward" (*mutakhalif*) or "primitive" (*primateeve* in Hebrew) to depict her own predicament and those she grew up with back in the village. She was well aware of the power such words held and, even more critically, the use and meaning of these terms in such places as the Western academy and Israeli planning offices. Rosa would use the term *turath* in discussing her community's social relations. On the other hand, she normally rejected *mutakhalif*, citing the ways it was typically deployed under racist and colonial forms of authority.

Discussing her own predicament as a woman who had spent her entire adult life fighting gender oppression, she once explained how she made sense of these terms.

> I sometimes use *mutakhalifeen* ["the backward ones"] to talk about my cousins and brothers and other Arab men. I use it with other [Arab] women I am close to as a way of attacking them [male family members]. But I don't tolerate an Israeli or a Westerner talking about my culture this way.

I read this remark as signifying the kind of ambivalence that men and women under foreign rule, like those I interviewed, felt on a continual basis. Rosa was certain that the Palestinian-Israeli conflict was a colonial one. Her dealings with the Israeli state and Israeli Jews never allowed her to forget the relations of domination that constrained her and other Palestinians in circumstances of intense institutional racism. But her experience with colonialism was, Rosa explained, not simply with Israelis. She complained about feeling silenced and unheard, but not only by certain patriarchal elements among her kin. Feminists from North America and Europe (and not a few from Israel), she told me, were forever interested in "unveiling" the oppression she suffered at the hands of her own society, "saving" her from the ills of patriarchal "backwardness."[10] Rosa had little time for these expressions of supposed solidarity no matter how well-intentioned many of these Western feminists were. With irony in her voice, she once told me:

> I always wondered when these American and European leftists came here, how they had *so* much time to worry about me and other Palestinian women. They had infinite time for me. You know, I'd think like, don't they have enough problems to deal with back in Italy or in New York? Don't they have their own men to fight? Or are their men perfect?

---

10. For insightful work that critiques particular Western approaches to Middle Eastern women and the assumptions that are so often implicit within them, see Abu Lughod (2002, 2013), Mahmoud (2005), Moallem (2005), and Mohanty et al. (1991).

They should make their own societies better before they start coming here to "liberate" me.

I routinely encountered this sentiment among the women I interviewed when these subjects were raised. The majority of those who had had contact with foreign nongovernmental organizations (NGOs) and scholars were able to offer a critique of the patronizing attitudes that have so consistently seeped into the "sisterhood is global" discourse of privileged Western feminists.

The Palestinian women I met made very few excuses for "their men." In fact, in front of me they were reluctant to defend the male members of their families and communities even slightly. I came to believe that this was probably the case because, as a man, they wanted me to understand as thoroughly as possible the strictures within which they were forced to deal. Rosa and several other women communicated (sometimes subtly, sometimes explicitly) that as a *male* researcher I was not outside of these relations—nor could I ever be. But I also witnessed how facile attacks against Palestinian men from those beyond their communities were not infrequently regarded by these women as ill-informed, ignorant, and even racist—as so often they were.

COLONIALISM, GENDER, AND THE PERSISTENT PULL OF PATRIARCHY

The experiences of Ghada, a woman in her late twenties, were in many ways similar to those of Rosa. She, too, was from a Palestinian town in the Galilee and had also constituted a life of relative autonomy and professional advancement in Jerusalem. But her situation was at variance with Rosa's in a number of respects, particularly since she maintained close ties with her immediate family and came from relative privilege and status. Ghada's relationships, goals, and tribulations in Jerusalem as a single woman mirrored those of other Palestinian women I met. She and other young women were individuals with professional goals who had also moved away from family and kin as much to advance themselves educationally as to achieve privacy and independence from their families. Like a number of middle- and upper-middle-class Arab women I spoke with, Ghada left her parent's house at age eighteen when she entered Jerusalem's Hebrew University.

"They [her parents] demanded that I get [a university] education," she told me. "And I wanted to study, too. But I also wanted to move to a place where everyone did not know me as someone from my family, as someone's daughter. The village is *very* small and the gossip surrounds you. Luckily," she smiled, "Israel is not building any colleges in the Arab areas. Otherwise, they [my parents] might have insisted that I go to school there, near them, and live at home."

Unlike Rosa, Ghada did not regard her departure from her wide web of "essential kin," as Carol Stack refers to such family members (1974, 43–44), as an "escape." Rather, she described her tight-knit familial ties in much the same way that Palestinian feminist Nadia Hijab does in her documentary when she refers to Arab family life as being often like a "warm blanket": at times oppressive during hot months but never something that she would want to discard when life became cold and lonely (Hijab and Luke 1985).

More than nine years after what had become a permanent move to Jerusalem, Ghada spoke feelingly about her kin and expressed an unmistakable affection for her parents and grandparents. As she grew more politically active in the city in her mid-twenties, she told me that she came to increasingly appreciate the predicaments of her parents' generation. These were the travails of the first Arab people subjected to Israeli colonial rule in the wake of the creation of the Jewish state. Two decades before the Palestinians of the West Bank and Gaza Strip, these communities lived for eighteen years under Israeli military rule *within* the state of Israel, regulations only lifted in 1966. During those years, tens of thousands of Palestinians had to obtain permission from those who occupied their land to even travel outside their own towns or villages.[11] Ghada's grandmother and mother did not have the option to attend university as Ghada did.

---

11. For one of the best accounts of those times for Palestinian citizens of Israel see Jiryis (1976).

The vast majority of women from that generation did not work in wage-labor jobs outside the homes, realms they characteristically managed with immense skill. Older generations of women who came of age in the 1950s and 1960s would commonly marry and have three children before they turned twenty-five years old.[12]

Their daughters and granddaughters in the 1980s, 1990s, and 2000s, however, progressively sought professional possibilities beyond the home. Ghada had a range of choices not afforded women from other generations, including remaining unmarried as long as she had. She was ambitious and serious about her career as a teacher and translator. The future she wanted for herself could not, she explained to me, be obtained in her family's village and perhaps not in Palestine/Israel at all.

Ghada had a number of Palestinian friends, women and men, who possessed similar interests in forging an independent existence in a much larger, more anonymous urban environment. However, in a few cases, as she, Rosa, and others of her generation would tell me, colleagues and friends ended up returning to their town or village (or to that of their spouse) where certain basic financial and social needs were more easily met. Sometimes these moves were permanent, sometimes not. But, as was routinely the case, these expressions of familial support came with a "catch." To decide to marry and make a life among a broader kin network was at times to walk back into someone else's home, with all of the expectations about proper gender roles, norms, and notions of family that patriarchal environments usually seek to sustain. Love and support, control and domination were not discrete phenomena but were bound together in a complex mixture of reciprocal obligations. I was reminded of the continued importance of the Second Wave feminist assertion (echoing Foucault) that "the personal is political" when I witnessed and heard how crucial the influence of familial forms of control were in the lives of most of the women I interviewed.

One of the criticisms Ghada and others leveled at those *ijaanab* (foreigners) who wished to "save" them was that these activists, scholars,

12. For an excellent discussion of familial life and natal and prenatal politics for Palestinians in Israel, see Kanaaneh (2002).

and "development people" from Western NGOs were unable to grasp the extent to which family, familial politics, and gender roles were not only a crucial dimension of many of their lives but also the ways they had shifted over time. This had happened, at least in part, because of the alternative futures these young women were working furiously to forge. I could understand why they would resent what they frequently regarded as these outsiders' patronizing views and behavior, even if well intentioned.

Changes in gender roles and advances in women's rights have never simply been mechanical reflections of heightened female labor participation or higher degrees of education. But I have come to believe, after scores of conversations with Arab women in circumstances similar to those of Ghada, Rosa, and others, that it would be difficult to make the case that these broader trends have not had a considerable impact on the consciousness and conditions of younger generations of Palestinians—women and men. Such increased professional and educational possibilities have certainly provided more economic autonomy from family, even for workers who faced discrimination and sexual harassment in the Israeli labor market. What began to come more plainly into focus for me was the fact that these women felt "shuttled," to use Spivak's (1988) image, between poles of chauvinism, just as Ghada and others were moved back and forth between Arab and Jewish neighborhoods in the city.[13]

Though already a few years older than the average age of marriage for Palestinian women in the late 1990s, Ghada did not feel particularly compelled to find a husband. Like her circle of close female colleagues in Jerusalem, she was immersed in the city's enriching cultural life, her schoolwork, and her job. Gregarious and beautiful, she enjoyed the company of countless friends and acquaintances, mostly Arabs, but also Israeli Jews—especially leftists—and foreigners. She rarely was without a boyfriend or male companion, having had a string of serious relationships with shorter ones in between.

13. The reference to shuttling or "violent shuttling" from Spivak's (1988) seminal piece describes a movement back and forth between the forces of colonial violence and native patriarchal authority.

Ghada's independence was striking to me. It was displayed in her dress, relationships, interest in Hebrew literature, and the manner in which she handled her parents on the phone. It was also made manifest in the ways she had fought for and won self-sufficiency from a vast web of kin expectations and obligations, from those family members like her mother who were less and less enamored by her unmarried status. But what I found equally important about Ghada's connections with her immediate family was how frequently—almost habitually—she would make the nearly six-hour round trip journey from Jerusalem to her parents' home in the Galilee, after a long and arduous work week teaching 120 teenage girls in a secondary school. These "paper-thin" weekends would entail her traveling by crowded Israeli bus, with two transfers. She would typically leave on a Friday morning or afternoon and return just after Shabbat had ended, once the Israeli buses began to run after sundown on Saturday.

Upon her return to Jerusalem, she commonly appeared quite tired and stressed as she unloaded the pickled vegetables and olives her mother had packed for her. And as she did, Ghada would unfailingly complain to me and other acquaintances about "home," as she readied herself for the week of teaching that would begin the next day at 7:30 A.M. What bothered her most, she told me, was her mother's incessant prodding about marriage. Her relatives would also chime in, carrying on about a matter she did not wish to discuss with them and that she regarded as none of their business.

Ghada detailed the ways in which she was beginning to be perceived in the village as a twenty-eight-year-old single woman. She wanted to be married and to be a mother someday, but not yet. And she reviled efforts to mold her into a particular kind of feminine subject, to position her in her "proper" familial place. That ambivalence, it seemed to me, wore on her at times. As she moved back and forth from city to village and back again, she was also drawn to and fro emotionally. The cost of fashioning a future at strong variance with her mother's trajectory was as evident to me as the sustenance she drew from the relations and family life from which she had distanced herself.

"I knew soon after I arrived at the university [in the early 1990s]," she once told me, "that I would never be going back *to live* in the village—just to visit. It would be easy to tell my parents 'I want to get married!' and have them start that process and go back and live there and raise a family. But I will never do it their way." This was a prevalent sentiment about village life among the young, single Palestinian women and men I spoke with during my fieldwork.

But there were also related concerns about national identity and growing levels of awareness that these unmarried adult Palestinians began to acquire while residing in Jerusalem. Nearly all mentioned suffering from a sense of having been marginalized within Israeli society, as citizens in a state that is—by Israel's own definition—not the state of all its citizens.[14] As non-Jews in the Jewish state they had been politically circumscribed, ideologically contained in a polity that denies their national identity. As one female Palestinian professional from the Galilee noted, "Before I moved to Jerusalem I was confused—my identity was confused. I did not know my [Palestinian] history. I did not know who I was."[15]

FINDING COMMUNITY AND HOUSING IN ARAB JERUSALEM

Though the women I interviewed typically moved into and out of a variety of areas in Jerusalem, the majority chose first to live in one of the dozen or so Arab neighborhoods in East Jerusalem. However, securing such a place had rarely been a simple task for several reasons. For one, Israeli authorities, as part of their efforts to control Palestinian population growth in the city, have severely limited the number of housing units

14. These principles are made clear in the Declaration of the Establishment of the State of Israel, May 14, 1948. http://mfa.gov.il/MFA/ForeignPolicy/Peace/Guide/Pages /Declaration%20of%20Establishment%20of%20State%20of%20Israel.aspx. For more on how they function institutionally see Davis and Lehn (1983).

15. Palestinians who grew up as Israeli citizens, and who came of age politically in Jerusalem, expressed this sentiment on myriad occasions. Forced to learn an Israeli-controlled curriculum in elementary and secondary school and isolated from the rest of the Arab world since 1948, the more than 1.7 million Palestinian citizens of the Jewish state have faced multifaceted issues around identity. Moving to Jerusalem, meeting other Palestinians from the West Bank and Gaza, and observing military occupation firsthand usually had a tremendous politicizing effect on them.

Palestinians are permitted to build in Jerusalem. This has led to a dearth of dwellings in Arab neighborhoods and contributed to significant over-crowding, as I will discuss at greater length in chapter 7.[16]

In the search for places to live in Palestinian East Jerusalem, female students and workers I spoke with generally encountered another set of social forces that they had hoped to leave behind in their villages or towns. Privacy and the desired latitude to live as they wished could often be limited in these neighborhoods. In these quarters, other residents sometimes discovered—through gossip or word of mouth—a good deal about these single women before they had even been introduced to them. This "talk" had particular gendered dimensions too. Further, there were assumptions among some neighbors about how these Palestinian citizens of the Jewish state might be different than the vast majority of Arab Jerusalemites who were not Israelis. This was somewhat surpris-ing to me but I did, in fact, hear this view expressed on more than a few occasions.

Two Palestinian women I came to know fairly well, Randa and Rania, had spent five years in Jerusalem as students and workers during the late 1990s and early 2000s. They followed a familiar circuit of travel for unmar-ried adult Arab women and were confronted with many of the same con-cerns that Ghada, Rosa, and others faced. As was true for fully half (22 of 43) of those I spoke with who made the journey to Jerusalem, these women had initially moved from their familial towns and villages to the dormi-tories of Hebrew University, where they matriculated as undergraduates. After a couple of years living in tiny dorm rooms, most decided to move to Palestinian neighborhoods in East Jerusalem.

16. In more upscale (and even more modest) middle-class Palestinian neighbor-hoods of East Jerusalem, rental costs by the late 1990s easily rivaled those in medium-sized U.S. college towns. As such, they were off-limits to most Palestinians. Instead, these properties were all too often rented to "internationals" who could afford them, including members of an endless wave of foreign NGO employees particularly present in Palestine in the 1990s. By the late 1990s it was not uncommon for foreigners to pay $1,000 a month for a two-bedroom place. This, in a city where local economists estimate that the average Palestinian household lived on less than $4,000 annually a year.

In their hunt for off-campus housing, they sought a place where they could easily get transportation to and from the university at night. This deeply restricted their search, since Israeli buses rarely run through Palestinian areas of the city and its environs. Further, the insufficient Palestinian-owned bus service did not stop at the Hebrew University nor run very often in the evenings. Even if female students were willing to walk the distance of several kilometers back and forth from school, it simply was not preferable after dark.

"I was told about a man who might have a place in Shu'afat [an Arab neighborhood 2 to 3 kilometers from the university]," said Randa. "He directed me to his father who, when he saw me and my friend—our clothes, our hair—obviously didn't want us [as tenants]."

"What *about* your clothes?" I asked.

"We didn't dress . . . the way they thought was acceptable. You know, modest."

Rania explained what transpired next:

Then his wife came into the room and asked who we were asking on behalf of. We said "us" and she said in a friendly way, "Oh, why do you want to live alone?" As if it were any of her business! And these are the kinds of questions that, if they are already asking before we even move in, then you know that this cannot work and that they are going to be looking into your life and constantly watching you.

The two were finally able to locate a flat in a Palestinian neighborhood a few kilometers from campus. There, encounters with the landlord were courteous. He and his family generally stayed out of their business. But Rania and Randa remained a bit of an oddity, since few single women were living alone in this quarter and nearly everyone in the vicinity knew or wanted to know their "story." Like in most other Palestinian residential areas, they were the only residents who were students at Hebrew University, the fortress-like structure that sat on the nearby hilltop. Their neighbors noticed what they did and that their lives diverged from the realities and rhythms of this congested neighborhood.

Both Rania and Randa believed that their independence, displayed in part by their comings and goings at all hours, might well have been interpreted by some of the young men of the neighborhood as signifying that they were sexually available. Perhaps because of this, they told me, they occasionally found themselves the objects of verbal harassment or catcalls as they strode by groups of *shehab* in the neighborhood. They and other women shared with me that they felt observed here, the objects of a near-constant gaze.

"And did you feel unsafe?" I asked.

"Hmmm, not so much unsafe as uncomfortable—looked at a lot," Randa replied.

More than eight in ten of the women I spoke with residing in similar circumstances in East Jerusalem talked about varying degrees of the same sort of social surveillance. Neighbors would from time to time peer out of doors and from behind half-drawn curtains to see what they were doing. Others in their same apartment complex seemed to pay attention to who their visitors were and when they came and went. Those I interviewed told of a sort of "social panopticon": even when the neighbors were not directly watching them, they could never be sure that there were not other sets of eyes on them. Like nearly every woman I spoke with, Rania told me that she had to engage in greater self-regulation than she wished to.

"You are always watching what you do here," Rania stated. "How you dress, who visits you. I have to censor myself a lot."

"Were there positive aspects about living here?" I asked.

"I guess," Randa said, unenthusiastically. She lit up a cigarette, adjusted the tiny space heater before us, and reclined in thought on her worn couch.

People in our culture see it as their duty to care about what is happening to other people. There is good intention in some of this [observation] and I have become friends with women in the neighborhood. It would be a great place to bring up children but it is just not where I am at this point. I want the freedom not to have to explain myself.

Though expressed in various ways, this was an opinion articulated by dozens of other single Arab women living in Jerusalem. As individuals in search of privacy and a place where they were able to make the principal decisions that affected their personal lives, they all too often bumped up against a patriarchy (*abuwiya*) similar to that which they wished to extract themselves from back home in their familial environment. As one interlocutor succinctly put it, "Sometimes the village is in the city."

CROSSING NATIONAL BOUNDARIES

A majority of the Arab women I interviewed decided at some point during their time in Jerusalem to explore housing options in particular neighborhoods where Israel Jews are the majority. Unlike Palestinians who grew up in the West Bank, East Jerusalem, and Gaza Strip, Palestinians from "inside Israel" possess not only Israeli citizenship but also fluency or near fluency in Hebrew. This, along with an often sophisticated knowledge of the Israeli social and political terrain, has permitted them to navigate their way through the procedures for finding apartments in Israeli neighborhoods.

Most of my respondents told me that the trend of crossing over into Israeli quarters where few Palestinians lived arose throughout the late 1980s and the 1990s. As the dearth of housing in East Jerusalem continued to intensify during the same period, it was sometimes cheaper to rent a modest place on the west side than on the east. Those Palestinian women I met who chose to live in West Jerusalem overwhelmingly sought out places more secular and middle-class. They regarded those who resided there to be more open-minded and less concerned with policing their movements than in other areas of the city like the ultra-Orthodox quarter of Mea Sharem mentioned above. This more "liberal" outlook, so the thinking went, would allay the possibility of both anti-Arab racism and gender harassment. But those I interviewed routinely came to understand that the city's social landscape was not as easily reducible to a "secular/liberal/safe" versus a "religious/chauvinist/dangerous" dichotomy.

The experiences of searching for apartments rented by Israeli Jews were usually tales of frustration and humiliation. Nearly every one of my

respondents could recall multiple incidents in which their Arab or Palestinian identity precluded them from residing in an Israeli neighborhood.
Would-be Palestinian tenants so often inquired about a long string of rent-
als advertised in Hebrew newspapers, on billboards at Hebrew University,
or on the walls of West Jerusalem commercial centers, only to have landlord after landlord disqualify them upon learning that they were Arab.
Some advertisements or fliers even stated a preference for "Jews-only" (a
perfectly legal practice in Israel). As one exasperated Palestinian female
student explained: "We call and ask about an apartment in Hebrew and all
is well until it comes time to give our name. When we do, we get a silence
on the other end. I've done this so many times I know what is going to
happen when I hear that silence."

Whether inquiries were made in person or over the phone, the signifiers of difference Israeli Jews routinely regarded as "dangerous," those
markers that indicated an unwanted presence, usually became apparent
once Palestinians provided their names or where they grew up or spoke
Hebrew with an accent that marked them as "Arab." As I have argued
throughout this book, one of the implications of living in a country as
segregated as Israel/Palestine is that the region, neighborhood, or town
that one resides in usually identifies one's identity.

Israeli landlords—men and women—would frequently ask coded
questions when the names Palestinians gave did not register as Hebrew
ones. Queries such as "Oh, where are you from?" or "Are you from Israel?"
or "What is your last name?" might follow, with the intention, it seems,
of ascertaining the caller's religious and national identity. And then there
were countless stories in which the Arab caller would be refused even
a viewing of the apartment because, as the Israeli landlord would awkwardly explain, "You would not be comfortable here."

Despite the generalized reluctance to rent to Palestinians, such movements across national divides did occur with increasing frequency until
the beginning of the Second Intifada in 2000–2001. They disrupted dominant Israeli efforts to create and perpetuate an order of strict communal
separation in the city between Arabs and Jews. I wish to turn to the gendered experiences of these circuits of travel in the following section.

ON THE MOVE WITH SUAD

Suad wanted a place of her own. In her twenty-four years, she had never once had her own room—certainly not her own apartment. Life with seven siblings in a cramped dwelling in her family's poor village just outside of Jerusalem afforded no such opportunity. Neither was she able to obtain the solitude and privacy that young writers and budding poets routinely require during her two years in the student dorms at Hebrew University. Carving out her own private realm in the Palestinian neighborhood that she had lived in for several months had proven unattainable. This was true despite the fact that her apartment was moderately priced, nicely appointed, and initially appeared to offer her a degree of seclusion and safety. Suad shared the flat with a Lebanese American roommate who studied at Birzeit University. The place became the hangout of dozens of other young artists and students on Thursday and Friday evenings, a site of quite lively gatherings, loud music, and the near-constant comings and goings of friends.

But as her time there progressed, those she lived among in this middle-class area simply became too intrusive, her neighbors too meddlesome, and some of the local *shebab* too obnoxious. When a "respectable" father of five, a few homes down the road, prevailed upon her open-minded landlord to stop her from having such noisy parties and male guests, Suad had had enough. Looking to expand her housing options and hoping to find a place that would permit her the anonymity and social latitude she desired, she initiated a search in a few different, more secular Israeli neighborhoods in West Jerusalem. After hunting for several weeks and making more than ten inquiries, nearly every Israeli landlord she spoke with refused to rent to her once they discovered that she was a Palestinian.

She finally found an affordable option agreeable to her and her roommate, another female Arab student in her early twenties. The Jewish owner was, Suad told me, "a wonderful woman" who taught at Hebrew University and who was totally opposed to Israel's occupation. She had no issue subletting to Palestinians and Suad sensed that her Israeli friend even preferred to rent her apartment to young Arab women over others. However, the flat, in the Jewish settlement of French Hill (Givat Shapira), was not exactly where Suad thought she would end up. The second settlement established in occupied East Jerusalem in the late 1960s, French Hill was home to roughly 7,500 Israeli Jews by the early 2000s.[17]

So spatially interwoven into West Jerusalem has this residential space become, that most Israelis probably do not even know that it was illegally built in Israeli-occupied East Jerusalem.[18] In fact, this fortress-like housing estate was, by the early 2000s, older than the majority of Palestinians and Israelis who resided in the city. Few I interviewed of any age could remember a time when the sight of its obtrusive beige towers, densely crowning one of Palestine's most beautiful hilltops, was not a part of the city's landscape.

French Hill, ironically, has a reputation for being a Jewish community more liberal in persuasion than most others. Though a settlement, it has been home to some of Israel's best-known liberal activists and civil libertarians, many of whom ironically state their opposition to "Jewish settlements." Despite the neighborhood's history as a site of colonial intrusion and its formal designation as a place reserved for Israeli Jews only, what it offers in the way of services, including reliable bus lines, well-lit streets, and easy shopping, has made it an attractive place for dozens of Palestinians. Its proximity to Hebrew University (a ten- to fifteen-minute walk away) makes it desirable for professors and students alike.

Palestinians are formally precluded from living here but sometimes are able to, provided they can persuade an Israeli Jewish occupant to sublet to them as was true in Suad's case. This increasingly happened in

17. The Israel Statistical Yearbook (2010) claims that there were nearly 9,000 people living in French Hill by 2009.

18. In a 2010 interview with an Israeli civil libertarian and human rights activist, Professor Jeff Halper, he estimated that no more than 10 percent of the Israeli Jewish population would regard this residential space as an "illegal settlement." The scenic hilltop where French Hill now stands was taken in part from the contiguous Palestinian village of Assiwiyya after the Jewish state conquered the east side in 1967. As Israeli "state land," much of it is officially reserved for the exclusive use and benefit of Jews only by the bylaws of the bodies that regulate land under Israeli rule.

the 1980s and 1990s as more and more Palestinians with Israeli citizenship (usually students at Hebrew University and fluent in Hebrew) sought housing near campus. Though the number of Arabs who rented here in the 1990s probably did not exceed 1–2 percent of the settlement's population, it was not uncommon to hear that a Palestinian had found a place on French Hill. By the early 2000s some local estimates claimed that the Arab population of French Hill was well over 5 percent. As with other Israeli residential realms, the majority of the Arabs I met who had lived or were living here were women with Israeli citizenship. Their ability to access such sites was greater than Palestinian men because of the gendered racialization of the "terrorist threat" and the fear of Arab males within Israeli society (of which I shall say more in the next chapter).

When I first arrived in Jerusalem to conduct fieldwork, I was as astonished as confused to learn that Palestinians would actually take up residence in this and other hilltop Jerusalem settlements (including in rarer cases in Ne've Ya'acov, Ramot Eshkol, and East Talpiot). That not a few of these were leftists or progressives, with a well-worked-out analysis of Israeli policies of exclusion, seemed horribly incongruous. It was as if, by some strange double inversion, Palestinians had penetrated realms that they should not be in, which in turn were places that the Israelis had wrested from them in violation of international law. Had Palestinians forgotten the illegality of this residential estate? Did their attempts to live on a settlement—however temporarily—represent a "selling out" or an act of national betrayal?

When I first met Suad, she jokingly—though not at all sheepishly—announced to me that she lived "on a settlement." I asked her if she knew that French Hill was a settlement when she decided to rent there.

"Of course."

"And did you know that these apartments were built on land stolen from [the Palestinian village of] Aissiwiyya?"

"I came to know this after I moved there," she continued.

"And you are okay with this?"

She shrugged her shoulders and started folding laundry.

"But it's a *settlement*, for god's sake," I persisted, perhaps a bit too indignantly.

Suad was silent for a moment as she continued to organize and build piles of socks and shirts. Then, as I continued to press matters, she explained slightly impatiently, "Ya Tuma, look . . . this is my land—all of it. I have the right to live anywhere. The way I see it is that I am liberating one housing unit on French Hill for the Palestinians." She went on to tell me that she had subletted there because these were the only apartments within walking distance of Hebrew University that also were on a bus line at night.

"I was tired of walking thirty minutes every night to get to my apartment in Shu'afat [a neighboring Arab quarter]. I had to pay for a cab *so* many times, which I couldn't afford and sometimes the driver would make [sexual] offers to me. And I was alone. Sometimes the same asshole would drive up after I ordered a cab and I would not even get in the car because I saw that it was him. As a man, you can't understand this."

"This happened a lot?"

"More than I wanted to deal with," she responded with a trace of annoyance. "On French Hill, it was mostly married couples. It was lighted and safe. There were sidewalks!" She laughed, feigning intense enthusiasm. "There were paved roads! And I could take the bus home almost right to my doorstep. And nobody was hanging out watching what time I came in and who entered my apartment and all of that."

This last statement, as she would later explain, actually turned out to be not entirely true. In fact, the manner in which she and her roommate were perceived as women and as Arabs contributed to the problems she would eventually face in this locale. Suad's difficulties began within a few months of moving in with her female roommate, a Palestinian student from a town in the Galilee not far from hers. Both related that, initially, life here was pleasantly uneventful. The Israeli Jewish residents of her building seemed indifferent to her. "They ignored us for the first few months we moved in. They did not invite us to the residents' association meetings or to any of their apartments. And that was *fine*, I did not move there to be part of them."

But the posture of a handful of their neighbors became more than simply one of indifference. After three or four months, Suad and her roommate, the only Palestinians in their building of perhaps 150–200 people, began to be accused of a series of supposed misdeeds, including the writing of Palestinian nationalist graffiti on the walls of their elevator on Israeli Independence Day. In the wake of this incident, the other residents of the apartment no longer left them alone as they had wished. There arose, from then on, palpable tension when they saw their Jewish neighbors in the hallway.

Both women would, from the moment of this allegation, have future conflicts with an Israeli male neighbor they referred to simply as *khara* (shit). His and other male neighbors' harassment included regular racist and sexist slurs after the graffiti incident. The hostility came to a boil one evening when this man tried to enter their apartment by violently punching and kicking their door after the women refused to answer questions he directed at them. It was this episode (and the women's reluctance to call the Israeli police for fear of being removed from their apartment) that led them to seriously consider leaving French Hill. These and other acts of aggression by Israeli neighbors became unbearable and demonstrated how everyday acts of racial hatred could arise very abruptly and decisively in contested areas of the city.

Like at least two dozen others I came to know in similar circumstances, Suad and her roommate spoke of their fundamental dilemma in the wake of the hostility leveled against them on French Hill. To remain in a setting of unwanted conflict and continual harassment was not preferable. Indeed, the fear and anger clearly had worn them down emotionally. But extricating themselves from their home would have exacted an emotional and political cost of another sort. There was, of course, the question of logistics: moving can be costly and anxiety-producing, particularly in this city of scarce and often expensive housing options. But, in addition, to leave the apartment early, they told me, to allow their Israeli neighbors to "chase them out," would have been a victory for the very chauvinisms they increasingly wished to struggle against and not bend to.

The majority of the unmarried Palestinian women I spoke with in the course of my fieldwork (more than 80 percent) mentioned that their main motivation for choosing to live in an Israeli Jewish neighborhood was to secure adequate and affordable housing. Fewer than one in five mentioned that their primary inspiration was to challenge the city's segregated social order—at least not initially. However, Suad and others' refusal to be pushed out of their homes *did* have an avowed political dimension, whether intended or not. Several respondents who also dealt with hostility in this and other Israeli neighborhoods described how they fought to remain *samud* (steadfast) in the wake of such abuse. These efforts, I argue, were not simply survival strategies but also acts of meaningful resistance.

A THIRD BOMBING AND THE AFTERMATH OF TERROR

I return now to the story with which I opened this chapter. As mentioned above, the third attack against the targeted Palestinian women of Musrara took place on an evening of national passions marking Israel's fiftieth anniversary. But in Jerusalem and across the country as a whole, only one national community was celebrating. The significance of the timing for the last bombing was not lost on the victims. These rituals have not simply been powerful assertions of religious and nationalist connection to a land many Israelis regard as God's bequest to the Jewish people but also expressions of exclusive entitlement to a city the Palestinians also regard as their national capital.

Eventually, after enduring threats to their lives throughout the year, the three Palestinian women from Musrara lost their apartment at the end of a twelve-month rental agreement in June 1998. The landlord simply refused to extend the lease. But in their struggles to remain steadfast, they had won tremendous gains as well. Not least, they explained, were the expanding degrees of independence and respect they were demanding and receiving from their parents, family, and communities. Those back in their familial realms—fearing for these women's lives—had unsuccessfully tried to get them to return "home" after the first bombing. Watching as their daughters and sisters ran the risk of serious injury no doubt produced immeasurable anxiety for all who loved them.

From New York and what I thought was an "Olympian" height of removed rationality, I pleaded with these women to move out and find a safer place to live. One cannot fight this kind of chauvinism, I told them, especially in a context where the state does not take your security seriously. Like all of their friends, I was fearful that this apartment would eventually become the scene of something even more horrible—serious injury or even death. My words, however, wisely went unheeded. Months later, awed by their tenacity and courage, I felt such the coward and came to appreciate that I had much to learn about resistance, struggle, and courage.

In remaining resolute during what became a terrifying set of circumstances, the targeted women communicated to Israelis that Palestinians would continue to struggle against racism and segregation. In confronting the violence and misogyny (sometimes violent misogyny) directed at them in their Jerusalem homes, they were also pushing back against patriarchal and sexist dictates and expectations within their own families and communities. When it became apparent that these women would not be forced out, family members they would never have expected got behind them. These assertions of respect and support, they told me, emboldened them. As Mona told me:

> When I went back to the village to visit during that year, right after the second bombing, everyone greeted me like a hero as I walked down the street. Even an old traditional man wearing a *hatta* [Arab headdress] jumped up off his stool on his veranda and came running up, limping on a bad leg, to shake my hand. So many people congratulated me and supported me. I knew after that trip home that I would *never* be forced out of that apartment. I was doing this for every Palestinian.

My concern in this chapter has been not only to identify the various forces of domination unmarried Palestinian women encounter under Israeli colonial rule but also to detail how such forces and forms of resistance to them operate spatially. I have sought to look at everyday life in a contemporary urban context where space and place are intimately bound up with identity and alterity, fear and hatred, purity and danger. The women whose stories I have concentrated on have fought to reconfigure their lives, to challenge the taken-for-granted assumptions of gendered and racial boundaries. In doing so, they have defied the broader practices and principles that have continually produced and reproduced Jerusalem as a place where Israelis and Palestinians have been compelled to live separate and unequal existences.

EPILOGUE

Four months after their departure from the targeted apartment in Musr-ara, Mona revealed to me one intriguing element of this tale of terror that she could not—for reasons of security—talk about during the year. After a protracted struggle between the women's attorney and the Israeli state, the police installed a tiny camera above the door of the flat after the second bombing. The hidden device captured the culprit who planted the third explosive device. The Israeli police told the women that he appeared to be an ultra-Orthodox Jewish man dressed in black.

The bomber, however, has not been apprehended and the victims do not believe that he ever will be. Though he is caught on tape, the authorities said that they can do nothing about it. With fantastic irony they explained that, though they have an image of a suspect, the appearance of the Haredi Jewish man makes him difficult to distinguish from other Haredi men. Trying to track him down, Israeli officials asserted, would be futile. The case of the bombings remains to this day officially unsolved.

6

Appropriate Places

Terrorism, Fear, and the Policing of Palestinian Men

And if charity does not move those who have everything to spare,
fear will. All the residents of the suburb wanted was for the animal
to be confined in its appropriate place, that's all, zoo or even circus.
They were prepared to pay for this to be done.

—NADINE GORDIMER, *Something Out There*

In Nadine Gordimer's novella *Something Out There*, a mysterious scourge terrorizes the white South African suburbs of Johannesburg. Residents live in fear as a spate of sightings of a nebulous creature are reported across apartheid's landscape of disquiet. The "security services" are marshaled to hunt the beast down but it eludes them. Though a few white citizens had fleetingly encountered it, all that could be said for certain was that no one had caught more than "a glimpse of something dark" (1984, 182).

The society Gordimer depicts is one in which racially subordinate communities are defined as different and dangerous, and on that basis consigned to their "appropriate places" within a profoundly segregated and violent social order. However, apartheid South Africa was also a country where oppressed groups thrust to the margins, to the squalor of Bantustans and shantytowns, so often journeyed back to locales of racial privilege to sell their labor power cheaply and occasionally to engage in acts of militant resistance.

The former South Africa and contemporary Palestine/Israel are far from identical places. Yet, many of the tales of terror and trepidation that Gordimer poignantly weaves together have analogous realities in Jerusalem and across the broader colonial landscape in which this fractured city is embedded. In fact, several prominent South African writers and activists (beginning with Gordimer, herself) have compared Israeli policies toward the Palestinians to the racism and state terrorism of apartheid in South Africa.[1]

In this chapter I examine the politics of fear that has defined in crucial ways the experiences of both Palestinians and Israelis in Jerusalem. I detail a range of spatial practices among both national communities that arise from being governed by trepidation, whether one is the occupier or the occupied, the colonizer or the colonized. For as Bertolt Brecht reminds us, "Fear rules not only those who are ruled, but the rulers, too" (1987, 297).

Fright and terror impact dominant and subordinate communities differently, to be sure. And one runs the risk of effacing the inequalities constitutive of colonialism by not sufficiently detailing the power differential present in Palestine/Israel. These disparities include not only the capacity to use violence but also the power to project particular understandings of violent practices and those who deploy them. Here, I focus on the gendered racialization of Palestinian boys and men in Jerusalem's public places, at military checkpoints that regulate movement into and out of the city, and aboard Israeli buses. I concentrate on the period between the signing of the Oslo Accords in 1993 through the years of the Second Intifada (2000–2005).

The majority of the roughly three dozen interviews I conducted with Arab men about these concerns were done between 1997 and 2012. This was a time when disillusionment pervaded Palestinian society as Israel swiftly

1. Echoing other South African progressives' critiques of Israeli human rights abuses, such as those of Nelson Mandela and Bishop Desmond Tutu, Gordimer has pointed out similarities between Israel and the former South Africa. In May 2008 she stated, "There is a similarity, alas, in the way Palestinians are being treated in the occupied territories, the brutal methods. The humiliation of people, moving people out of their homes, keeping them on one side of the wall while their sustenance, their crops and grain, are on the other. It is indeed comparable to what happened in South Africa" (quoted in the *Jerusalem Post*, May 22, 2008, 4). See also the statement by Bishop Desmond Tutu (2002) in support of the movement for boycotts, divestment, and sanctions and that of Nelson Mandela (1997): http://www.e-tools .co.za/anc/mandela/1997/sp971204b.html, accessed November 29, 2013.

put into place an ever more rigid regime of separation (*hafrada*) between Arabs and Jews. This was also an era when hopes for an end to Israeli military occupation, a sentiment that arguably peaked in the wake of the signing of the Oslo Accords, began to diminish nearly as rapidly as it arose.

Anxieties about "security" and "terrorism" have been pronounced among successive Israeli governments and their backers abroad. However, they are routinely spoken about as if these concerns were solely those of Israeli Jews. Further, in the mainstream U.S. media violence against Palestinian and Israeli civilians has rarely been measured by the same yardstick since 1948. Very few mainstream U.S. commentators on this conflict, for instance, refer to even the most egregious violations of human rights by Israeli soldiers or settlers as "terrorism." Bombs dropped by Israeli warplanes on civilian population centers or laser-guided missiles fired by U.S.-made Apache helicopters that have killed thousands of Palestinian and Lebanese civilians are routinely justified as "self-defense," "retaliation," or "antiterrorism" measures by mainstream Western media sources.[2]

But hidden within these concerns with security are other logics. I argue that Israel's proliferating "security" regulations used to control the movement of millions of Palestinians over the last two decades have not principally been about stopping the next act of militancy. Rather, these practices and their accompanying discourses are most often deployed to justify an intensifying order of separation between Arabs and Jews.[3] The fueling of fear within Israeli society has, I submit, been vital to sustaining these spatial realities and the privileges that inhere to them.

THE GENDERED RACIALIZATION OF PALESTINIAN MEN

During interviews with Palestinian men, it was rare to find someone who had not experienced abuse or humiliation at the hands of Israeli soldiers,

---

2. For specific statistics on civilians killed in Palestine/Israel see B'Tselem (2013).

3. As mentioned in earlier chapters, Israeli discourses around the "Arab threat" have, over the years, continually referred to the dangers Arab populations are said to represent to the Jewish "character" of the state.

police, or civilians. Even when interviewing Palestinian women, the particular problems associated with being a Palestinian male would routinely arise. One Palestinian grandmother, Jamila, who hosted international delegations at the human rights organization she worked for in the city, recounted in 2002 the abuse her two sons had been subjected to over the last several decades of military rule. She described one instance in the late 1970s in which Jewish settlers brandishing wooden sticks attacked these boys, then twelve and fourteen, on their way home from school. The youth, she told me, were beaten so badly that they could hardly walk and slowly limped home, crying in pain.

"Can you imagine what a *mother* feels?" her calm giving way to a palpable anger.

> You know, I meet [foreign] delegations who come here in solidarity with us. But I don't even tell them the worst things because nobody would believe me. They would think I was lying.

It was not always dramatic forms of physical abuse that those who lived under occupation emphasized when talking about these concerns. More often than not Palestinians would relate quotidian acts of cruelty at the hands of the occupying forces. And, not inconsequentially, it was the loved ones of the abused who in the retelling of these incidents expressed more anger and sadness than those whose bodies had been physically violated.

Dozens of Palestinian men, nearly every one I spoke to about this subject, told me about being detained and humiliated by Israeli soldiers or police. With the advent of the Second Intifada in 2000, that harassment became even more prevalent than in previous decades. Young Arab men who traveled across this urban center alone or in groups were "moving targets" of harassment and profiling measures.

"At least here [in East Jerusalem] you have others [Palestinians] around you. Over there [in West Jerusalem] you are surrounded," explained Nidal, a Palestinian man of twenty-five. As we stood at midday along the hectic and congested Salahadin Street in East Jerusalem, he told me about this vulnerability between heavy draws of cigarettes. He spoke about working and "hanging out" in West Jerusalem. But as he did, his words were marked by a perplexing ambivalence. Though he was from time to time hassled in that part of town, he went there routinely—and not just to wash dishes in an upscale Israeli restaurant. Nidal and other young men like him seemed undeterred by the potential abuse or profiling they knew they might experience on the west side. I was witnessing, I thought, a performance of macho bravado, both in their refusal to be contained in their "appropriate places" in East Jerusalem as well as in their denial that they felt fear.

Among the disturbing dimensions of social life on the west side was the sight of Israeli soldiers and civilians with automatic rifles slung over their shoulders or pistols in holsters. This was particularly unsettling given that only one national community was permitted to carry arms throughout the country and those with the guns at times looked a bit on edge. These "weaponized" public places reminded me of images from other twentieth-century colonial urban centers, like Algiers or Nairobi.

EXPLOSIVE OCCURRENCES

My unease about spending extensive time in West Jerusalem was magnified by events in Palestine/Israel during the mid-1990s and again, for several months, in 2001–2003. The city was unusually tense during these periods due to a generalized rise in violent acts between Palestinians and Israelis. Among these were a spate of Palestinian bombings of Israeli buses and public places. In February and March 1996, at least seven bombings took place in Israeli cities, resulting in the deaths of roughly sixty-one Israeli Jews and four Palestinians. At least four of these attacks were on Jerusalem buses.

The government of Shimon Peres's March 1996 bombardment of Palestinian refugees at Qana, Lebanon, in which the Israeli air force killed 105 civilians in one evening, eventuated in a heightened military and police presence in Jerusalem. Heavily armed Israeli police and soldiers in helmets and riot gear were present in hefty numbers, some walking in groups of six, particularly in Palestinian neighborhoods. During the Second Intifada in the early 2000s intercommunal attacks reached new heights. During the most severe times, the city's west side commercial districts were all but empty during normal business hours as residents feared militant attacks. Innumerable clubs and cafés in West Jerusalem hired security guards to staff their front entrance and check the bags of all who entered. Men and boys thought to be Arab were particularly scrutinized as they moved through the city.

Nowhere, as far as I could tell, was such profiling more intense than on Israeli buses, at bus stations, and at bus stops. Tens of thousands of Jerusalemites use such public transportation on a daily basis and these zones became sites of intense apprehension. I noticed that riders would frequently gaze at others on the bus as they apparently sought to discern if their surroundings were safe or if someone they deemed suspicious had boarded. Seeing was not a passive exercise for those who took public transportation in those years, whether Israeli, Palestinian, or internationals like me.

There were innumerable ways in which those of us who relied on buses during these tumultuous periods tried to make ourselves feel more at ease. Rationalizations were devised to settle the nerves:

"There had never been a bomb placed on *this* bus line and so it was probably safe."

"Bombers never strike on Tuesdays, but often did on Sundays."

"This bus line went near or briefly through Arab East Jerusalem and, therefore, wouldn't be attacked."[4]

When I asked Israeli and Palestinian friends why they did not walk or take cabs in this dangerous age, one woman responded, "We can't stop our lives. I need to get to work across town and can't keep paying for cabs." In these circumstances, rationalizations became necessary to survive and carry on in a city where, as one Israeli friend remarked, "it's safe until it isn't."

The bus bombings were chilling events. They could typically be heard from several kilometers away, along with the blaring sirens of ambulances

---

4. Certain bus lines that had been targeted on previous occasions (such as the #1 or #18) were often all but empty on subsequent days and subsequent Sunday mornings. But recognizing patterns never ensured that one could evade an attack. Those patterns shifted, too.

that would wail in their wake. The attacks terrified Israelis in realms similar to the fortressed zones of white privilege that Gordimer (1984) describes in the story that opens this chapter. The bombings were initiated within a year of the signing of the Oslo Accords in September 1993, with the first major attack occurring in the fall of 1994.

For the next six or seven years, members of certain politically active Islamic organizations were the primary perpetrators.[5] These were groups that had, until the signing of the Oslo Accords, directed the bulk of their militant activity against Israeli soldiers and settlers in the Gaza Strip and West Bank. Armed actions such as these against the forces of military occupation were for the most part abandoned around 1994. This, despite the fact that they were both popular among Palestinians and usually seen as legitimate forms of resistance by the international community. Elements within Hamas and the Islamic Jihad now turned toward indiscriminate attacks in Israeli cities, mostly targeting civilians. Among their goals was to jettison the Oslo Accords and the rule of their rival Yasser Arafat's embryonic state structure, the Palestine National Authority (PNA).[6] Their message to Israelis seemed to be that as long as Palestinian civilians were killed under military occupation, Israeli citizens would face retribution.

Until my research stay in 1997, I had never related to these attacks in the ways I was compelled to while living for a short period of time in West Jerusalem. East Jerusalem had been my home when the first suicide bombing occurred in Tel Aviv in the fall of 1994. I was due to leave from a summer of Arabic study in the city the very day a bus was blown up near a Jewish settlement in Jerusalem on August 21, 1995. However, I never rode Israeli buses in those days. Though I always opposed these attacks, they were then for me the dramatic consequences of forty years of Israeli

---

5. I refrain from the use of "fundamentalist" and "fundamentalism" throughout this work because I believe that the terms have become more ideological than analytical and often preclude a proper understanding of the character of these organizations. I believe that "political Islam" is a far more illuminating term.

6. For a superb analysis of the political realities of the 1990s in Palestine/Israel, see Usher (1995, 1999).

military occupation. They were not a source of apprehension or a direct personal threat. They happened elsewhere and to others I did not know.

It was only now, residing as I was in West Jerusalem with Palestinian and Israeli friends who were also endangered, that I was compelled to view these acts and the dire threats they posed from an altogether different location. I lived less than a kilometer from places where three suicide attacks occurred, and I commonly traversed areas and neighborhoods where past explosions had taken place. A café I frequented with friends near Rehavia, Moment, a two-minute walk from my apartment and just up the street from the Israeli prime minister's house, was the site of a 2002 bombing that left a dozen dead, including the bomber.

By the time I returned to the city for more fieldwork in 2002 and 2003, small monuments of the sort I detailed in chapter 3—sometimes just an unobtrusive plaque or wreath—had been placed at several of these locales. Standing at the precise location where violent attacks had recently taken place reminded me of the dangers of life in the city. I feared for Palestinian and Israeli friends who rode public transportation. I feared for myself, too.

Mainstream Israeli and U.S. media who reported on the region seemed decidedly more concerned with the welfare and security of Israelis than Palestinians. "Security," in fact, was spoken of almost as though it were the exclusive need of Israeli Jews. In most accounts from Western mainstream media sources, "terrorism" was, by definition, any act of violence if committed by an Arab or Palestinian against Israeli Jews.[7] Reports of bombed Israeli buses were often front-page stories with accompanying images of grieving Jewish victims. Israeli assaults against Palestinians and Lebanese, with explosives from the air, were not uncommonly relegated to four inches of text on page six of a newspaper.

Examining the statistics on the number of Palestinians and Israelis causalities since the beginning of the Second Intifada reveals some vital findings. During the years between 2000 and 2012 there were nineteen

---

7. Even the Israeli Jew who assassinated Israeli Prime Minister Yitzhak Rabin in 1995 was not referred to as a "Jewish terrorist."

months in which Israelis killed more than seventy-five Palestinians. During that same period there was only one month in which Palestinians killed that many Israelis. The total numbers killed on each side during the same period were, according to the Israeli human rights organization B'Tselem, 6,792 Palestinians and 1,102 Israelis.[8] This disparity of death operated alongside a disparity of empathy from those who reported on this conflict.

PROFILING A THREAT

While living in Jerusalem I became, like countless Israelis and Palestinians, reliant on Israel's Egged bus system, one I grew to know, if not to love. I put to memory several of the city's two-dozen-odd routes that I utilized on a regular basis. Critically, I learned which routes came the closest to the Palestinian neighborhoods in East Jerusalem where I pursued the bulk of my research.[9] Riding public transportation in the Jerusalem of the mid-1990s and early 2000s meant traversing spaces of fear and uncertainty. One had always to imagine what *might* happen while simultaneously trying to put it out of one's head. I felt relief upon alighting, especially in West Jerusalem, and walked away from crowded public places as quickly as I could.

Riding Israeli buses in the days of the bombings was for Palestinians a doubly dangerous endeavor. For one—and this was generally ignored by Western commentators who reported on these attacks—Palestinians who boarded these buses were subjected to exactly the same perils as Israeli Jews. Though militants nearly always struck in areas where Israeli Jews predominated, their assaults were fairly indiscriminate. Anyone on targeted routes or in the vicinity of a bombing could be killed. Three or four of the victims of the February and March 1996 attacks, for instance, were Palestinians, and several other Arabs—one or two whom I knew—were injured or nearly averted death in these hits.

---

8. See www.btselem.org/statistics, January 30, 2013.

9. The closest, I say, because in Israel's "united capital," Palestinian residents of the city are generally unable to access these buses in their neighborhoods.

But Palestinian passengers, particularly Arab men, faced another sort of peril, particularly during the years of the Second Intifada (2000–2005). They were subjected to noticeably more pervasive policing efforts. Those I interviewed reported being subjected to increased surveillance, profiling, humiliation, and repression along Jerusalem's streets. These were degrees of abuse not seen since the years of the First Intifada in the late 1980s and early 1990s.

This was especially true in Jerusalem's main commercial areas in the wake of these attacks. With heightened fervor, Israeli forces began checking "Arab-looking" men as they boarded buses, pulling them aside in public places and detaining them on streets. It was a policing based substantially on profiling. Anyone assumed to be Arab could be accosted, questioned, detained for hours, and even beaten.

The sound of the Arabic language (and those who spoke it) increasingly became a signifier of danger in realms where it was thought to be incongruous, unwanted, or out of place. Few Israeli Jews are fluent in Arabic, but the majority certainly recognizes it when they hear it. If Arabic were detected on a bus—if, for instance, a Palestinian woman or man were heard talking on his or her cell phone to another Arabic speaker—Israeli riders would not uncommonly stare with some concern at the individual. This visible discomfort and fear could be routinely witnessed on public transportation. I even occasionally observed scared-looking Israeli riders moving seats, or even alighting. And very occasionally there was physical or verbal abuse leveled at Palestinian riders.

Undercover agents might suddenly appear and demand identification from one deemed "suspicious." Unarmed Palestinians, involved in no wrongdoing, were occasionally forced off of buses or questioned simply for riding or walking while Arab. This was true even if they were citizens of Israel. I personally witnessed at least a half-dozen such cases. In interviews with Israelis and Palestinians I was told of this happening more often than I would have imagined. Arab men or boys were randomly detained. Sometimes they were ordered to stand against walls with hands held high at gunpoint. These were rituals of docility and domination that comprised everyday life in Jerusalem like few others.

THE SEMIOTICS OF RACISM:
LOOKING FOR THE FACE OF TERROR

It was during these periods of heightened violence that Israeli buses became what Robin Kelley (1994, 57), in the context of the Jim Crow U.S. South, refers to as "moving theaters" of resistance and racism. Several Israeli Jews I interviewed explained what taking buses in that age was like. They related that as they did they would regularly find themselves trying to determine if there might be a bomber in their midst by panning across the riders on the bus and looking for "Arab men."

An anti-Zionist Jewish colleague of mine, Yael, described how she feared riding public transportation while living in Jerusalem. Though she seemed a bit embarrassed telling me how she felt, this leftist who has since left Israel admitted that not only was she constantly looking out for "suspicious" people on buses but also that her attention was drawn more toward what she perceived to be "Palestinian-looking" men. With irony in my voice, I asked her what a "Palestinian-looking man" looked like exactly. She had no answer and, somewhat sheepishly, apologized: "It was wrong to say that . . . I don't know what a Jew 'looks like,' and wouldn't be too happy if someone said that [about Jews]."

The attacks in Israeli towns and cities numbered roughly a dozen in 1996 and 1997. There would be a lull in such bombings, but they would resume during the Second Intifada beginning in 2000 with even greater force as the repression under Israeli military rule escalated. Unrestrained to a significant extent by the Bush administration, the government of Ariel Sharon (2001–2006) used torture, Apache helicopter gunships, and F-16 aircraft against the civilian population of Palestine, at least 99 percent of whom had nothing to do with the planning of these bombings. This is what human rights groups condemned as collective punishment.

After a bus bombing, Israel would invariably "seal" the West Bank and Gaza Strip (excluding East Jerusalem). The more than 3–3.5 million Arab inhabitants of these areas at the time could not move freely, sometimes even to the next town. Jerusalem would be closed off to nearly all Palestinians, keeping them away from their center of commercial, religious, and social life. This form of collective punishment made life under military occupation all the more onerous. By the early 2000s, travel to Jerusalem for the vast majority of Palestinians was forbidden in the name of "Israeli security."

These "security" measures further subverted an already feeble Palestinian economy and created growing pools of unemployed youth increasingly precluded from entering the Israeli labor market many had become dependent on. The proliferating desperation and poverty in villages, towns, and refugee camps became the cauldron in which assaults against Israelis were produced.[10] According to several estimations by Israeli and Palestinian scholars, by 2001–2003 these acts were committed almost as regularly by those *not* from Islamic organizations as by those who were.[11]

DISGUISING DIFFERENCE

Profiling Palestinian men and other racist policies have not proven effective in stopping attacks against Israeli civilians. One dimension of these militant actions underscores this. By 1996, it had become clear that the bombers—in nearly all cases—had not come dressed in the ways that Israelis might imagine an "Arab" or "Arab terrorist" would. Rather, they had begun to don ever more sophisticated disguises, their appearances altered in ways that defied Israeli profiling schemes.

In March 1996 one bomber, whose body was torn asunder by the blast, was found to have actually dressed as an Israeli soldier. He wore an authentic army uniform and carried a rifle. To further evade authorities, he had dyed his hair blond and even wore an earring to further subvert

10. See Israeli security specialist and former Shin Bet agent Ami Ayalon (2002) on the flawed logic of Israeli security. Such a critique has been strengthened in recent years as elements within Israel's military establishment have acknowledged the limitations of racial profiling for ending militant attacks.

11. An Israeli economist and opponent of his government's occupation of Palestinian land, Yoav Peled, remarked in a 2002 interview I did with him at the height of these bombings that "we, Israelis and the Palestinians, need to come to terms with the fact that about half of the suicide bombings happening today are being done by people who used to support the Oslo Accords, who are not part of *Hamas* or Islamic Jihad."

the operative profiles against Palestinians. In this instance, the assailant's head, decapitated by the blast, was discovered near the actual site of the bombing. Israeli investigators had to be forensic in new ways as they pieced together the corporeal clues of dismembered bodies.

Other Hebrew-speaking militants dressed as Haredi Jews planted themselves deep within Jerusalem's ultra-Orthodox neighborhoods in 2003. On yet another occasion in the summer of 1994, two fair-skinned Palestinian cadres entered West Jerusalem wearing casual clothing, brandishing submachine guns strapped over their shoulders, and reportedly wearing yarmulkes. As they opened fire on a row of open-air restaurants near Ben Yehuda Street, they managed to kill two people before being killed themselves. These and other bombers had appropriated the most Israeli of Israeli signifiers as part of their masks. In doing so they were able to carry out their operations more deftly and stealthily. In doing so they also made murkier an already ambiguous semiotic environment. For not only were these militants able to elude detection, but in at least one case, they shot Palestinians that they misrecognized as Israeli Jews sitting in a café in West Jerusalem.

This phenomenon of disguise, confusion, and subterfuge, I believe, laid bare the futility of Israeli profiling schemes and the random checks of "Arab-looking" men. It also exposed the flawed assumptions on which these practices have been based. One might reasonably have concluded that if the purpose of this heightened policing was the one that Israeli officials claimed (namely, to apprehend those who might be on their way to attack their citizens), then they would have to begin randomly checking and curtailing the movement of men who resembled Israeli soldiers or Hasidic Jews.

A further point worth mentioning is one all-too-often forgotten when assessing whether particular policing or military action makes Israel (or any other country) safer. Successive Israeli governments and the majority of Israeli Jews might well believe that this is the principal question, perhaps the only one worth answering. However, I submit that it is certainly not the principal *ethical* question. This book has been arguing that even if attacks against Palestinian civilians and policies of collective punishment had made Israelis safer in some demonstrable way, it would not, for that reason alone, justify them. Ethnically cleansing the entire Palestinian population from the West Bank and Gaza Strip might conceivably enhance the Jewish state and its settlers' security. That would not, however, warrant the practice of mass expulsion. This is a point often more easily understood when put in opposite terms: If detaining Israeli Jewish civilians, indiscriminately bombing their cities, and restricting the movement of people because they were Jewish could be shown to improve Palestinian security, would these human rights abuses be justified?

Israel's practices of indiscriminate bombing, imprisonment, and torture seemed to amplify Palestinian attacks on Israeli civilians. There continued a pronounced dialectic of violence and counter violence until 2005, when suicide attacks against Israeli civilians in Israeli cities almost completely ceased. So why did the Israeli state continue to pursue often draconian "security" policies that violated the human rights of Palestinians? I want to suggest that, as with the so-called war on drugs or war on terror in the United States, Israeli security measures have been in a sense performed to help mitigate the fear and channel the rage of much of their citizenry. Further I argue that these policies are meant to inject heightened distress and anxiety into the communities they have sought to subjugate. They are intended to constitute a deterrent, to quell resistance to Israeli military occupation.

Living and detailing life in the city during this period led me to the conclusion that these actions against a largely unarmed population might be many things but they are generally not related to security. They have not, after all, provided anything like safety or well being to Israelis or Palestinians. Instead, they promote a façade of safety, a "fix" of well-being, in the face of increasing demands for harsher policies against the Palestinians articulated by dominant Israeli political parties and their growing constituents.

In the period that I am focusing on in this chapter, and indeed throughout Israeli history, there has existed a myth that the Israel Defense Forces (IDF) could finally end or substantially reduce Palestinian resistance or militancy by "cracking down" ever harder on civilian populations. In this way, the Israeli state is not alone among governments of the world. And it appears that the majority of the Israeli population, in the words of Gordimer (1984, 147), have been "prepared to pay for this to be done." But what has that meant for Palestinian boys and men? How have their very movements into and through Jerusalem been increasingly more circumscribed?

I want to turn now to the question of how Israeli officials' production of a "terrorist" threat is a gendered construct. In the next few sections I explore this more thoroughly. Toward that end I begin with a fieldwork moment that speaks to these questions in Jerusalem. The incident occurred one late fall afternoon in 1999 in the center of West Jerusalem near the main post office on Jaffa Street. As the sun began to set and the streetlights gradually illuminated the busy thoroughfares, a friend of mine, a young Muslim woman dressed in a *hijab,* and I were accosted by two Israeli policewomen in their twenties. At the sight of us moving toward them, they literally jumped out of their seats on the edge of a concrete-encased flowerbed. It seems that they had their suspicions piqued by what could only have been a Muslim woman, accompanied by a bearded man chatting in Arabic, in West Jerusalem.

I was only rarely stopped by the police or military when I walked the city's streets, especially when I was dressed in shorts and a baseball cap, as I was that day. But on this occasion the policewomen approached me with concern and demanded that I produce identification.

"Show me your ID," one of them ordered in Arabic.

"Why?" I objected curtly in English, wanting them to know that I was an American.

The second woman asserted aggressively, in highly accented English and her voice rising, "Where are you coming from? Where do you live in Israel?"

"I don't live in Israel," I responded, "I live in East Jerusalem."

This did not quicken the process. They delved further into my purpose in the country for another five minutes or so and even demanded to search my backpack. But to my amazement they made no queries into the identity of my Palestinian Muslim colleague. They simply ignored her. This, despite the fact that it was she who was the clear "giveaway," the one so obviously *not* an Israeli Jew. Her veil was the bright light that drew the "security moths" to the potential danger that I, the assumed Arab or Muslim man, posed. The assumptions here were many, I believe. Among them was that a Muslim man would most probably be walking with a Muslim woman—and being a Muslim man was for them a source of concern.

In the course of this back-and-forth exchange, another Palestinian friend of mine, an Israeli citizen, happened to come upon us. She sussed out what was taking place and began, in perfect Hebrew, to demand answers from the policewomen.

"Why are you stopping him?" she asked pointedly, walking right up to us. "It's because he is Arab, right?" The young policewoman seemed taken aback by this intervention, probably believing that this Palestinian with exquisite Hebrew was an Israeli Jewish woman. She sheepishly mumbled something and then handed my passport back and walked away.

This encounter underlined the fact that the Israel-defined "terrorist threat" is grounded in a variety of assumptions about Palestinian women and men. Arab women, while the objects of sexist or racist behavior in Jerusalem as discussed in chapter 5, are usually not seen by Israeli officials as representing a *terrorist* threat. These gendered assumptions have gendered implications. Palestinian women usually have more options than Palestinian men as they seek to live and move through urban spaces. They are not singled out nearly as often for random questioning at checkpoints or while walking in public places as are their male counterparts. But mired as my Muslim female friend was in the dangers that I was seen to potentially pose, these circumstances speak to the myriad ways in which men's and women's conditions in Palestine are bound up together under Israeli rule.

PROFILING, CHECKPOINTS, AND "SECURITY"

Palestinians can be harassed and detained anywhere under Israeli control. They can even be profiled by Israeli officials in European and American airports en route to Ben Gurion Airport in Tel Aviv. But acts of racism and cruelty occur perhaps most commonly at permanent army checkpoints that are positioned where the Jewish state has unilaterally defined and redefined the boundaries of Israel's "eternal capital." During the course of my time in Palestine/Israel, I crossed these checkpoints literally hundreds of times. Traveling through them was essential if one wanted to better understand the relations of spatial domination that impinge on Arab Christians and Muslims under an expanding colonial project.

In 1992 and 1993, the government of Prime Minister Yitzhak Rabin (1992–1995) established a series of permanent army emplacements between Israeli-defined Jerusalem and the rest of the occupied West Bank. These positions began to foreclose entry into the city for an increasing number of Palestinians residing in the West Bank and Gaza Strip. Until the signing of the Oslo Accords in 1993, these communities were generally able to travel to Jerusalem as they wished, especially during the day. Before the checkpoints were erected, a typical journey from the Old City of Jerusalem to the center of Ramallah could take as little as fifteen minutes by car. Once these barriers were instituted, the trip could easily take an hour or longer during the Second Intifada. During the morning and evening rush hours, Palestinian automobiles would routinely back up 100 to 200 meters from a slow-moving army checkpoint.

Only months before the signing of the Oslo Accords, more stringent restrictions were placed on Palestinian workers wishing to cross the Green Line and enter the Israeli labor market.[12] This more intense spatial separation was instituted, I believe, at least in part, to assert to Palestinians, to the international community, and to Israelis themselves that unlike other areas of the West Bank that the Jewish state might return to the Palestinians, East Jerusalem was the exclusive province of Israel and would never be ceded or shared.

In the age of Oslo, Palestinians interested in traveling to and within Jerusalem frequently took what were known as *services*: a shared cab or

---

12. It was at this time that the Israeli government began to replace roughly 150,000 regular Palestinian workers from the territories occupied in 1967 with guest workers from Thailand, Turkey, Romania, and Nigeria. By some estimates, these non-Israeli citizens would surpass 200,000 by the early 2000s.

minibus that could hold eight to ten people. In the 1990s, these cars were either beat-up, secondhand Mercedes sedans or dilapidated yellow or white vans with four rows of ill-upholstered seats that were only vaguely secured to the floor. At that time, the one-way trip to and from Jerusalem to neighboring Bethlehem or Ramallah cost 2–3 Israeli shekels (roughly 75 cents at the time). Those unable to afford this mode of travel made use of the underfunded Palestinian bus system, a fleet of weathered jalopies with rusted exteriors that took longer to arrive at any particular destination than a shared cab. I normally took services, riding in them literally hundreds of times during my time in the city.

As Palestinians sought to enter Jerusalem in the age of the checkpoints, a set of rituals would be engaged in by Arabs and Jews alike. As cars approached Jerusalem's outer perimeter, occupying authorities required that they queue up and wait to be inspected. As shared cabs neared the *hawaajez* (checkpoints), Palestinian male riders within these cramped quarters—bodies pressed together—would begin to reach for their identification cards (*hawiyya*) in wallets or vest pockets.

Once at the front of the line, an Israeli soldier would open the car door or reach through the window for the driver's papers. Another young conscript, sometimes clearly irritated, would examine male passengers' identification cards or Israeli-issued permission-to-enter documents. The soldiers, wearing knife- and bulletproof vests, would sometimes gaze at these IDs with the intensity of one analyzing a complex piece of writing. On other occasions such moments of verification would be so perfunctory as to completely belie Israel's stated concern for security. There were even occasions when some of the men in the car or the driver were not required to produce papers at all. The papers of women and younger boys were generally not asked for. Soldiers rarely checked bags or purses, and they searched the compartments or trunks of vehicles even less often.

On those occasions when a Palestinian male passenger in the cab was found not to possess Israeli permission (*tasriih*) to enter Jerusalem, soldiers would extract him from the vehicle and send him back by foot, sometimes physically or verbally abusing him before doing so. By the end of the Second Intifada, those found trying to enter the city without the authorization of military forces faced far worse treatment, including imprisonment and severe beatings. Every so often, cars, cabs, and buses would be kept at checkpoints and emptied of their male passengers. Those staffing these nodes of control would typically order men and boys to stand in a line while being questioned. On innumerable occasions I witnessed Arab men and women, boys and girls, being told aggressively and rudely to "go home!" (*ruuh ala beit*) as they sought to enter Jerusalem by foot.

These barriers, built on land that nearly the entire international community calls on Israel to withdraw from, constituted disruptions in the lives of those who were forced to pass through them. These nodes of control grew to more than 500 during the height of the Second Intifada. In 2011 the UN reported that there were still over 500 checkpoints throughout the West Bank, though not all of them were used as regularly as they had been in the early 2000s.[13] They affected not only those who would cross them but also those who waited for friends and family on the other side. Detention or physical abuse was a daily threat for the thousands of Palestinians who sought to move across these barriers, particularly young men.

But these sites of regulation also revealed something altogether different in their quotidian dimensions. It was in these face-to-face encounters with soldiers that one could occasionally see the fear in those ordered to staff these borders. It was important for me to remember that most of these soldiers were conscripts. I was reminded of that as I came to know several Israeli men who refused service in the IDF, members of the groups Yesh Gvul and Breaking the Silence. Many of them were sent to prison for repudiating what in Israel is widely regarded as a "national duty" and a rite of passage for Israeli Jewish men. Though the behavior of individual soldiers was frequently arrogant and racist, I challenged myself to direct my irritation principally at the institutional forces that had erected the checkpoints in the first place.[14]

13. For more on this, see "Movement and Access in the West Bank" (United Nations Office for the Coordination of Humanitarian Affairs Occupied Palestinian Territory 2012).

14. Generally compelled to serve in the military for three years, these Israelis, some just eighteen years old, were injected into a regime of military occupation that, by the 1990s, was usually older than they were.

What had militarization done not only to Palestinians but also to these Israelis, many of them youth if not children? How had the IDF shaped them ideologically? How were they subjected to the vast masculinist socialization processes that those in armies and militarized societies the world over all too often undergo?[15] It is, of course, difficult to see the humanity in those who humiliate and injure others. However, amid cruelties of various kinds, I witnessed from time to time the intervention by one soldier in an effort to stem the excesses of another. And when this happened, it underlined the point that I had always been able to accept in theory: namely, that we need to acknowledge the extent to which conscripts in any army are used in the service of elites.

One standard encounter that was especially difficult to watch would occur between soldiers and aged Arab men and women, some old enough to be their grandfathers or grandmothers. These sometimes fragile elders, rarely speakers of competent Hebrew, were at times treated shabbily or ordered to and fro. Not infrequently these Palestinians would be yelled at in Hebrew or with Arabic phrases the Israelis had learned, including commands of one sort or another, like "come here!" "stand over there!" "line up!" or "wait!" Palestinians, young and old, were frequently spoken to as though they were disobedient children. At times, they were laughed at or patronized in degrading ways. Sentiments of anger and frustration were rarely expressed verbally between Arab passengers during these moments of waiting. What, after all, was there really to say about circumstances so routine and obviously absurd? But it is difficult to imagine that this kind of treatment did not leave very deep traces on the minds and memories of those compelled to endure it.

TECHNIQUES OF THE BODY: NECESSARY POSTURES

Though not immediately apparent to me, certain uses of the body became gradually more visible as I watched Palestinian males traverse spatial

15. For an excellent examination of gender, militarization, and Israeli society see Sharoni (1995).

and social boundaries in Jerusalem. Marcel Mauss's (2007) theorizing of what he refers to as "techniques of the body"—the manner in which actors carry themselves, utilize their bodies, gesture, and identify themselves through corporeal performances—provide insights into broader colonial dynamics that impinge on Palestinians and Israelis. Mauss (2007) along with Bourdieu (1977), Butler (1993), Peteet (1994), and a range of other scholars have sought to explore the political dimensions of bodies in motion in the production of gender and sexuality. What Bourdieu refers to as the bodily *hexis* is central to my analysis. *Hexis* includes a set of gendered norms and roles that are

> realized, embodied, turned into a permanent disposition, a durable manner of standing, speaking, and thereby of feeling and thinking. (Bourdieu 1977, 93–94)

During my time in Jerusalem, I witnessed Palestinian men exhibit contrasting postures. There were slight but occasionally noticeable discrepancies between the way the *shebab* traversed East Jerusalem versus the manner in which they carried themselves in their interactions with soldiers. I noticed the reactions of Palestinian drivers, usually men in their twenties and thirties, as they dealt with those who regulated their movement. These were encounters, it should be remembered, in which one side was armed and held near absolute power over the other.

Palestinian cab drivers, especially those who crossed checkpoints, regularly displayed tremendous aggression on the roads. Few I knew who had spent even a week in Palestine failed to notice this. Speeding and honking their horns were common practices that both defined and flouted the rules of the road. These drivers would frequently wave their arms out of the window to help move around other cars, curse other drivers moving too slowly for them, and shuttle through traffic as though they were involved in a high-speed chase.

However, as these men stopped at Israeli checkpoints to answer questions and present their papers the "rules" changed. Their movement, temperament, and tone frequently shifted. Conversations with soldiers usually took place in Hebrew or a superficial Arabic. Drivers would not uncommonly partake in friendly small talk with their questioners. This sometimes appeared to be done with a forced, nervous smile that betrayed their vulnerability. They might try to deal with the gatekeepers by speaking and joking in Hebrew with the hope that a nonconfrontational attitude might facilitate their movement through the barrier. Occasionally there were bribes given to the soldiers, as the Arab men who Amiry (2010) journeys with across this policed landscape and others report. Some soldiers and drivers could encounter each other as often as five times a day at particular nodes of control. What impact did these rituals of dominance and submission have on both parties as they sought to get through their respective days?

"SECURITY THEATER": MAKING A SHOW OF IT

"Saah! [Go!]," yelled the Israeli conscript as he slammed shut the sliding door of the rickety van. Those in the car were deemed "passable," and this was the driver's cue to move through the checkpoint and proceed. Once, in the summer of 2002, while driving away from a protracted and senseless interaction with particularly arrogant soldiers, I turned toward a rotund, middle-aged Palestinian man in the car, pressed up against me in the back row of seats, and asked a rhetorical question loudly enough for others in the cab to hear.

"Do they think this makes them safer?" I inquired angrily, slightly jarring him out of thought. He shrugged his shoulders somewhat surprised, as others in the car were, by my intervention. Realizing that I was a foreigner, he proceeded to explain matters as he saw them for the rest of the ride. "You know," he responded, "there is no way to shut off the border between us [Israelis and Palestinians]. Do you know how many ways there are to go around these borders?"

As mentioned in the first part of this chapter, the Israeli state's public rationale for policing entry into and through Jerusalem is to "increase security" and to keep out "terrorists." But in fact these barriers, erected long before the spate of suicide bombings in 1996, have not been shown to mitigate militancy. Israeli officers might well instruct their underlings that these Palestinian cars seeking to enter Jerusalem might potentially contain the next suicide bomber. However, it is unlikely—based on the perfunctory ways in which soldiers routinely performed their duties—that they believe their jobs to be so vital.[16] As mentioned above, I contend that the bulk of the military and political leadership continue with the façade of "fighting terror" in an attempt to foster the idea among Israelis that they are meeting the security threat properly. As these rituals are reenacted each day, hegemonic notions within Israeli society about the threat that Arabs—as Arabs—pose to the Jewish state seem to be solidified.

In the late 1990s, I witnessed on several occasions hundreds of Palestinian workers openly circumventing these points of inspection at six or seven o'clock in the morning. This they did in plain sight of soldiers at checkpoints standing but a few dozen meters away. These Palestinian laborers did not possess Israeli permission to enter Israeli-controlled Jerusalem or they would have crossed through the checkpoints. But they were being allowed to evade Israeli "security" by those who staffed these barriers. They could be seen clearly getting on transportation provided by Israeli employers who then drove off with them to work sites in Israel.

This perplexed me until I figured out what was happening. These workers were among the dwindling number of Palestinian men who daily sold their labor power cheaply in Israeli plants and at construction sites. Israeli employers were generally quite keen on hiring these workers but found it increasingly difficult to do so as the age of the checkpoints and the policy of accelerated separation intensified. To satisfy simultaneously the demands of capital as well as those of anxious Israeli citizens, this informal measure had been undertaken. Very few of the hundreds of thousands of Palestinian day laborers had been involved in any major act

16. The proliferating *hawaajez* that began to envelop the city in the 1990s did not prevent bombings inside Israel. It was during the most intense closure of the Palestinian territories in February and March 1996, a time when nearly all Arab residents of the West Bank and Gaza were formally forbidden to enter Israel and Jerusalem, that two of the four bus bombings described above took place in Israeli population centers. All of the several dozen suicide attacks against Israelis have occurred despite the existence of these checkpoints.

أهلاً وسهلاً بكم في نقطة المراقبة "معبر هزيتيم"

– إنت على مدخل منطقة عسكرية. قبل دخولك.
إقرأ هذه التعليمات وتقيّد بها لأجل المرور السريع
ومنع التأخير الزائد.

– الرجاء تحضير وثائقك للفحص والتقدّم نحو
الموقف الفارغ.

– يجب الانصياع لتعليمات الفاحصين.

– المرور فردي.

– حافظوا على النظام والنظافة.

تتمنى لك يوم سعيد!

ברוכים הבאים לנקודת הביקורת "מעבר הזיתים"

– הנכם נכנסים לשטח צבאי. טרם כניסתכם,
אנא קראו והישמעו להוראות אלו לשם מעבר
מהיר ולמניעת עיכוב מיותר.

– אנא הכינו תעודותיכם לבדיקה וגשו לעמדה
הפנויה.

– יש להישמע להוראות הבודקים.

– המעבר בבודדים.

– שימרו על הסדר והניקיון.

המשך יום נעים !

WELCOME TO "HAZEYTIM" CHECK POINT

YOU ARE NOW ENTERING A MILITARY AREA. TO MAKE
YOUR TRANSIT EASY AND TO AVOID UNNECESSARY DELAY
FIRST READ THESE INSTRUCTIONS AND THEN OBEY THEM.
PLEASE PREPARE YOUR DOCUMENTS FOR INSPECTION AND
APPROACH AN INSPECTION POINT WHEN IT BECOMES FREE.
FOLLOW THE INSTRUCTIONS OF THE INSPECTORS.
PASS THROUGH ONE BY ONE.
PLEASE KEEP THIS TERMINAL CLEAN.
Have a good day !

12. An Israeli military checkpoint known as "HaZeytim" on the far eastern reaches of Jerusalem, 2006. It is a major node of control into the city used by Israel to regulate Palestinian movement.

of violence against Israeli civilians since 1967.[17] But the policy and official discourse (particularly under the Israeli Labor Party in the 1990s) was to rapidly produce a more intense order of apartness between Arabs and Jews, or, as Prime Minister Rabin famously noted during his 1992 election campaign, taking "Gaza out of Tel Aviv." This necessitated reducing the number of Palestinians in the Israeli labor market.[18]

POLICING THE STREETS OF JERUSALEM: EVERYDAY EXPRESSIONS OF RACISM

Military checkpoints are predictable sites of racism and abuse. But there are other locations throughout Jerusalem where Palestinians also face harassment. Along the streets of this city, east and west, Israeli police and soldiers travel daily on patrol. Their presence in any particular locale, neighborhood, or market can be unpredictable. In Jerusalem's public places, the ambiguities of social and racial difference exist more deeply than they do at checkpoints where the color of license plates and an apartheid-like road system for Jewish settlers had begun in the mid-1990s to funnel Palestinians and Israelis into and through ever more separate spatial realms.

As Israeli Jews and Palestinians make their way through urban areas like Jerusalem, a more complex dynamic exists between occupiers and occupied in which other elements of difference are seen and unseen, read and misrecognized. A Palestinian would not necessarily be regarded as such in particular areas of the city where both peoples mix and move. This is due to the dynamic I refer to as "blending," a phenomenon discussed somewhat in Chapter 5 and which I shall say a little more about toward the end of this chapter. "Blending" is that set of cultural dynamics and

17. Suad Amiry's (2010) superb work provides perhaps the most brilliant account of Palestinian workers crossing borders in the age of the checkpoints and the everyday traumas associated with these crossings.

18. As Graham Usher (1995) notes, "Even Rabin, in an unguarded moment in December 1992, mused before an American Jewish delegation that he wished Gaza would 'disengage itself' from Israel and then 'sink' into the Mediterranean" (8).

signifiers that, at times, permits Palestinian women and men to evade racial-profiling efforts. As opposed to efforts to "pass," blending happens not necessarily through conscious, active efforts of hiding one's "true" identity but because the ethnic and racial lines that divide and mark Palestinian and Israeli are frequently very fine.

While walking Jerusalem's busy streets, I routinely witnessed a range of interactions between Palestinian men and Israeli soldiers. These modes of contact were usually not violent in the strict sense of the term. But even when the latter were "just checking" the IDs of the former, the humiliation and abuse that took place in the course of such encounters was readily apparent. Once, while descending the steps of East Jerusalem's central post office along one of the busiest thoroughfares, Salahadin Street, I spotted four soldiers, each heavily armed, surrounding a tall, pencil-thin Palestinian man of no more than twenty-five years old. He had just come down the same staircase I had, having been in the post office.

What unfolded was at first inexplicable. The soldiers in loud and aggressive voices suddenly surrounded the young man and began to question him. Then, while holding his ID card, they ordered him to take his shoes off. The soldiers then told him to jump up and down for several minutes in the middle of the road while hundreds of Palestinians shopped and strolled through the area. Those who detained him stood in a tight semi-circle and laughed raucously as if at a frat party. The Palestinian detainee's head rose and fell rhythmically above theirs for a few minutes.

The young man finally ceased springing up and down, physically unable to continue. But no sooner did he stop to rest than he was commanded to carry on by these uniformed Israeli men, one of whom shoved him slightly. He started jumping again for several more seconds and when he plainly could not go on, he bent over in exhaustion, breathing heavily, hands on knees. As the Palestinian sought to reach for his shoes, the soldiers slapped him on the back in mock appreciation as they left the scene. The entire time this spectacle unfolded their army jeep, parked awkwardly at an angle in the middle of Salahadin Street, all but impeded the midday traffic, which piled up behind it. The game was over, for now.

The young Palestinian man continued to catch his breath, hands on knees, and eventually put his shoes back on. I stood just a few feet away and wanted to say something to him, to inquire if he was all right. But I did not know how to express my concern without making him feel any more embarrassed than he probably already did. He finished tying his shoes and then, after a few more moments of rest, stood up straight and disappeared rapidly down the crowded street. The object of the soldiers' abuse did not seem physically injured. But I wondered what damage this public humiliation had done to him emotionally. I thought then and since about the traces of hatred and anger that might have been left on this young man. What might his child, his parent, or his sibling have felt had they witnessed this done to their loved one? How quickly or slowly does the effect of such an experience dissipate, if at all?

Palestinians who also observed this incident or who I later told about it did not seem astonished. Several I spoke to found it abhorrent but related that they had seen far worse along this very thoroughfare and elsewhere. One East Jerusalem merchant I interviewed and came to know quite well commented that he thought these kinds of rituals of humiliation were about "Israel reminding us that *they* are in control. They don't have to break our bones to do this." Pointing out the front door of his store toward Salahadin, he added, "Look what they do out here *every* day."

ARAB-JEWISH ENCOUNTERS IN THE YEARS OF "HOSTILE INTIMACY": 1967–1987

In the twenty years between the advent of Israeli rule over East Jerusalem in 1967 and the rise of the First Intifada (1987–1993), Israeli Jews and Palestinians described intercommunal relations as somewhat at variance from those since. Though marked by hostilities typical of that between colonizers and the colonized, these earlier times were also characterized by increasing levels of mixing and positive encounters between Arabs and Jews in the public places of West and East Jerusalem. Middle-aged and elderly Palestinian shopkeepers in Jerusalem were always the segment of the population who had the greatest, most sustained contact with Israeli soldiers and civilians. Overwhelmingly men, they proved to be the best raconteurs of these encounters, both before the First Intifada and since. Small business owners with whom I spoke remembered when Israeli Jews would routinely travel to the Arab business districts in East Jerusalem in substantial numbers. The big day was Saturday—Shabbat—when stores are generally closed in West Jerusalem and the Jewish settlements on the east side.

Israelis were not averse to crossing over on other days, too, and they did, sometimes brandishing weapons, sometimes not. They were frequently in search of less expensive commodities and excellent food (things rarely found in West Jerusalem). Any fears they had of Palestinians were not powerful enough to keep them away, particularly since their army and police were a prominent presence throughout these business districts. By the mid-1980s in this segregated city, both peoples were traveling to the neighborhoods and commercial zones of the other like never before—or since.

However, with the advent of the First Intifada in late 1987, spatial relations and social encounters began to shift. Locales in this urban center where Palestinians and Israelis had interacted and mingled did not evaporate. But in a matter of months, they became zones of rising fear and hostility. Palestinians I spoke with told me that their travels to West Jerusalem did not drop off that much in those years. This was, after all, where thousands of them worked on a daily basis. But it was widely noted that Israeli Jews increasingly refused to drive their cars anywhere near the center of East Jerusalem by 1988. Israeli bus routes were altered to skate around some of the areas of dense Arab population concentrations.

As mentioned, by the late 1980s and early 1990s, roughly 150,000 Palestinian workers from the West Bank and Gaza Strip—mostly men—entered Israel to work each day in low-wage jobs.[19] However, the Jewish state made it illegal for these day laborers to stay within the "Green Line" overnight. If caught in Jerusalem past the 11 P.M. Israeli-imposed curfew without a pretext, Palestinian men could be detained or, as some described, taken for "a ride." This expression referred to an act well known to several Palestinian men I spoke with. It involved Israeli soldiers handcuffing an Arab they saw walking in the city (usually at night), loading the individual into a jeep, and then beating the detainee as the jeep drove around.

19. When general strikes were called during the First Intifada, the Palestinian workforce would stay home, bringing Israeli industries, like construction, to a near halt.

Ashraf, a man now in his early forties, told me about the time this happened to him during the First Intifada.

> I remember they [the soldiers] blindfolded me and were laughing and yelling like they were at a football game while they were hitting and kicking me. They really found it a good time and they would blare loud music. Then they would dump you somewhere, just dump you in the middle of the city at night and you did not know where you were and had to walk home.

Twelve years later, he recounted this and other similar incidents casually and without emotion between sips of Arabic coffee. His manner was strangely reserved, and I was surprised that he detailed these tales of torture and terror with such calm—even interspersing them with humor and irony. But equally confounding were his stories about how Palestinian men would, despite these dangers, continually return to West Jerusalem, Tel Aviv, and other Israeli-majority areas. He and his male friends would travel there not only to work, which was a necessity, but also for leisure, to go to the beach, and to visit Palestinians who lived in Israel. What would draw them to realms potentially so dangerous, I wondered? If the *shebab* were interested in crossing over into West Jerusalem for amusement, why would they continue to defy the curfew and risk being caught?

Ossama, a contemporary of Ashraf, spoke of those stakes during one interview. He told me of a time on New Year's Eve in 1988 when he and two of his fellow Palestinian revelers were caught in West Jerusalem after the curfew. They were spotted leaving West Jerusalem after 1 A.M. in a car with blue license plates, at the time the color Israel earmarked for West Bank Palestinians. They were pulled over by the Israeli police and detained. Guilty only of staying beyond the 11 P.M. curfew, they were taken to the local headquarters, slapped around, threatened, and held in jail for the entire night.

"But the worse thing was that we were not allowed to call our families," he related. "And remember, this was the middle of the Intifada when people [Palestinians] were being killed every day by soldiers and settlers. They [Palestinians] were disappearing and were being found dead.

Imagine what my parents were thinking when I didn't come home." Such an experience highlighted the ways fear has intersected the families of targeted Arab men under military rule.

One illustration of the heightened antagonisms that surfaced during the First Intifada was the week of mob violence against Palestinians in Jerusalem in August 1990, following the disappearance of two Jewish youths from Jerusalem. Hundreds of Israeli Jews, assuming that those responsible were Palestinians, embarked on what two Israeli civil libertarians referred to as "pogroms" against Arab civilians. These two Israeli eyewitnesses, civil libertarian Israel Shahak and Witold Jedlicki, wrote that the content of the mobs' Hebrew slogans "included the traditional 'Death to the Arabs' . . . increasingly replaced by 'Murder to the Arabs.'" The crowd, according to these observers, could also often be heard screaming, "Kill all Arab babies" and "Rape all Arab Women" (Shahak and Jedlicki 1991, 3–6).[20] Three Palestinians were killed by the rampaging mob and at least two dozen others were seriously injured.

In a few cases, a man believed by the Israeli crowds to be Arab, and accordingly beaten, turned out to be an Israeli Jew. The rioters rampaged through Palestinian commercial areas in East Jerusalem, smashing property. What was peculiar about these incidents was the disturbingly racist principle that motivated them. The mob was driven by the idea that in seeking "retribution" against alleged acts of "Arab terrorism," a completely innocent Palestinian—sometimes any Palestinian—could be attacked in "retaliation." If they could not apprehend the actual perpetrator, any Arab would do. I was confronted with these discourses and practices throughout my research. They remain, I believe, a consistent and abiding dimension of Israeli colonial racism.

THE AMBIGUITIES OF DIFFERENCE

The distinction mentioned above between what I am describing as "blending" and what is regularly referred to as "passing" in other racial contexts

20. See Shahak and Jedlicki (1991). For another account of this violence see Chesin, Hutman, and Melamed (1999).

is important to address in Palestine/Israel. The identities of those who "blend" in Palestine/Israel are simply missed or misrecognized by dominant communities because of assumptions they so often have about what the other must certainly look like. Palestinians who are not initially perceived as Arab by Israeli Jews are not, I assert, generally trying to hide their identity. Instead, given the dangers of being recognized as Arab, they have not gone out of their way to announce that fact.[21]

Nearly every Palestinian man I spoke with had tales of abuse that he had undergone at the hands of Israeli soldiers, settlers, or civilians in West Jerusalem. However, I also met a handful of men who had never once been hassled or detained while in Israeli-majority areas like West Jerusalem or Tel Aviv. In most cases, while traversing public places and riding public transportation, these Palestinians who "blended" were assumed to be Jewish or internationals by Israeli Jewish citizens. Their appearance and presence raised little if any suspicion with soldiers or police, at least not in surface encounters.

In the final pages of this chapter I offer a few emblematic experiences of Palestinian men under Israeli colonial rule in and around Jerusalem in the late 1990s and early 2000s and of the politics of racial and ethnic signifiers of otherness.

"Blending" in Jerusalem: Sami's Story

Sami is a Palestinian man, originally from the northern West Bank town of Nablus. Though he resided and worked in Jerusalem during the period when I conducted my research, he did so "illegally," that is, without Israeli authorization. If found to be living in the city, those who transgress

---

21. I am not arguing that there is an "Arab" look or an "Israeli Jewish" look, only that both dominant and subordinate communities possess cultural assumptions about what an Arab or a Jew typically "looks like." That imagination, in turn, has an impact on how individuals are treated. Mizrahim and Ethiopian Jews, a number of Mizrahi community activists told me during my stay in Jerusalem, not uncommonly utilize religious symbols—yarmulkes and Stars of David, particularly—in public spaces to create ethnoreligious clarity about which religious and national community they belong to.

Israeli law in this way can be imprisoned for months or years. Sami was fair-skinned with dark blonde hair and piercing green eyes. A fashion-conscious man of thirty-eight when I first met him in the late 1990s, he had become fairly well off even by Israeli standards. The commitments to political struggle that he once held in his teens and twenties had been mostly supplanted in his thirties by a dedication to his successful business.

I sometimes kidded Sami that he looked more Norwegian than *Naabilsi* (a term referring to those from the Palestinian town of Nablus). He "blended" when he was in West Jerusalem and other Israeli contexts like few other Arab men could. It might be said that he routinely flew under the "racial radar" of colonial rule. Though he emphasized that he never tried to pretend he was an Israeli Jew or *ijnabi* (foreigner), his fluent Hebrew, Western-style clothing, and somatic features generally created the impression among both Israelis and Palestinians that he was not an Arab. When Sami walked through Palestinian commercial areas in the Old City, Arab merchants routinely called out "Shalom!" to him, thinking he was an Israeli or a tourist. Israelis commonly addressed him in Hebrew, too, particularly in areas like West Jerusalem or Tel Aviv. Sami told me that he usually went along with this, responded in Hebrew, kept his cool, and kept on moving.

Given the risks that loom for Palestinians under military occupation, I could hardly fault him. However, his ability to "blend" rarely assuaged the concerns he harbored of being incarcerated in Israeli prisons. Sami was, after all, a former political prisoner and torture survivor. Though not readily recognized as a Palestinian, he had a "record" and was a known quantity to Israeli intelligence: he was, so to speak, in their "system."

"I never get stopped in West Jerusalem—never, never, never. Sometimes they [Israeli soldiers or police] look at me for a long time as I approach them," he explained, "and I just try to stay cool. But they don't ask to see my ID. They just nod, sometimes say something in Hebrew and nod." Palestinians like Sami who do not "stick out" or who are not immediately regarded by the dominant national community as "matter out of place" cannot sustain this ambiguity in more substantial interactions with Israelis (e.g., in job interviews, in the search for housing, or in longer conversations with Israeli security). An individual's "real" identity in these instances almost always comes to the fore eventually. This can happen as discussed in chapter 5 when one's Arabic name is given, when one's domicile is made known, or when longer conversations in Hebrew take place.

The Limits of "Blending": Jamal's Story

Jamal, a Palestinian born and raised in the Jewish state, also made his way through much of Israeli society without typically being identified as an Arab. Though it is written on his Israel-issued ID card that he is Muslim, his Israeli citizenship allowed him the right to be nearly anywhere at any time in Jerusalem. His experiences, however, illustrate the tenuous social location that Palestinians with Israeli citizenship generally confront in a state where full rights do not flow from citizenship but rather from being a Jewish citizen.

A friendly, immensely intelligent, and politically sophisticated man of about thirty years old in the early 2000s, Jamal had studied at Hebrew University and worked in Jerusalem for seven years. He told me that as an Israeli passport-holder, his status was distinctively different from Palestinians who grew up in the West Bank and Gaza. There was, he related, a kind of "in-betweenness" that he lived. This was especially true while he was a student at the Hebrew University. Jamal was neither fully Israeli to many Israeli Jews nor fully Palestinian to some Palestinians from the West Bank and Gaza.

When I asked him about life in the city and at college, he spoke of being pulled persistently between wanting to express his Arab identity and his nationalist politics, on the one hand, while wishing to fit in with the Jewish-majority student population on the other. "I wanted both," he related. "I wasn't trying to avoid either [group]." Jamal was not averse to mixing with Jews, and over the course of several years and dozens of conversations I never once heard him make an anti-Semitic statement. Socially skilled and gregarious, he attended the parties of Jewish friends and dated Jewish women—Israeli and American. However, during his four years of college, Jamal came to understand that avoiding anti-Arab racism was next to impossible. He was continually made to feel unwanted or not quite at home in the Jewish state, despite the fact that his family had lived in Palestine for generations before Israel had been founded. Jamal related how budding friendships with Jewish students were all too often broken-off when they learned he was Arab.

> "I got to know some of the Americans [Jewish students] at Hebrew University. Okay, this is funny, because their Hebrew was so bad they could not tell by my accent that I might not be a [Israeli] Jew. They assumed I was. I look like I could be. But they did not even know that 'Jamal' was an Arab name! So we would talk and hang out and sometimes we really got along. But the second they found out I was Palestinian, they would *never* have anything to do with me again. They would never talk to me again. They might acknowledge me when we'd pass each other on campus but they would keep away. This happened *so* many times!"
>
> "Not all of them reacted this way, right?"
>
> "No, of course not."
>
> "So, how did you deal with it?
>
> "Well, it really made me mad—*really* mad!" He exclaimed in English. "These fuckers!" his voice rising, his hand smacking the table for emphasis. "It is the worst kind of racism ['*unsuriyye*]: you know, they like you and then when they find out who you are they don't like you. They stop talking to you—are afraid of you—*only* for that reason."

Jamal's experiences of being "found out" and then discarded would invariably arise during our conversations. These incidents revealed a precarious condition that Palestinian students at Israeli universities mentioned feeling in various ways. Having the latitude to mix with Israeli Jews, particularly in institutions like universities where a Palestinian might wish to establish himself or herself professionally, had its parameters. When Arabs bumped up against such limits, there were clearly emotional injuries that produced anger and sadness. These social impediments, these barriers that were sometimes opaque and at other times translucent, would continually (re)clarify the boundaries of racial privilege for Palestinians living in contemporary Jerusalem across class and gender.

Disclosing Fear: Munir's Story

Palestinian men I spoke with whose bodies had been the sites of torture and physical abuse were usually not averse to describing this maltreatment. However, the more I listened to these narratives the more I noticed that something was missing. Though Palestinian males readily told of moments of brutalization, only seldom did they express feelings of fear. One might have thought by listening to some of them that they were afraid of nothing. I observed among countless men gradations of a macho intrepidness and proud bravado. Surviving the violence and beatings of settlers and soldiers have been, as Julie Peteet (1994) perceptively documents, "a rite of passage" for Palestinian males as they entered adulthood and sought to claim particular masculine identities and status.

Women in these same homes would with great regularity relate their worries and apprehension about male family members' safety. They would frequently turn attention to their trepidation for the well-being of sons, brothers, husbands, or fathers. But rarely did the Palestinian men I came to know acknowledge that they themselves were afraid. They may have done so among their close friends and comrades. But with me and other internationals I spoke with such disclosures were very rare.

Munir, a man in his thirties in 2006, was different. A corpulent and gentle dark-skinned Arab who studied in Jerusalem, he had the unenviable task of having to ride the Israeli bus system for several hours a week as he navigated his way to work, to school, and to friends' homes throughout Jerusalem. The eldest son of a Bedouin family of modest means, Munir's appearance powerfully announced his ethno-racial identity. Both Palestinians and Israelis, he told me, almost always identified him as an Arab. This was underscored by the harassment that he dealt with on Israeli buses and other public places. In these realms, Munir consistently attracted the gaze of police and soldiers. He told me that he routinely felt knife-like stares as he boarded buses and experienced nonverbal expressions of hatred and disgust among Israelis. This wore on him and I could understand why.

Perhaps because Munir was unlike other Arab men I knew or maybe because he faced the threat of serious bodily harm and needed my help, he once revealed his fear to me. It happened late one summer evening in

2006 after I had hosted him and a half-dozen other friends at my residence in East Jerusalem. As our night of political discussion and mirth-making concluded around 2 A.M., and as other mutual colleagues strangely departed for other destinations without asking if Munir needed a ride, he somewhat sheepishly inquired if he could sleep at my place that night. To walk home at this late hour to his apartment in the Old City, he related, was a risk he did not wish to take.

The roughly two-kilometer journey by foot, through the desolate streets of East Jerusalem, was for him a decidedly worrisome prospect and that worry showed on his face. Out there, beyond the safe confines of my house, were soldiers and perhaps armed settlers roaming "their" city. A group of settlers from a right-wing organization had provocatively taken over an Arab-owned home in his neighborhood in the Muslim Quarter of the Old City in recent months. They, like the soldiers, were known to harass Palestinian men with impunity under the cover of darkness, detaining them and sometimes doing much worse. Any Palestinian man out at night, particularly this late, could attract suspicion.

Having to ask to sleep at my home was plainly a bit embarrassing for Munir. It should not have been, but it was. We had just met a few weeks earlier and were only beginning to get to know one another. I felt ashamed for not having thought of his predicament and offering him my spare bedroom before he felt a need to ask. Because he had broached the subject, he then wished to explain the basis for his request. Munir described the everyday sorts of harassment he had to contend with under Israeli rule:

> There are weeks when I am stopped two or three times and told to present my ID. On the bus today, in fact, just on the way over here, I was sitting and reading an Arabic newspaper and an Israeli policewoman approached me and demanded to see my *hawiyya* [identity card]. I gave it without any protest and kept reading the paper as if nothing happened.

The Arabic newspaper in this instance, he figured, helped draw attention to him instantly. But his skin color and "profile" as a Palestinian were routinely things that marked him as potentially dangerous in the Israeli imagination.

"Look how stupid this is," Munir continued. "If I had been involved in something, would I be reading an *Arabic* newspaper on an Israeli bus in the middle of West Jerusalem?" These measures, he had no doubt, were not about security, they were about racism. "Security," however, was not only that magical discourse that stoked fear and suspicion of Arabs among Israeli Jews. It also served to justify the violations of their civil liberties and human rights in the name of an "antiterrorism" that was, itself, quite terrorizing to Palestinian men like Munir.

"Humiliation [*izlaal*] is not an easy feeling to deal with," he continued. "When it happens . . . you know, it is something that makes me upset for the rest of the day, for a long time. I spend so much of my time just being angry."

Blackness as Metaphor and as Signifier

Like Munir, "blending" or moving through Israeli society undetected and unmolested has never been a possibility for 'Azmi. A dark-skinned Palestinian whose family came to Jerusalem from Central Africa more than 200 years ago, his genealogy points to the remarkable cultural diversity and mixture that has comprised Palestine in the modern period. But attached to those histories are the distinct racial signifiers that have marked him in potent ways. He is recognizable from far away and is easily picked out of crowds—both in Arab and Jewish locales. If 'Azmi walked my streets in the United States, sought to catch a cab, or drove his car through particular neighborhoods, he would certainly have experienced the racial profiling that African Americans have always been subject to. Though a real *qudsi* (a dyed-in-the-wool Jerusalemite who had spent his entire life in the city), Israeli authorities treated him as though he did not belong in their "eternal capital."

'Azmi was well known, even legendary in Palestine for his history of militancy. Until the mid-1980s, he was a political prisoner in Israeli jails. For more than a decade he remained incarcerated for planting explosives in a West Jerusalem commercial district. He once told me that he did this after Israeli death squads had assassinated a string of Palestinian comrades, deep in the occupied West Bank, in the months after its conquest in June 1967.

"I did it," he related softly but with a degree of discernible pride, "to send a message to the Israelis that as long as their government brutalizes us they will have to face this kind of retribution." It was no surprise that once caught he was, like tens of thousands of other Palestinians, tortured. During the years of his imprisonment he learned Hebrew and refined his Marxist analysis. As his incarceration grew longer and he watched thousands of others set free while he remained, he became an elder in the prison, one who instructed younger Palestinian prisoners about the finer points of politics and national liberation. His status was bound up with his masculinity, his valor, and with the fact that he was a torture survivor and a militant.

'Azmi acquired his freedom in a prisoner exchange in the mid-1980s. But as he added in the same breath, echoing other former detainees, he only entered into what he regarded as the "larger prison" of Israeli military rule. After his release, 'Azmi began to have problems with alcohol. Though a brilliant, poetic, and charismatic man, those who knew him related observing his increasingly volatile and disturbing behavior. His interactions with comrades and enemies alike grew erratic, his relations with friends and family increasingly belligerent.

The story of this political elder was one that always struck me as particularly tragic, from his initial assault against civilians, through his long detention, and into the post-prison constraints of colonial rule. His tribulations were especially difficult because of the manner in which soldiers and Jewish settlers continually harassed him along the streets of Jerusalem, years after his release. He was, in a sense, still very much confined, still subject to the gaze of Israeli "security" like few others I met.

Soldiers and settlers were able to spot him fairly easily in public and occasionally would call out racist slurs that referenced his skin color and phenotypes: "nigger," *shvartze* (a derogatory Yiddish word for dark-skinned people), *kushi* (derogatory Hebrew word for dark-skinned people of African origin), or *hayawaan* ("animal" in Arabic). Like nearly all other communities, Palestinians are not immune to racism. The prestige

'Azmi held as a legendary political prisoner intersected racial hierarchies among Palestinians that diminished that status among some. But he had never been physically assaulted by other Palestinians because of his racial assignment. At least twice since being released from prison, Israeli soldiers on patrol had severely pummeled him. On one occasion, they broke his shoulder blade and injured his head in the course of throwing him to the ground. Though 'Azmi did not express fear to me, he did describe what it felt like to be as vulnerable as he was.

"They can see me anywhere because of my color," he related stoically. "Because I'm black, I stick out." Even from far away, 'Azmi continued, sometimes before he can see roaming groups of soldiers, they notice him. As we traversed the crowded alleys of the Old City he told me, "Some of them [soldiers] know who I am, my history." He stopped to shake hands with a local merchant or two who clearly had great fondness for him. With irony in his voice, this former militant added:

> They are still afraid [of me] because they know what I did. And they feel they can do anything to me. And there is so much hatred in their eyes. I don't shy away from them. I always look them right in the eyes and when I look at them that is what I see—total hatred.

CONCLUSION

In this chapter I have analyzed some of the enduring dangers that "dangerous" Arab men and boys have experienced under an Israeli regime of colonial surveillance. The period I have chronicled with greatest emphasis, the mid 1990s to 2012, was one where intensifying forms of separation between Palestinians and Israeli Jews were created across wide swaths of Palestine/Israel, not simply in Jerusalem. Fear and racism have helped sustain and bolster this spatial order of apartness, one that shows little sign of receding.

What is all too commonly ignored about the national struggle in Palestine/Israel are the quotidian effects of broader "security measures." This chapter has sought to detail some of the everyday dimensions of terror and terrorism as lived by occupier and occupied, alike. In the last decade this has included a range of dehumanizing practices that I feel must surely impact in significant ways those who perpetrate this violence, not simply its victims. What, after all, might be the implications of Israeli soldiers inscribing identification numbers on the foreheads and forearms of Palestinian detainees as they did in the early 2000s? One mainstream Israeli Knesset member at the time, Tommy Lapid, thought it troubling enough to publicly demand that the IDF stop such practices. His appeal was powerful: "As a refugee from the Holocaust," he stated, "I find such an act insufferable."[22]

In the last ten years or so there have been reported cases in which Palestinian boys and men were not only detained and beaten at checkpoints but also publicly stripped and made to stand naked at gunpoint at these nodes of control in front of hundreds of others. This, as the Israeli soldiers mocked them. In recent years, there has arisen a growing phenomenon in which soldiers post pictures of blindfolded Palestinian prisoners, humiliated in a range of ways, on Facebook and other social media. Such stories surface routinely in the Hebrew press and elsewhere and then seem to disappear without much comment or accountability.

The gendered manifestations of colonial racism in this continually shifting urban center are innumerable. And faced with the enormity of these expressions, I and other researchers are left with a range of only partially answered questions. To what extent, for instance, did the abuse visited upon these men and boys contribute to their own violence in their households and communities? What were the ramifications of brutality, torture, and sexual humiliation on the psyches of the violated? And, as mentioned, what impact did such degradation have on the Israeli men and women who meted it out? As abuse and humiliation from the street is brought back home to places most intimate, the effects do not simply dissipate in an environment of love and compassion. Palestinian and Israeli feminist organizations and community psychologists have, in fact, examined and fought the pernicious links between the effects of military occupation and the phenomenon of domestic violence in the homes of Palestinians and Israelis.

22. Associated Press (2002).

Among the oppressed, the colonized, even the forced laborer in the Nazi death camp, there are responses to oppression that propel innocent victims into the victimizers of others. Primo Levi's (1988) challenging account of such realities in what he refers to as the morally ambiguous realm of the "Gray Zone" speaks to these manifestations of militarism. But in discussing them, it is crucial to remember what Alessandro Manzoni, quoted in Levi's work, poignantly remarked about these most inhumane of conditions: "Provocateurs, oppressors, all those who in some way injure others, are guilty, not only of the evil they commit, but also of the perversion into which they lead the spirit of the offended" (Levi, p. 44).

Traveling across Jerusalem's colonial landscape, one is confronted with layers of racism and cruelty. If one listens and observes sensitively enough, it is possible to witness some of the hidden perversions to which Manzoni refers. I offer here an initial glimpse into the abiding impact of the criminalization of Palestinian boys and men in Jerusalem and the costs associated with Israel's goal of keeping "dangerous" Arabs in their "proper" place.

7

Up from the Ruins?

Demolishing Homes and Building Solidarity in a Colonial City

The right to the city is far more than the individual liberty to access urban resources: it is a right to change ourselves by changing the city. It is, moreover, a common rather than an individual right since this transformation inevitably depends upon the exercise of a collective power to reshape the processes of urbanization.

—DAVID HARVEY, "The Right to the City"

While walking the contemporary urban landscape of Israeli-occupied East Jerusalem, from realms poor to privileged, I would occasionally come across peculiar mounds of ruin. These piles of crushed concrete, broken bricks, and twisted iron were usually the remains of hundreds of Palestinian homes in Jerusalem demolished by Israel since 1967. The owners of these destroyed dwellings rarely have the resources to clear away these remains—so they remain. They "stand" as silent monuments to the force of Israeli colonial authority and its efforts to impose the rule of one national community over another in contemporary Jerusalem.

Each razed structure possessed multiple stories of despair, I came to learn, layers of hidden hardship and humiliation. Interviews with family members who had witnessed the cruel felling of the places most intimate to them revealed anguish and anger that dissipated very slowly. Those sentiments were compounded all too often by the loss of movable property buried beneath the rubble. These were belongings that the Israeli authorities would not let families remove before dismantling their homes: a mother's jewelry, an adolescent's artwork, a student's photographs or books, family heirlooms, a grandfather's cane.

In this final chapter, I continue my examination of spatial and racial politics in contemporary Jerusalem by analyzing the centrality of homes to the national struggle between Israelis and Palestinians. I focus on the specific ways in which colonial violence impinges on the land and housing of Jerusalem's Arab communities. But I also highlight how Palestinians and Israelis have constituted an array of small-scale forms of resistance to military occupation, particularly around housing justice. Over the last fifteen years I have researched the efforts of several activist organizations in Palestine/Israel. The preponderance of my time has been spent with the Israeli Committee Against House Demolitions (ICAHD), a human rights collective founded in 1997 and based in West Jerusalem. Members of this group and their proliferating supporters internationally have been involved in a range of political projects whose overarching aims are, in their own words, "to end Israel's occupation over the Palestinians."[1] To both its admirers and detractors within Palestine/Israel and abroad, ICAHD has become perhaps best known for acts of creative civil disobedience. These efforts have grown significantly in the last decade and have often (though not always) involved Israelis and Palestinians working together to impede nonviolently the destruction of familial places.

This chapter is based on forty-one interviews with Palestinians, Israelis, and internationals committed to housing rights activism in Jerusalem and elsewhere. In addition, I spent several months engaging in participant observation at three of ICAHD's annual summer work camps and on roughly 20 tours organized by this and other human rights organizations from the late 1990s until 2012.[2] Chapter 2 highlighted the more mixed and less hierarchical Arab-Jewish relations during the era of British colonial Jerusalem (1917–1948). As I conclude this book, my analysis in a sense comes

1. See Halper (2010) as well as the ICAHD web site: http://icahdusa.org/. Accessed November 20, 2012.

2. These include the inaugural ICAHD work camp in 2003, as well as those in the summers of 2006 and 2012.

13. A Palestinian home demolished by Israel in the neighborhood of 'Anata, 2006. An Israeli military tower near the illegal Jewish settlement of Pisgat Ze'ev is in the background.

full circle as I detail constructive interactions and antiracist encounters in the city among Palestinians and Israelis involved in a budding movement for the right to live safely in one's own home. What might these expressions of solidarity offer toward the transformation of a city premised on equality and social justice rather than on separation and inequality?

Over the last several decades, anthropologists and other scholars have detailed the ways in which familial places represent complex social and cultural locales. They have explored myriad ways in which kinship ties, domestic networks, and relationships most intimate are constituted, negotiated, and contested.[3] And as these writers have done so, they have emphasized the importance of not romanticizing familial realms with all of the

3. For innovative anthropological analyses of these dynamics see the work of Stack (1974), Joseph (1999), Johnson (2006), Collier, Rosaldo, and Yanagisako (1997), and Taraki (2006b).

hierarchies, instances of oppression, and quotidian cruelties that permeate them cross-culturally. My experiences with those whose homes have been wrested from them have made me appreciate the fact that without the ability to feel secure within one's own dwelling—or in the absence of a dwelling at all—the possibilities for healthy communities and families diminish substantially. Possessing basic shelter in Jerusalem or anywhere else might be thought of as a necessary but not sufficient condition for peace and justice.

THE POLITICS OF HOUSING
UNDER ISRAELI COLONIAL RULE

This book has documented various inequities between Palestinians and Israeli Jews under Israeli governance. But there are few more prominent than those found in the areas of residential space. Since the advent of military occupation in East Jerusalem in 1967, Israel has built over 50,000 housing units for Jewish settlers on this side of the city. By 2012 the settler population had risen to nearly 200,000 in East Jerusalem's nine major residential settlements. Over the same period, governing authorities have, through a private Palestinian developer, constructed only 500 units for the more than 325,000 Palestinians of East Jerusalem. Compounding the pressures produced by these vast disparities in the construction of homes is the enduring practice of demolishing Palestinian dwellings. The United Nations, ICAHD, and other human rights organizations estimate that from 1967 to 2012, Israel destroyed roughly 25,000 Arab homes and other structures in the West Bank and Gaza Strip.[4] Several thousand of these demolitions have been carried out in the Jerusalem area alone.

Demolitions continued unabated throughout the age of the Oslo Accords in the 1990s as did the construction of housing units for Jewish settlers. Between the signing of the Oslo agreements in 1993 and 2012, the

---

4. This estimate is based on UN reports; Israeli, Palestinian, and international human rights groups' data; and figures that come from the Israeli government. See United Nations Office for the Coordination of Humanitarian Affairs (OCHA) 2012; and ICAHD (2012).

Israeli government more than doubled the number of settlers in the West Bank (including East Jerusalem) from about 275,000 to close to 600,000. Within the Israeli-defined boundaries of East Jerusalem the settler population jumped from about 120,000 to 200,000 over the same period.[5]

During the early phases of my research, I was intrigued by how many Palestinians and Israelis involved in housing rights activism saw the need to educate Americans about their government's role in reproducing Israeli military occupation. That has, in fact, been a crucial component of what organizations like ICAHD regard as their mission. Toward that end, activists urged me to see the conditions of enforced "apartness" that they experienced in Jerusalem in equivalent American terms. The challenge was to imagine a contemporary U.S. racial landscape that had not eliminated Jim Crow laws, de jure segregation, and legally sanctioned racial covenants.

In a 1998 interview I conducted with the late Israeli civil libertarian and Holocaust survivor Israel Shahak, he posed this question: "What would the reaction in the United States be if the government said 90 percent of the country was only available to Christians? You need to talk to Americans in this way about what is happening here. Put it in *their* terms." Doing what Shahak suggests yields startling figures about housing in Palestine/Israel. It would be as if 1.8 to 2 million homes in the United States had been destroyed in the last four decades by a foreign government internationally recognized as illegally occupying the United States. That number would be enough to house the entire populations of municipal Detroit, Boston, and Washington, DC.

What motivates such policies to constrain Palestinian home building in Jerusalem? The answer lies in that most central feature of colonial governance: concerns with race and racial difference and the classifying and counting of colonizer and colonized, alike. As discussed in previous chapters, since 1948 Israelis have expressed anxieties about rising Palestinian populations and "demographic time bombs," particularly in Jerusalem. Concerns over "Arab population growth," "too many Arabs," or

5. See B'tselem 2012 Report on Settlements, http://www.btselem.org/topic/settlements. Access date November 24, 2012.

dangerously high Palestinian birthrates are racial discourses that under-gird Israel's continued appropriation of Palestinian land.[6]

HOUSING RIGHTS ACTIVISM
IN CONTEMPORARY JERUSALEM

Activist struggles around housing politics have been compelling and suc-cessful in a number of ways but not principally because of their capacity to substantially impede these demolitions. Those involved in housing rights activism have, in fact, salvaged relatively few Palestinian structures slated for destruction. Instead, as Jeff Halper, the founder of ICAHD, explained during a 2003 interview about the new organization's capacities:

> We slow the Israeli Army down. If we do civil disobedience at a house they [Israel] want to demolish, then we can make the government's job more difficult. We take up more of their time and maybe, instead of destroying four houses that day, they will only destroy two.

Whatever local triumphs ICAHD and other housing rights organizations have had (and there have been many), they have been unable to rebuild even 1 percent of the structures Israel has demolished. According to its principal organizers, ICAHD has built or rebuilt about 190 homes since 1998. This figure is not insignificant and hundreds of Palestinians have been directly helped by this dimension of the group's efforts. But activ-ists not only acknowledged but also emphasized that their work has not mainly been humanitarian or charitable in the narrow sense of the term. They have not, for instance, had the resources to reconstruct thousands or even hundreds of homes since the late 1990s, and doing so would not

6. A principal finding, described in previous chapters, is that Israel has sought to explicitly regulate the demographic realities in the city, hindering Palestinian population growth while engaging in efforts to bolster the number of Jews in Jerusalem. The former Israeli mayor of Jerusalem, Teddy Kollek, stated at a Jerusalem Municipal Council Meet-ing on June 17, 1984: "Like all of us here, it seems to me, I am worried about the balance of power and about Arab growth within and around Jerusalem" (cited in B'Tselem [1997]).

alone achieve their goal of ending Israeli military occupation. Their organizing is most meaningful for reasons beyond their capability to provide
shelter to those in need. International educational and outreach campaigns have been ICAHD's major thrust, with an emphasis on work in
Europe and the U.S.

However, running concurrently with the growth of these political projects have been ever-greater degrees of separation between Israelis and Palestinians in Jerusalem. This, as discussed in previous chapters, has become
increasingly the case since the early 1990s (and with particular force since
the early 2000s). Affirmative forms of contact and shared movement-build-
ing have, therefore, in some ways been more and more challenging to forge.
Israel, with the backing of the United States government, has made it next
to impossible over the last two decades for the majority of Palestinians
from the West Bank and Gaza Strip to live in or even visit Jerusalem. Israeli
Jews who might have traveled to Arab areas of East Jerusalem in the 1990s
have become more fearful about doing so after the outbreak of the Second Intifada in 2000. Further, beginning in the early 2000s, Israel increasingly enforced a 1990s prohibition barring their own citizens from entering
most major Palestinian towns (what are still regarded in the Oslo Accords
lexicon as "Areas A"). It surprised several of those I spoke to in the United
States that there are today actually Israeli checkpoints that stop Israeli Jews
from driving into Ramallah and other Palestinian towns.

An additional challenge has faced activists in recent years. As several involved in this organizing told me, in the last five years or so it
has become progressively more difficult to promote these forms of joint
Arab-Jewish struggle in the local and international press. Though print
and radio media were once reasonably attracted to the political work of
ICAHD and other groups, like the Israeli antiwar group Women in Black,
they have found this political organizing far less intriguing than they did
in the early 2000s.[7] Much of these movements' sheen, it seems, has worn
off in the eyes of journalists.

7. One ICAHD activist who has done a good deal of the group's media outreach
related to me in 2012 that when she had tried in recent years to get reporters and writers

CITY OF RUINS: BURIED FRAGMENTS

Most of the Palestinian parents I spoke with whose homes had been destroyed would raise the issue of the emotional toll taken on their children. These young people had not uncommonly been traumatized by the violent and sudden elimination of their dwellings. Activists and family members related how in many instances they were familiar with the Israeli demolition crews who would arrive at night or early in the morning when residents were asleep. Converging on these sites deemed "illegal" might be as many as two dozen armed men, accompanied with loud bulldozers or powerful pneumatic drills, yelling orders for the family to leave and violently expelling those who resisted these commands.

This damage was lasting and few of these mostly working-class and working-poor families had access to the resources needed to address the trauma produced by the razing of homes. Hearing these narratives reminded me of those I discussed in chapter 4 about the night the Moroccan Quarter in Jerusalem's Old City was eliminated in June, 1967. The demolition of Palestinian familial places represented a certain continuity of spatial dominance, one linked to an abiding Israeli governmental vision for Jerusalem and by particular racial notions about the Arab communities they ruled over.

In the majority of cases I became familiar with since the late 1990s, those whose homes had been destroyed had been taken in and aided by others in their neighborhood or community. In the course of interviews with members of about 29 different displaced families, 21 (70 percent) had found refuge with other Palestinian families for varying lengths of time. These networks, these "webs" of support, were not unlike those that Carol Stack (1974) describes in her analysis of domestic networks in poor and segregated African American neighborhoods. The demolition of a shelter could affect—and usually did—the victims' friends and extended

---

from the foreign press to cover their annual work camp, one sympathetic journalist told her that unless someone was shot or seriously injured, editors would not deem it newsworthy enough to cover.

kin. These networks were typically mobilized and, in Stack's words, they proved to be "elastic"—a good thing, too, I thought, since they certainly were stretched.

Sorrow and fury emanated from the experiences of those made homeless into broader kin groups and communities, like concentric circles of a stone dropped in a pond. Relationships with those who took in the displaced would not uncommonly fray, and the tensions and violence experienced would at times disrupt others who sought to help them but who could not do so indefinitely. A scarcity of resources could precipitate friction between those previously quite close. These were what might be referred to as "the hidden injuries" of colonial rule.[8] I became confident that these realities could move countless Israeli Jews and others internationally if only they were made aware of them.

As I was becoming more familiar with these human rights concerns and as I traveled to several of these sites of demolition, I became nearly as disturbed by the economic conditions that enveloped these razed structures as I was by the demolitions themselves. Embedded in at times immense poverty, particularly in relation to the relative privilege that Israeli citizens generally possess, the rubble of destroyed homes usually sat along vaguely paved streets. These narrow, pothole-ridden threads ran through densely populated Palestinian quarters where the occupying power has sought to preclude needed construction and capital improvements.

An Arab neighborhood like 'Anata on the fringes of Jerusalem resembled the conditions found in several refugee camps I visited in the West Bank. Children living there typically played amid the dust and fumes of cars and trucks that traversed these ghettos. As the Palestinian population of East Jerusalem expanded at a rate of 3 to 4 percent a year since 1967, few new classrooms, parks, or community centers were built—and rarely if ever by the Israeli authorities.

After spending several months in this divided urban center, east and west, it struck me that Jerusalem's *least*-serviced Jewish residential areas

8. I borrow this term from Sennett's (1993) wonderfully evocative formulation, "hidden injuries of class."

were better equipped and cared for by the Israeli government than the *best*-serviced Palestinian quarters. The city's poorest Israeli Jews are not wealthier than the richest Palestinians. However, even the most destitute among the Israeli Jewish population typically lived in neighborhoods with better public services than the Palestinian quarters of East Jerusalem.[9]

THE MAKING OF A LANDSCAPE OF APARTNESS

Beyond these expressions of discrimination in access to housing exists another interrelated dimension of inequality between Arabs and Jews: the politics of movement in and around contemporary Jerusalem. By this I mean not simply who is permitted by Israel to enter Jerusalem, but the very infrastructure of roads made available to Israeli-Jews as opposed to Palestinians. In the last twenty years, Israel has spent hundreds of millions of dollars paving new "bypass" roads and other infrastructure for the Jewish settlers. They have been designed so that Israelis are able to evade the Arab towns and villages upon which these residential estates are so frequently built.[10] This vast network connects outlying settlements to the center of Jerusalem and elsewhere, sometimes through tunnels that burrow under Palestinian population centers and fortressed bridges built

9. It should be noted that poor and working-poor Israeli Jews in an increasingly neoliberal Israel have typically only been able to find decent and affordable housing once they move to subsidized Jewish settlements built on Palestinian land. One example of this disparity in the provision of services can be seen in the crisis of adequate housing for poor ultra-Orthodox communities in Jerusalem. Faced with overcrowding in such neighborhoods as Mea Sharem, the Israeli government built a new settlement in East Jerusalem, specifically for them, in 1994. Ramot Shlomo (Heights of Solomon) sits on the land of the neighboring Palestinian villages Shu'afat and Beit Hanina, and it is now, according to the Israel Statistical Yearbook (2010), home to over 18,000 people.

10. For a superb analysis of how the Israeli state appropriated Palestinian land in the West Bank after 1967 see Shehadeh (1988).

over Arab population concentrations. Of all the spatial metaphors observable under Israeli rule, this road system was among the most telling.

In the last ten years, a further policy meant to divide colonizers and the colonized has arisen in every corner of Jerusalem. This is the much-discussed Israeli "separation wall." Condemned by the International Court of Justice (ICJ), the highest judicial body in the world, and prominent human rights organizations, this barrier has torn through several thousand acres of Palestinian territory. Dozens of Arab homes and hundreds of thousands of Palestinian olive trees have been destroyed to make way for the wall. It has not only further split Israelis from Palestinians but also Palestinian families from their lands and relatives.[11]

I raise the issues of the wall and the bypass roads because they cannot be seen as separate concerns from those of housing. Instead, each is bound up with the other in a number of ways. For one, these highways and barriers have eliminated dozens of Palestinian homes and buildings that obstruct their inexorable paths. By 2012, the wall was nearly complete in the Jerusalem area. As its final contours are solidified, it has expanded still further the de facto boundaries of Israeli-controlled Jerusalem. The most recent alterations now encompass territory well beyond the Israeli-drawn municipal borders of 1967. The abiding principle of Israeli racial policy and planning (considered in previous chapters) can be seen in the efforts to use the wall to appropriate the maximum amount of Palestinian land with the minimum number of Palestinians.

---

11. The Israeli state and its supporters abroad routinely assert that the barrier (typically an electrified fence in rural areas) is built roughly along its internationally recognized borders. Any examination of its route, particularly in the Jerusalem area, demonstrates the falsity of such a statement. Around Jerusalem, in particular, the wall drives deeply into territory recognized as illegally occupied Palestinian land by every other country in the world. For an illustration of the barrier's route, see the maps and documents of the United Nations Office for the Coordination of Humanitarian Affairs (OCHA), http://www.unocha.org/ocha2012–13/opt. Accessed November 20, 2012. For more on the ICJ's ruling see: http://www.icj-cij.org/docket/?p1=3&p2=4&k=5a&case=131&code=mwp&p3=4. Accessed October 1, 2012.

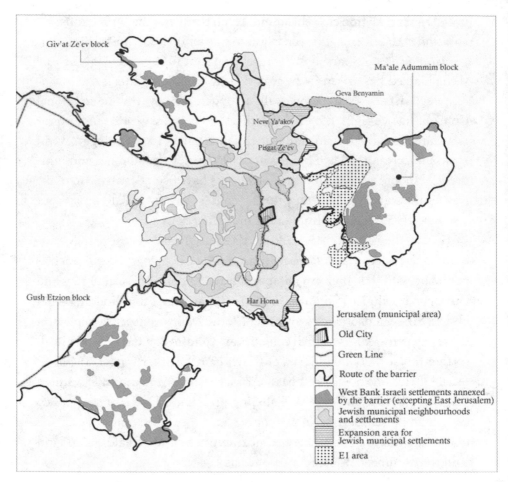

Map 5. Jerusalem, 2011, increasingly defined by the "separation wall" enveloping Israeli-occupied Jerusalem. Note that the path of this barrier circumvents and excludes major Palestinian population concentrations as it expands the city's borders further into the West Bank in violation of international law. Courtesy of Francesco Chiodelli, reprinted with permission.

These varied measures, policies, and visions converge in ways that have contributed to tens of thousands of Palestinians leaving Jerusalem for neighboring areas like Ramallah and Bethlehem, where they are able to build homes without being harassed. Colonial authorities have stripped thousands of other Palestinians of their Israeli-issued "residency permits," as well, essentially removing them from the city.[12] In dozens of conversations with those affected by Israel's manufactured housing dearth, I met few who did not comprehend how these policies operated and with what demographic designs.

One Jerusalemite I spoke with about these concerns was May, a middle-class Palestinian mother of two. She and her family were in the midst of packing up and moving from Jerusalem's Shua'fat neighborhood to Ramallah when I visited her in 2006. Their primary motivation for leaving the city was that the governing power would simply not let them build a home for their expanding family.

"It is *so* expensive here [Jerusalem]," she explained to me. "You know this and you have a western salary. They tax us and we get nothing—not even sidewalks. We applied for a permit to build [a home]. We paid them [the Israeli municipality] about twenty thousand shekels [roughly $5,000]. They took our money but never gave us a permit." She continued, "Not only is our land taken, but the little we have left, we can't build on."

The "little" land that May referred to amounts to the roughly 12 to 14 percent of East Jerusalem that Palestinians are allowed to inhabit. This area Israeli authorities refer to as "yellow" land. The balance of East Jerusalem has been coded as "red" and "green" zones. "Red" land (about 40 percent of East Jerusalem) has been appropriated from Arab Christians and Muslims and reserved for the use of Jewish-only settlements and military emplacements. Land zoned "green" (roughly 45 percent of the east side) is territory upon which the municipal authorities permit no construction. The Palestinian property redefined by the Israeli state as "green" has very little market value or exchange value because little or nothing productive can be done with it.[13]

According to ICAHD, Israel has rejected more than 90 percent of Palestinian home-permit applications since 1967, strictly limiting the number

12. The Jerusalem-based human rights organization, Hamoked: The Center for the Defense of the Individual, has published several important studies on Israel's attempts to remove Arabs from the city through these bureacratic means. For one of the most recent and thorough analyses of these questions, see HaMoked (2013).

13. See Kaminkar (1997) and Halper (2010) for further insights into Israel's administration of land under their control.

of structures Arabs are able to construct for the needs of their families. Israeli officials have, therefore, made construction they regard as "legal" next to impossible for Palestinians to engage in. This they have done while criminalizing the thousands of structures that Palestinians have built on their own land (mostly in the meager and highly bounded places regarded as "yellow" zones).[14] By 2010, Arab homes deemed "illegal" by Israeli authorities numbered in the thousands.

LIVING UNDER, AROUND, AND WITHIN FEAR

The Israeli state's policy of demolishing homes is illegal under international law, specifically the Fourth Geneva Convention relating to the treatment of civilians under military rule. When a state in possession of conquered lands does this on a mass scale, these actions can rise to the level of war crimes or crimes against humanity. However, simply defining these practices in technical legal terms can elide the actual human costs associated with losing one's dwelling. The microdimensions of these violations, the hidden traumas and fears that arise from simply the threat of demolition, need also to be discussed.

It is not simply resources and access to housing that are unequally distributed under Israeli colonial rule in Jerusalem but fear and vulnerability, too. The majority of the roughly three dozen Palestinians I spoke with who had been served demolition orders or who have resided in homes deemed "illegal" expressed feeling a continual, low-intensity trepidation—even, at times, terror. It is what Toufiq, an inhabitant of one such targeted household and a jovial, chain-smoking man of about forty years old, described to me as "fear on simmer." Hearing endless accounts of how it felt to constantly live within such straits helped explain why so many of Palestine's adult population have become two-pack-a-day smokers.

Several thousand other homeowners who have been served demolition orders reside in a similar between-and-betwixt condition of uncertainty.

14. See Kaminkar (1997) and Chesin, Hutman, and Melamed (1999).

They are compelled to live with the prospect that one day—they know not when—they may awake to the sounds of demolition crews. The prospect of losing one's shelter, even if it does not happen, affects plans to travel abroad, to educate children, and to construct a blueprint for survival and advancement. The terror and the "state of emergency" that Walter Benjamin (1973b, 257) refers to as being the "rule not the exception" seemed to me precisely what Palestinians living in targeted dwellings that had been served demolition orders were contending with.[15]

YUSUF'S HOUSE OF PAIN

I visited Jerusalem in the summer of 1994, months after the signing of the Oslo Accords and in the days immediately following the return of the exiled Palestinian leader, Yasser Arafat to the West Bank and Gaza. Amid the maelstrom of tentative hope and abiding despair that accompanied those times, a Palestinian journalist and I went to the site of a recently demolished Arab home. The location was on the far eastern edges of Jerusalem, just beyond the Mount of Olives. Here, the terrain is dramatic, plunging from incredible heights crowned with church spires, towers, and forests down sharply toward the arid Dead Sea and Jordan Valley, the world's lowest point, just 35 kilometers away.

The razed structure that we traveled to see, once fairly spacious and nicely designed, was now an enormous pile of debris. It had been the handiwork of Yusuf and his family who had combined the funds of two middle-class households to build the two-story, five-bedroom abode. But just a few days before they were to move in, with only an hour's notice, Israeli authorities had brought down the walls of the dwelling crushing everything inside. The demolition crew had not even let the owners get their belongings out before they flattened it. A variety of new appliances and furniture were buried beneath its remains.

---

15. I am indebted to the writings of Michael Taussig (1991, 1992, 2006) for his illuminating work on Walter Benjamin's ideas about fear and terror.

Yusuf owned a pharmacy in the East Jerusalem business district. A man in his early fifties by the advent of the Oslo Accords in 1993, he and his wife had spent their entire adult lives under military rule. He was soft-spoken, gentle, and decent. His demeanor did not betray any rage I imagined he certainly must have possessed in the wake of this catastrophe. I could, however, still see grief in his eyes—an abiding grief. Yusuf had supported the Oslo Accords and had hoped that it would lead to the end of the occupation and some semblance of normal relations with Israelis. But in the days and weeks after the loss of his home he expressed a singular lack of confidence that Israeli rule would end. "There can never, ever, ever be peace here," he stated categorically.

Yusuf and his family needed a larger living space and they had put the money together to build such a dwelling. However, the Israeli authorities refused to give them permission to construct one. This father of three, therefore, like hundreds of other Palestinians, had taken a sizable risk when they decided to break ground anyway. In one final irony, the owners, traumatized by having watched their savings and shelter dissolved in one morning, were then billed for the demolition of their house by the Israeli authorities.

"Where can we build?" Yusuf's brother demanded rhetorically, his voice full of exasperation, as we slowly traversed the property now strewn with the wreckage. "Where can we live, if not on *our* land? Where can we live, where can we live?"

THE MONTAGE CITY

Later that week, I returned to speak further with the family in the home that they had been set to move from, and which they shared with another group of relatives. In one segment of their nicely appointed living room were boxes of belongings, packed up and stacked, which they had intended to transfer to their newly built residence not 20 meters across the street. The locale that held out the promise for a more comfortable existence would now only haunt them on a continual basis since they were forced to encounter it daily. Nobody was moving anywhere now. How agonizing would it be, I asked myself, to now have to unpack those boxes and put everything back? What would it be like to have to observe your demolished property across the street as you left each day for work and when you returned? As Yusuf explained the genealogy of the family's housing predicaments, others of his kin sat silently with blank, cheerless faces, as if in shock.

In the distance, on a sprawling hilltop a few kilometers away and perceptible from the site of the remains of this family's demolished abode, lay Ma'ale Adumim. One of the largest Jewish settlements in the West Bank, its lofty watertower rises eerily above densely packed, boxlike housing units with red roofs.[16] This veritable fortress has occupied these heights since the late 1970s. The growth of its population was accompanied by the construction of impressive recreation facilities, a few commercial areas resembling American strip malls, and broad, well-paved boulevards lined with Israeli flags and billboards in Hebrew. Some 22,000 Jewish settlers resided here at the time Yusuf's home was destroyed in 1994. By 2010 the number was closer to 33,000.[17]

Dwellings in this and other illegal settlements are never demolished, they only proliferate. On this densely populated ridge, surrounded on several sides by steep gray precipices, recent Jewish immigrants from places such as Russia or North America are subsidized to move. The grounds were well kept, and possessed in abundance what one British landscape architect who toured the site with me in 2006 described as "very-water-intensive" plants and flowers. Palm trees and metallic green grass could also be seen as one traversed Ma'ale Adumim's main thoroughfares. These elements were in stark contrast to the lack of services found in nearly every Palestinian neighborhood in Jerusalem.

The visual montage across this city's rapidly shifting colonial landscape was astounding. One witnessed poverty residing within view of

16. Ma'ale Adumim is Hebrew for "red ascent"; the name is taken from the Book of Joshua 15:7 and 18:17.

17. For population figures of this and other areas under Israeli control, see the very comprehensive Israeli Central Bureau of Statistics (2010).

first-world services. It was possible to observe Palestinian neighborhoods and villages separated from but occasionally rubbing up against the fortressed barriers of illegal settlements. Well-lighted and freshly painted living environments for one people are visible from the rust and poverty of another. During the scorching summer heat, there were Olympic-sized swimming pools alive with mirth in settlements like Ma'ale Adumim while, simultaneously, an Israeli-manufactured water shortage was created in adjacent Palestinian neighborhoods, villages, and refugee camps.

Four years after my initial visit to the site of Yusuf's destroyed dwelling, I returned to pay the family a visit. They were still in their original home, still doubled-up with relatives. The ruins of the razed structure still remained. After spending the afternoon with Yusuf's kin, I returned to the Jerusalem home of my Palestinian hosts, a family I had known for several years. They were successful businesspeople with progressive and nationalist politics who had taken me under their wing since my early days of research. I thought that they would express surprise and outrage at the news I shared of Yusuf and his family's travails. But for those living under military rule, stories of this sort have ceased to cause a great deal of amazement. Upon hearing what I had observed at dinner that evening, one person declared nonchalantly, "They shouldn't have built it. They shouldn't have pumped all that money into a house without a permit."

"But the Israelis wouldn't *give* them a permit," I protested. "They needed to build for their growing family, it's their land, they were living in cramped conditions."

Everyone at the table was well aware of these facts. No one was unsympathetic or thought the demolition justified. However, they also understood the perils of defying what Palestinian legal scholar Raja Shehadeh (1988) has referred to as the "occupier's law." In retrospect it seemed that there were simply limits to how much anger those who dealt with military rule as a way of life could express on a regular basis. Perhaps for Palestinians, surviving emotionally in a context where one's land, home, water, and even family members could be taken from you in arbitrary ways demanded a discipline and equanimity that outsiders like me could only begin to fathom.

DESTRUCTION ON THE PERIPHERY:
THE CASE OF THE JAHALIN BEDOUIN

Jerusalem's chasms of opportunity exist not only between Israeli Jews and Palestinian Arabs but also within each national group. In the last two decades there have arisen within Palestinian society remarkable class differences and status distinctions that are attributable in large part to dynamics unleashed by the Oslo Accords. Not a few millionaires have been made in the crucible of Oslo and within the corrupt structures and institutions of the Palestinian National Authority. This wealth has been created as the majority of Palestinians remain poor, unable to access the Israeli labor market, and without much political or economic hope in an emerging neoliberal Palestine.[18]

One particularly marginal set of communities are the two dozen or so Arab Bedouin groups who reside on the fringes of East Jerusalem in an area contiguous to the current, Israeli-drawn municipal boundaries. This territory, which the Israeli state has sought to confiscate and add to an enlarged Jerusalem, is known as "E-1" (see map 5). The seminomadic Bedouin of the area had utilized the region's hilly, sun-baked terrain for decades before settlements like Ma'ale Adumim were established in the area in the late 1970s atop the highest hills.[19] When visiting these communities over the last twenty years, one could see, and indeed hear, some of the hundreds of Israeli settler cars that zoomed by at top speed each day on the bypass roads. These nicely paved highways circumscribed ever more tightly these families' tiny shanties, the generators they rely on for electricity, and their herds of goats. Observers of Palestine and Israel too often forget the histories and challenges of Jerusalem's Bedouin. Their situation is particularly tenuous today since they reside overwhelmingly on

18. For more on the making of these post-Oslo economic realities see Linda Tabar and Sari Hanafi (2005).

19. For more on the condition of these Bedouin populations, see the report by the UN Office for the Coordination of Humanitarian Affairs (2011).

land the Israeli state wishes to annex to an expanded "greater Jerusalem." Once again, the land is desired and its Arab inhabitants are not.

Members of these groups explained to me how they had sought over decades to reconstitute and sustain their kin networks under conditions of displacement. But they have done so not in the densely packed squalor of refugee camps or urban ghettos but across the dramatic and largely barren hills just east of Jerusalem. They have moved principally on the outer edges of Palestinian society, socially and spatially. Though some of the young men and women have begun to work in Jerusalem's service sector or in construction, a good deal of the community still continued to engage in goat- and sheepherding.

In the late 1970s when Ma'ale Adumim and other neighboring Jewish settlements arose, several thousand Bedouin discovered that they were residing on lands the settlements wished eventually to encroach upon, territory Israel had redefined after 1967 as "state land." This was another case not of Palestinians crossing borders but of the borders, in a sense, crossing

14. Jerusalem-area Jewish settlement, Ma'ale Adumim, in 2006. It was built by Israel on appropriated Arab land in the mid-1970s. By 2010 it was home to over 30,000 settlers.

them. It was not four years into the Oslo period that the Jewish state commandeered a long-targeted piece of territory used by the Jahalin Bedouin. This area was expropriated for the expansion of Ma'ale Adumim. Refusing orders to leave, the Jahalin were physically removed from this place in a matter of hours one morning in 1997. Bulldozers swept away their small dwellings of corrugated metal, plastic tarps, and wool rugs as dozens of armed soldiers evicted the families and their animals. When members of the community returned to protest, they were expelled again, and some of the men were beaten and imprisoned.

Israeli authorities refer to this expulsion as the "relocation" of these Bedouin families. Palestinian and Israeli human rights groups described how the appropriation of this residential area would permit the construction of an elementary school for the children of the settlers. Walter Benjamin's notion of "cultural documents" and "documents of barbarism" were again seen converging on one site in real time (1973b, 256). Those who govern East Jerusalem and the rest of the West Bank resettled the Jahalin near a sprawling municipal trash dump on an even more remote patch of territory on Jerusalem's southeast edge, part of what Mary Douglas (1966) might regard as the dominant power's "pollution behavior," or its response to the presence of unwanted people on land coveted by the Jewish state.[20]

On visits to the relocation site contiguous to the garbage dump, I witnessed the effects of the forced sedentarization on the Jahalin. There was great hardship here but also abundant humiliation felt among the "relocated." Daily deprivations were evident, for instance, when Bedouin men and women, boys and girls were seen scavenging the piles of refuse at the Israeli trash dump only a few hundred meters from the place to which they were now consigned. In the early 2000s, I came across a disturbing photo from about that time and printed in a leftist Israeli journal. The image,

20. One Israeli military spokesperson present at the eviction of this Bedouin community is quoted in a documentary entitled "In Search of Palestine" (Said 1998b). He defends the removal of this community on these very grounds. For more recent information see the publication of the United Nations Office for the Coordination of Humanitarian Affairs (OCHA) (2011).

which still haunts me, was part of a story about these Bedouins' plight and forced eviction. In it, a young Arab man, perhaps in his early twenties, stands atop an expansive pile of refuse almost as tall as he. The young, "relocated" Bedouin man peers down at the photographer standing below and with an expression of surprise holds up in one hand an intact egg, unearthed while rummaging through the garbage.

The Israeli authorities have proposed moving an additional 2,000 to 3,000 Bedouin from more than a dozen other communities in or around "E-1" to this peripheral site near the dumping grounds. The Palestinian governing authorities, insulated from their own people in Ramallah and living and working in guarded mansions and fortressed military redoubts, have had little if anything to say on these Bedouins' behalf. Did the Palestinian government even regard these communities as those they represented? If, on this marginal, barren hillside on the outskirts of Jerusalem, the Israelis had deemed it appropriate to dispose of the "dirt"—both the human and the nonhuman—did Palestinian elites see these families, the poorest of the poor, as those with whom they were in solidarity?

RACHEL

It was in the late 1990s that the work of ICAHD and other Israeli and Palestinian initiatives grew significantly in the realms of housing rights activism. These included a marked increase in educational tours of the city, cross-border partnerships, and other projects that brought Israelis and internationals into the daily, lived challenges of Palestinians under military occupation.

That Palestinians and Israelis live today in progressively more separate and set-off places is certainly true. However, as I familiarized myself with activist life across the country, I began to meet dozens of Israeli-Jews who *would* travel to Palestinian towns and neighborhoods in an effort to help end military occupation. One such person who came down from her fortressed residential estate to engage in the most politically committed of ways with Palestinian Jerusalemites was Rachel. Her life as a community organizer and Israeli city planner represented both what solidarity work could mean as well as how individuals, locked largely into positions of dominance vis-à-vis another national community, could wrest themselves from the exigencies of privilege.

"When I drive home from work," remarked Rachel in 1999, "every day I look down at 'Assiwiyya [the neighboring Arab village]. And I see that my Palestinian friends are building homes without permits. They are all considered 'illegal' and I totally support this."

Rachel spoke of observing this Arab neighborhood from the heights of her home on the East Jerusalem settlement of French Hill, mentioned in previous chapters. Though technically a settler, she oddly stated an unequivocal opposition to "the settlements." A transplanted New Yorker from Manhattan's Upper West Side, she arrived in Israel in the late 1960s as a city planner, exuberant about the Zionist project.

"I moved to Jerusalem and bought it all!" Rachel once conveyed to me about her initial acceptance of Israel's prevailing myths. She became a major player in efforts by the Jewish state to "reunite" Jerusalem's east and west sides soon after the 1967 war. "I was asked by [then Israeli mayor] Kollek to be part of the planning of East Jerusalem. But it became clear to me that the municipality did not want plans that would help their [the Palestinian] neighborhoods to develop."

By the time of her death in 2003 her political perspectives had become more progressive. She became a prominent member of the Israeli Zionist left and was close to the Meretz political party. My interviews and conversations with her in the late 1990s and early 2000s were as illuminating as her housing rights activism was inspiring. This woman in her sixties was a walking archive of information about the city's past and present planning strategies. A former member of the Jerusalem City Council in the late 1980s, Rachel became increasingly critical of Israeli governance in Jerusalem and what she regarded as the state's discriminatory housing and land policies. And after she raised the issue of these practices during her first term in office, she was summarily voted off the council in the next election.

This seasoned urban planner then channeled her energies into grassroots organizing, working for greater equality between Palestinians and Israelis. In the course of conversations with her in the mid- and late 1990s, I gathered that she did not see Israeli rule as colonial rule, at least not in

Jerusalem. Further, Rachel was not opposed to the notion of a Jewish state, nor was she against Israeli Jews living in occupied East Jerusalem. After all, Rachel had done so for more than three decades. But she would fight against her government's policies until Palestinians were treated equally and with dignity—words she would constantly use.

This community organizer was not, when I pressed the issue, opposed to a reality in which Palestinians and Israelis lived together in the same neighborhoods. Unlike other Zionists, she was not of the belief that Arabs and Jews must be kept apart for their mutual benefit or to sustain some "natural" social order. However, she could not see it happening in the near future and thus wanted to help create as much justice as possible given the contemporary realities. That meant minimally the equalization of services in Arab and Jewish neighborhoods. "Yes, yes, we want to get there [to a city without segregation]," Rachel once said earnestly. "We want to get there for sure. But people are suffering *now* and we need to address their basic, immediate needs *now*. If you only accept a solution of total integration immediately, it will never work. You'll get nothing." Rachel understood as well as anyone the logic behind her own government's delineation of the city's borders, ones she acknowledged had been drawn to purposely exclude non-Jews. However, her critique of Israeli policy was less directed at the historical making of these frontiers as it was at the persistent discrimination and racism within them.

In a city of proliferating ironies, it was only fitting perhaps that one of Israel's most dedicated community organizers and important voices against the occupation lived in one of the oldest Jewish settlements in the West Bank. French Hill (or Giv'at Shapira), as mentioned in previous chapters, was actually built in part on the land of a neighboring Arab village. Rachel, curiously, had very cordial dealings with Palestinian activists from this very village and was in regular contact with them.

I traveled with this Israeli activist on three occasions to 'Assiwiyya and other Palestinian neighborhoods in occupied East Jerusalem. It was evident that her aim was to go right to the grassroots of Palestinian society. She took groups of Israelis and internationals to visit with local Arab community organizers engaged in housing rights issues and to hear about the challenges they faced. Palestinians I interviewed had generally quite kindhearted things to say about this Israeli woman precisely because she did what many felt someone in her circumstances was reasonably able to do within the strictures that impinged on her. In that embrace of this Israeli by Palestinian activists, perhaps the prospects for a more just and less segregated Palestine/Israel could be witnessed.

KAFKAESQUE PALESTINE

I met ICAHD's founder and principal organizer, Jeff Halper, in the summer of 1999. And it was not long after our first meeting, one early morning in late October of that same year, that I accompanied him and my sister, a Chicago-based journalist, to witness the legal machinery of Israeli colonial rule. We traveled north by car from Jerusalem to an Israeli military court located within the Jewish settlement of Beit El, a few kilometers north of Ramallah. Jamal, a Palestinian man in his late sixties, had been summoned to appear there as a defendant that morning. The three of us came in solidarity.

The Israeli soldier guarding the front entrance to Beit El spoke to us in a mixture of Hebrew and fluent, British-accented English. Because Jeff was an Israeli driving a car with a yellow Israeli license plate, we were permitted to enter this militarized housing estate by car and not by foot. The three of us proceeded along the settlement's empty streets, parked, and then made our way to the site of the trial by about 8am. There we came upon another soldier, armed with a long, unruly automatic weapon slung over his shoulder. He guarded the entrance to the makeshift courthouse in a building that resembled a doublewide mobile home.

With no one else around and in an attempt to break an awkward silence, the conscript began to ask us questions, again in perfect English. The settler told us that he actually lived on Beit El, in an apartment about a kilometer down the road. His commute to work was short these days but his original journey to Palestine/Israel had been somewhat more involved. He and his wife had moved to the Jewish state from Chicago ten years previously. When we inquired in a perfunctory way as to how he liked living here, he responded enthusiastically and without a pause, "Love it! Love it!" But he did not sound entirely convinced by his own words.

There he stood, a man from the Rogers Park neighborhood of Chicago, tasked with regulating the entry of Palestinian defendants into the court. We sat in the separate place where Israelis and internationals were permitted to wait before entering. Just then, we observed those we had come to meet on the other side of the fenced-in "Palestinian" area. Jamal, wearing a traditional *hatta* (or headdress), was accompanied by his middle-aged son. He stood accused by military authorities of building an illegal home. When the Israelis destroyed it the first time his family rebuilt it. For this, Jamal was charged with violating Israeli law and faced a hefty fine if not imprisonment. Once we spotted one another, they and we approached the high partition that separated us and leaned close to the fence to talk. We greeted each other and spoke until the defendant was instructed to enter the courtroom a few moments later by military officials.

However, having made sacrifices to arrive by 8 A.M., Jamal was told by an Arabic-speaking Israeli soldier that he and his son had come on the wrong day and would have to return in a week's time. In the course of their exchange, the soldier, a head taller than the defendant and probably in his thirties, stood over him, his voice rising somewhat as he answered the elder Palestinian's questions about the apparent mixup in dates. Jamal maintained his composure even as the official spoke to him as though he were a disobedient teenager. He needed to read the Hebrew court documents more carefully, the Israeli communicated in a no-nonsense way. This was a thin, almost frail grandfather who had traveled the nearly two hours by foot and by multiple cabs to get to the court from his home on the southern fringes of Jerusalem. Now he was scolded for not following directions and sent away.

The dimensions of this single encounter were emblematic of broader realities that have comprised Israel's regime of military occupation. For one, authorities had the power to command Palestinians who were not Israeli citizens to appear before an Israeli judge. They controlled the spaces Jamal and his son traversed, making them move through gates, turnstiles, and checkpoints under the watchful eyes of soldiers and settlers, some newly arrived from Britain and the United States. The military regime could define the actions of a man building a home for the needs of his kin on his own land and with his own money as "criminal" and could punish

him in the ways they saw fit. Furthermore, they had the power to humiliate him before family and friends, underscoring how dominance and
subordination, superiority and inferiority are integral to quotidian intercommunal relations and encounters in colonized places like Jerusalem.

A week or so later, I joined a handful of Americans and Israelis from
ICAHD and other groups in a solidarity visit to Jamal's demolished
home. It was a miserable day in November, a time when Jerusalem begins
to become rainy, overcast, and blustery. The cold wind whipped across
the all-but-barren ridge where Jamal's family and perhaps forty others
resided. We observed the makeshift dwelling that he and his sons had created once the original house had been demolished a few months before.
The family now found refuge in a 15-by-15-foot tent, whose plastic flaps
were thrashed about by the tumultuous weather that morning.

We drank tea as the cold rain subtly tapped the top of the temporary
shelter. Water, brought to this dwelling from a spigot 20 meters away, was
heated by a tiny kerosene burner the size of my laptop. On the far side of a
fairly deep valley, not a quarter-mile away, there were densely built structures of a vastly dissimilar stock. They comprised a settlement, conspicu-
ous by their red roofs and other distinctive signifiers: landscaped grounds,
an armed presence, a gated perimeter, and paved roads. This residential
area was totally off-limits to Arabs unless they worked there as day laborers. Palestinians were sometimes permitted to enter this and other settlements to assemble homes for future settlers but were forbidden to deploy
these skills to build even the most meager shelters for themselves and their
kin. Jamal and his family remained steadfast in ways that were astounding to me and others. Our solidarity visit came to an end and we rose to
shake hands with our hosts. As we did so Jamal affirmed resolutely, "if
they destroy our home again, we will rebuild it again—again and again
and again."

SOLIDARITY ACROSS BOUNDARIES

By the summer of 2003, the activism of ICAHD had attained such levels
of success and attention that dozens of individuals from around the world
had signed up to participate in the organization's first two-week summer

work camp. Those who journeyed to Jerusalem came in solidarity not only with Palestinians whose homes had been demolished but also with the roughly four million who continue to live under one of the longest-running military occupations in the world. The denial of housing rights was, camp organizers emphasized, only one dimension in a broader system of spatial regulation. Rebuilding homes was not enough, they stressed; the entire machinery of Israeli occupation had to be dismantled for the good of both peoples.

Participants that summer worked to reconstruct—for the fourth time—a home in the Palestinian neighborhood of 'Anata. This structure, known as "Beit Arabiya" (named for the mother of the family whose house it was), had become a symbol of defiance for the local community. The volunteers with ICAHD's 2003 work camp would finish assembling it by the end of the two-week program. As of the completion of this book, Israeli authorities had demolished the house six times, the last of which was on November 1, 2012. And just as many times it has been rebuilt.

By the fourth camp, in 2006, more than three dozen other homes had been rebuilt with contributions and donated labor. Participation in these forms of civil disobedience began to rise markedly, including among growing numbers of Israeli Jews. The first day of the 2006 camp was a sweltering hot July morning, with temperatures already reaching 90 degrees by 9 A.M. A human chain of forty-odd people was swiftly fashioned between a massive stack of off-white cinderblocks and the rudiments of a reassembled home.

This skeletal structure was not yet a familial place and looked like it was weeks away from occupancy. Deep in 'Anata, a dusty and impoverished Arab neighborhood on the fringes of Jerusalem, this dwelling had been destroyed in recent months by Israeli forces. But it was not only the "illegality" of the house that was at issue; Israel also regarded efforts to rebuild it as unlawful. Those of us taking part were, in fact, involved in "criminal" activity in the eyes of the Jewish state. Though we, with foreign passports, would probably not be attacked if Israeli soldiers arrived to break up the work, as they did once or twice that summer, the Palestinians there could quite easily have been arrested and beaten.

Inside this reemerging familial place, professional carpenters, electricians, and brick layers—all local Palestinian men—were involved in the more skilled dimensions of construction. We, the unskilled laborers comprising the human chain, moved concrete blocks, lifted heavy iron reinforcements, and, perhaps as importantly, bore witness to the incessant cruelties of colonial violence. Participants were usually in need of rest and water within an hour. The bricks and tiles were not light and by midday, several retreated to the shade, unable to carry on the work. Literally thousands of cinderblocks and other items would pass through these links of solidarity over the next two weeks. And, as has been the case during each of the ten annual work camps, by the end at least one, sometimes two, destroyed structures had risen up again from the rubble.

Over the last decade, hundreds of activists have arrived in Jerusalem to rebuild homes with ICAHD and learn firsthand about conditions of life under military occupation. They have ranged from men and women in their early seventies to college students in their late teens. They have been millionaires from Great Britain and penniless Arab American and Jewish radicals from Berkeley and Manhattan.[21] And then there are the Israeli Jews who have come in small but significant numbers. By 2006, ICAHD organizers sought to have at least one Israeli Jew present at the camp at all times in the event that the military arrived. The general feeling was that a Jewish Israeli was best able to confront their own regime and that their presence would be the best assurance against army violence.

On my first day at the 2006 camp in 'Anata, I stood next to just such an Israeli, a high-school teacher from West Jerusalem named Uri. He was in his sixties and had a surprisingly good grasp of Arabic. Activists younger and more radical than he took up positions all around him in the human chain. Four or five of them, all in their early twenties, had already formed a clique. They were all thin and sprightly, some with impossibly pale skin that looked like it would roast under the scorching sun by the first water break.

---

21. Even a former British MP and minister in Tony Blair's government, Claire Short, participated in recent years.

These fledgling leftists—European and American—began to partake in a blistering critique of the U.S. government's role in arming Israel and in the demolition of Palestinian homes. Their rhetoric was high, and it seemed as though they had worked out to their complete satisfaction the way the entire imperial order was fashioned and how they would deconstruct it (perhaps by the second water break). After listening for some time, Uri interjected and remarked that the work we were involved in was "not political." "This," he declared, "was just about homes and human rights."

The younger activists who heard him did not acknowledge the distinction he was trying to make. A few of them scoffed at his words in ways that I thought were ungenerous to say the least. While homes and human rights in Jerusalem, I believe, are nothing if not political, convincing Uri otherwise did not seem to me even remotely as important as acknowledging and supporting the actual work he was involved in. He was, after all, in his modest way actually *doing* something that challenged the human rights abuses of his own government. In interviews with Israeli participants in the ICAHD camp, particularly in the early years, it became clear that while a good deal were radical activists—some even militantly anti-Zionist—there were several like Uri with a simple notion of justice who were not afraid to cross the frontiers of fear that circumscribe millions of Israelis and Palestinians.

Nearly every day of the camp that summer, the sound of jackhammers and heavy equipment reverberated in the valley below our worksite. They were operated by Israeli men young enough to be Uri's grandchildren. This Israeli construction crew, guarded by three soldiers, laid out the course for the emerging "separation wall" that would within a year or two virtually divide this Arab population from segments of Jerusalem that the Israeli state wished to hold as theirs exclusively. When I returned to this site in 2012, the wall around much of 'Anata had been nearly completed. It was as physically obtrusive as it was aesthetically revolting; it represented the perpetually moving edge of Israeli colonial power.

Chapters 3 and 4 described how, in the weeks immediately after the conquest of East Jerusalem in June 1967, Israel rid Jerusalem of thousands of its Palestinian inhabitants. Unlike the wholesale expulsion of the city's Arabs in 1948 from the western neighborhoods, in 1967 tens of thousands of Palestinians were excluded from the city through the deft gerrymandering of borders and denial of residency. The Israeli state still regards these forty-seven-year-old boundaries as the official ones. However, since about 2003, the concrete separation wall has begun to be erected around Jerusalem in ways that, as mentioned above, unilaterally expand the future contours of Israel's so-called unified and eternal capital (see map 5).

Since the early 2000s the path of the wall has not only *taken in* hundreds of additional acres of Palestinian territory but also *left out*, on the other side of the barrier, about 70,000 additional Palestinians recognized even by the Israeli authorities as legal residents of Jerusalem.[22] These are Arabs with Israeli-issued Jerusalem residency permits, but they comprise a perceived "demographic threat" to the Jewish state. If Israeli planners can keep them on the other side of the wall, they can more easily abandon these unwanted populations and strip them of their Jerusalem residency permits in the future. Local activists, Israeli and Palestinians, were universally in agreement that this was the aim of governing authorities.

By the mid-1990s, when Yusuf's family, the Jahalin Bedouin, and hundreds of other Palestinians were contending with the loss of their homes, there was no ICAHD. There were, of course, instances of local Palestinian resistance that had confronted Israeli human rights abuses such as home demolitions for decades, most famously and effectively during the First Intifada, from 1987 to 1993.

There had also begun to emerge Israeli groups involved in exposing human rights abuses under military occupation, including members of Women in Black and Yesh Gevul. But there was little joint Palestinian-Israeli direct action that could have been mobilized to resist the destruction of Palestinian familial places. This has begun to change over the last decade fairly substantially. However, these shifts in activist energy have

22. For an insightful analysis of these contemporary Israeli urban planning aims in Jerusalem, see Chiodelli (2012).

15. Israel's separation wall running through a Palestinian neighborhood in East Jerusalem, 2006.

begun to happen, ironically, in an era when Israel's colonization of the territories occupied in 1967 is becoming increasingly irreversible.[23]

Though these practices of resistance and expressions of solidarity were heartening to witness, I rarely found a way to be sanguine about the broader political circumstances around land and housing in Palestine/Israel. In a city of proliferating monuments, each demolished home was a memorial to dispossession, and their numbers rose with each passing month. But amid such ruins there have been meaningful small-scale expressions of joint struggle. These are, I have come to believe, necessary

23. In the wake of the formation of ICAHD, other sites where Palestinians and Israelis worked in concert emerged in the early 2000s. These were nodes of struggle that sought to contest the policies of Israeli expansion (e.g., the protests against the "separation wall" in places like the Palestinian villages of Bil'in, Budrus, or Nabi Saleh or against the theft of Palestinian homes in Sheikh Jarrah). In several instances, nonviolent actions have met with fairly intense repression from Israeli soldiers and settlers at these and other flashpoints.

16. A plaque framed and presented by ICAHD participants to the Palestinian residents of Beit Arabiya after it was rebuilt for the fifth time in 2012. The plaque commemorates the home's first rebuilding in 1999 and honors the Palestinian-Israeli cooperation that has reestablished this family home five times.

but not sufficient conditions for the construction of a more egalitarian future across this fractured landscape.

CONCLUSION

Instances of political commitment across Jerusalem's sharply drawn internal frontiers are essential to acknowledge. These efforts in the realms of housing rights have not uncommonly proven to be exemplars of courage and antiracism in a city where innumerable forces operate to keep Palestinians and Israeli Jews separate and unequal. Joint activism of the sort organized by ICAHD persists across progressively more fortressed national divides. These expressions of resistance have continued to challenge Israeli colonial rule and many of the prevailing principles and beliefs that sustain it. Among them is the notion that Palestinians and Israelis, Arabs and Jews are "eternally" at odds and that intercommunal mixing and shared residential life threatens to disrupt a "natural" order of apartness.

Struggles and forms of solidarity from below, of the kind examined in this chapter, may well be the foundation for constructing a social and spatial reality in Jerusalem that is different in meaningful ways from the prevailing apartheid-like arrangement. But it is equally important to recognize that the structural inequalities that shape this abiding, decades-old arrangement of apartness cannot be broken down simply through annual work camps or educational tours. Neither can iron-fisted expressions of domination be eliminated through individual friendships across borders, however vital and heartening those may be.

As South African writer, Nadine Gordimer, remarked at the height of apartheid in her own country, those who struggled for justice there had to grasp the difference between empathy for oppressed groups and truly transformative political mobilization on their behalf. Both are vital but as she astutely observed, "You can't change a regime on the basis of compassion. There's got to be something harder" (Lazar 1997). Her insight speaks precisely to the limits of some of the political projects discussed above, which, however noble, are only beginnings. Israelis and Palestinians involved in this collaborative activist work generally understood this as well as anybody. They also understood that beginnings are important.

I have been arguing throughout this book that the Palestine/Israel conflict needs to be studied and situated within a framework of colonialism and anticolonialism. But the forms of resistance I have discussed in this chapter have also helped me see that taking decolonization and antiracism seriously cannot be premised on the elimination of either of these two national communities. I have come to believe that the futures of Palestinians and Israelis, colonizers and the colonized in this narrow strip of contested land are bound up together inextricably. And this makes a place like Jerusalem and the broader landscape within which it is embedded a distinctive sort of colonial conundrum. For this reason and many others the boundaries of the mind seem every bit as material as the checkpoints, walls, and bulldozers that proliferate across this fractured urban space. In colonial cities like Jerusalem, it was ever thus.

Works Cited · *Index*

Works Cited

Abowd, Thomas. 2000. "The Moroccan Quarter: A History of the Present." *Jerusalem Quarterly* 7 (Winter): 6–16.

————. 2006. "Present and Absent: Historical Invention, Ideology, and the Politics of Place in Contemporary Jerusalem." In *Cities of Collision: Jerusalem and the Principles of Conflict Urbanism*, edited by Philip Misselwitz and Tim Rieniets, 328–336. Basel: Birkhäuser Architecture.

————. 2007. "National Boundaries, Colonized Spaces: The Gendered Politics of Residential Space in Jerusalem." *Anthropological Quarterly* 80, no. 4: 997–1034.

Abu El-Haj, Nadia. 2001. *Facts on the Ground: Archaeological Practice and Territorial Self-Fashioning in Israeli Society.* Chicago: University of Chicago Press.

Abu Lughod, Lila. 1986. *Veiled Sentiments: Honor and Poetry in a Bedouin Society.* Berkeley: University of California Press.

————. 2002. "Do Muslim Women Need Saving?" *American Anthropologist* 104, no. 3: 783–790.

————. 2013. Do Muslim Women Need Saving? Cambridge: Harvard University Press.

Abunimah, Ali. 2010. "NY Times' Jerusalem Property Makes It Protagonist in Palestine Conflict," The Electronic Intifada, March 2. http://electronic intifada.net/content/ny-times-jerusalem-property-makes-it-protagonist -palestine-conflict/8705. Accessed November 2, 2012.

ADALAH. 2010. NGO Report to the UN Committee on Economic, Social and Cultural Rights Regarding Israel's Implementation of the International Covenant on Economic, Social and Cultural Rights (ICESCR).

Aderet, Ofer. 2011. "A Stir over Sign Language." *Ha'aretz*, July 29. http://www .haaretz.com/weekend/week-s-end/a-stir-over-sign-language-1.375919.

Ahmad, Aijaz. 1996. *Lineages of the Present.* New Delhi: Tulika.

Alatar, Mohammed, dir. 2007. *Jerusalem: The East Side Story*. Produced by Palestinian Agricultural Relief Committees.

Alsultany, Evelyn. 2012. *Arabs and Muslims in the Media: Race and Representation after 9/11*. New York: New York University Press.

Amiry, Suad. 2010. *Nothing to Lose But Your Life: An 18-Hour Journey with Murad*. Doha, Qatar: Bloomsbury.

Anzaldua, Gloria. 1999. *La Frontera/Borderlands*. San Francisco: Aunt Lute Press.

Arab Centre for Human Rights in the Golan Heights. 2007. Jan 25. http://www2 .ohchr.org/english/bodies/cerd/docs/ngos/almarsad.pdf.

Arendt, Hannah. 1969. *On Violence*. New York: Harcourt, Brace.

Armstrong, Karen. 1996. *Jerusalem: One City, Three Faiths*. New York: Harper Collins.

Asad, Talal. 1991. "Afterword." In *Colonial Situations*, edited by George Stocking, 314–324. Madison: University of Wisconsin Press.

———. 1993. *Genealogies of Religion*. Baltimore: Johns Hopkins University Press.

Asad, Talal, and Roger Owen, eds. 1983. *Sociology of "Developing Societies": The Middle East*. New York: Monthly Review Press.

Asali, K. J., ed. 1989. *Jerusalem in History*. London: Scorpion.

Associated Press. 2002. "Prisoner ID Numbers Outrage Nazi Victim." *Bangor Daily News*, March 13, A2.

Association of Americans and Canadians in Israel (AACI) Website. 2011. http:// www.aaci.org.il/.

Atran, Scott. 1989. "The Surrogate Colonization of Palestine 1917–1939." *American Ethnologist* 16, no. 1: 719–744.

Ayalon, Ami. 2002. *Christian Science Monitor*, April 11. http://www.csmonitor .com/2002/0402/p01s04-wome.html.

Badil Publication. 2005. Centre on Housing Rights and Evictions (COHRE), Resource Center for Palestinian Residency & Refugee Rights.

Balibar, Etienne. 1991a. "Is There a Neo-Racism?" In *Race, Nation, Class,* edited by Etienne Balibar and Immanuel Wallerstein, 17–28. London: Verso.

———. 1991b. "Racism and Nationalism." In *Race, Nation, Class*, edited by Etienne Balibar and Immanuel Wallerstein, 37–67. London: Verso.

Bardenstein, Carol. 1999. "Trees, Forests, and the Shaping of Palestinian and Israeli Collective Memory." In *Acts of Memory: Cultural Recall in the Present,* edited by Mieke Bal, Jonathan Crewe, and Leo Spitzer, 148–168. Lebanon, NH: New England University Press.

Barthes, Roland. 1957. *Mythologies*. New York: Hill & Wang.

Behar, Moshe, and Zvi Ben-Dor Benite. 2013. *Modern Middle Eastern Jews: Writings on Identity, Politics and Culture (1893–1958)*. Waltham, MA: Brandeis University Press.

Bellow, Saul. 1976. *To Jerusalem and Back*. New York: Penguin Classics.

Ben-Ami, Shlomo. 2007. *Scars of War, Wounds of Peace: The Israeli-Arab Tragedy*. Oxford: Oxford University Press.

Benjamin, Walter. 1973a. "The Work of Art in the Age of Mechanical Reproduction." In *Illuminations*, edited by H. Arendt, 217–251. New York: Collins Fontana.

———. 1973b. "Thesis on the Philosophy of History," In *Illuminations*, edited by H. Arendt, 253–264. New York: Collins Fontana.

Benvenisti, Meron. 1976. *Jerusalem: The Torn City*. Jerusalem: Isratypeset.

———. 1996. *City of Stone: The Hidden History of Jerusalem*. Berkeley: University of California Press.

———. 2002. *Sacred Landscape: The Buried History of the Holy Land since 1948*. Berkeley: University of California Press.

Benziman, Uzi. 1976. *al-Quds: Madinah bila Aswar*. Translated into Arabic by Muhammad Madi. Jerusalem: 'Arafah Agency (Arabic).

Bhabha, Homi. 1983. "The Other Question." *Screen* 24, no. 6: 18–36.

———. 1994. *The Location of Culture*. New York: Routledge.

Bible. King James Version. http://quod.lib.umich.edu/k/kjv/.

Bishara, Amahl. 2012. *Back Stories: US News Production and Palestinian Politics*. Palo Alto, CA: Stanford University Press.

Blake, William. 1804. "Jerusalem." http://www.bbc.co.uk/poetryseason/poems /jerusalem.shtml.

Bourdieu, Pierre. 1977. *Outline of a Theory of Practice*. New York: Polity.

———. 1990. *The Logic of Practice*. New York: Polity.

———. 1991. *Language and Symbolic Power*. Cambridge, MA: Harvard University Press.

Brecht, Bertolt. 1965. "The Exception and the Rule." In *Bertolt Brecht: The Jewish Wife and Other Short Plays*, edited by Eric Bentley, 109–143. New York: Grove.

———. 1987. *Poems: 1913–1956*. New York: Routledge.

Brodkin, Karen. 1999. *How Jews Became White Folks*. New Brunswick, NJ: Rutgers University Press.

Brown, Wendy. 2006. *Regulating Aversion*. Princeton: Princeton University Press.

B'Tselem Report. 1997. "A Policy of Discrimination: Land Expropriation, Planning and Building in East Jerusalem."

B'Tselem Report. 2013. www.btselem.org/statistics.

B'Tselem Report on Settlements. 2012. http://www.btselem.org/topic/settlements.

Bunton, Martin. 2007. *Colonial Land Policies in Palestine 1917–1936*. Oxford: Oxford University Press.

Butler, Judith. 1993. *Bodies That Matter*. New York: Routledge.

———. 2009. *Frames of War: When Is Life Grievable?* London: Verso.

Cesaire, Aime. 1972. *Discourse on Colonialism*. New York: Monthly Review Press.

Chatterjee, Partha. 1993. *The Nation and Its Fragments*. Princeton: Princeton University Press.

Chesin, Amir, Bill Hutman, and Avi Melamed. 1999. *Separate and Unequal: The Inside Story of Israeli Rule in East Jerusalem*. Cambridge, MA: Harvard University Press.

Chiodelli, Francesco. 2012. "The Jerusalem Master Plan: Planning into the Conflict." *Jerusalem Quarterly* 51 (Autumn): 5–20.

Chomsky, Noam. 1987. *The Chomsky Reader*. New York: Pantheon.

Cohen, Stanley. 2001. *States of Denial: Knowing about Atrocities and Suffering*. Cambridge, MA: Polity.

Cohn, Bernard. 1996. *Colonialism and Its Forms of Knowledge: The British in India*. Princeton: Princeton University Press.

Collier, Jane, Michelle Rosaldo, and Sylvia Yanagisako. 1997. "Is There a Family? New Anthropological Views." In *The Gender/Sexuality Reader: Culture, History, Political Economy*, edited by Roger N. Lancaster and Micaela di Leonardo, 71–81. New York: Routledge.

Comaroff, John. 1997. "Images of Empire, Contests of Conscience." In *Tensions of Empire: Colonial Cultures in a Bourgeois World*, edited by Frederick Cooper and Ann Laura Stoler, 163–197. Berkeley: University of California Press.

Comaroff, John, and Jean Comaroff. 1991. *Of Revelation and Revolution: Christianity, Colonialism, and Consciousness in South Africa*. Chicago: University of Chicago Press.

Cooper, Frederick, and Ann Laura Stoler. 1997. *Tensions of Empire: Colonial Cultures in a Bourgeois World*. Berkeley: University of California Press.

Crapanzano, Vincent. 1985. *Waiting: The Whites of South Africa*. New York: Random House.

Crenshaw, Kimberle. 1996. "The Intersection of Race and Gender." In *Critical Race Theory: The Key Writings That Formed the Movement*, edited by Kimberle Crenshaw, Neil Gotanda, Garry Peller, and Kendal Thomas, 358–368. New York: New Press.

Davis, Angela. 2012. "Dismissal of Palestinians Is Reminiscent of Jim Crow Days." Special to *The Mercury News*, October 5, http://www.mercurynews.com /opinion/ci_21707875/angela-davis-dismissal-palestinians-is-reminiscent -jim-crow.

Davis, Uri. 2004. *Apartheid Israel: Possibilities for the Struggle Within*. London: Zed.

Davis, Uri, and Walter Lehn. 1983. "Landownership, Citizenship, and Racial Policy in Israel." In *Sociology of "Developing Societies": The Middle East*, edited by Talal Asad and Roger Owen, 145–158. London: Monthly Review Press.

de Certeau, Michel. 1984. *The Practice of Everyday Life*. Berkeley: University of California Press.

Declaration of the Establishment of the State of Israel, http://mfa.gov.il/MFA /ForeignPolicy/Peace/Guide/Pages/Declaration%20of%20Establishment% 20of%20State%20of%20Israel.aspx. May 14, 1948.

Deeb, Lara. 2006. *An Enchanted Modern: Gender and Public Peity in Shia Lebanon*. Princeton: Princeton University Press, 2006.

Derrida, Jacques. 1981. *Positions*. Chicago: University of Chicago Press.

Dirks, Nicholas B. 1996. "Forward." In *Colonialism and Its Forms of Knowledge: The British in India*, ix-xviii. Chicago: University of Chicago Press.

Douglas, Mary. 1966. *Purity and Danger: An Analysis of Concepts of Pollution and Taboo*. London: Routledge.

Doumani, Beshara. 1994. "The Political Economy of Population Counts in Ottoman Palestine: Nablus, circa 1850." *International Journal of Middle East Studies* 26, no. 1: 1–17.

Dumper, Michael. 1997. *The Politics of Jerusalem since 1967*. New York: Columbia University Press.

Eagleton, Terry. 1991. *Ideology: An Introduction*. London: Verso.

Eliachar, Elie. 1976. "I Know the Arabs." *Journal of Palestine Studies* 5, nos. 1/2: 183–185.

———. 1983. *Living with Jews*. London: Widenfield & Nicolson.

Fadlalla, Amal Hassan. 2007. *Embodying Honor: Fertility, Foreignness, and Regeneration in Eastern Sudan*. Madison: University of Wisconsin Press.

Fanon, Frantz. 1963. *The Wretched of the Earth*. New York: Grove.

Foucault, Michel. 1980. *Power/Knowledge: Selected Interviews and Other Writings, 1972–1977*. Edited by Colin Gordon. New York: Pantheon.

Ghannam, Farha. 2002. *Remaking the Modern: Space, Relocation, and the Politics of Identity in a Global Cairo*. Berkeley: University of California Press.

Gilbert, Martin. 1996. *Jerusalem in the Twentieth Century*. New York: Random House.

Gordimer, Nadine. 1984. *Something Out There*. New York: Viking.

————. 2008. "Interview." *Jerusalem Post*, May 22, 4.

Gregory, Derek. 2004. *The Colonial Present*. Malden, MA: Blackwell.

Gregory, Steven. 1998. *Black Corona: Race and the Politics of Place in an Urban Community*. Princeton: Princeton University Press.

Grigg, Edward. 1945. Cabinet Memorandum: Palestine, April 4. CAB 66/64/14, National Archives, Kew Gardens, London.

Hadawi, Sami. 1957. *Land Ownership in Palestine*. New York: Palestine Arab Refugee Office.

————. 1990. *Bitter Harvest: A Modern History of Palestine*. Essex, UK: Scorpion.

Halbwachs, Maurice. 1992. *On Collective Memory*. Chicago: University of Chicago Press.

Hall, George H. 1946. Cabinet Memorandum: Long Term Policy in Palestine, July 8. CAB 129/11/9, National Archives, Kew Gardens, London.

Halper, Jeff. 2010. *An Israeli in Palestine: Resisting Dispossession, Redeeming Israel*. London: Pluto.

HaMoked Report. 2013. "Residency in Jerusalem under the Shadow of the Temporary Order." December 1. http://www.hamoked.org/files/2013/1158070 _eng.pdf.

Harvey, David. 2008. "The Right to the City." *New Left Review* 53 (September-October): 23–40.

Hasso, Frances. 1998. "The 'Women's Front': Nationalism, Feminism and Modernity in Palestine." *Gender and Society* 12, no. 4: 441–465.

Hasson, Nir. 2012. "Rare Photograph Reveals Ancient Jerusalem Mosque Destroyed in 1967." *Ha'aretz*, June 15, http://www.haaretz.com/news/national /rare-photograph-reveals-ancient-jerusalem-mosque-destroyed-in-1967. premium-1.436593.

Herzl, Theodor. [1896] 2006. *The Jewish State*. London: R. Searl.

Hijab, Nadia, and Colin Luke, dir. 1985. "Family Ties." Documentary film. Vol. 3 of *The Arabs: A Living History*. Falls Church, VA: Landmark Films.

Hiyari, Mustafa. 1989. "Crusader Jerusalem, 1099–1187." In *Jerusalem in History*, edited by Asali, 130–176. London: Scorpion.

Hobsbawm, Eric, and Terrance Ranger. 1992. *The Invention of Tradition*. Cambridge: Cambridge University Press.

Honig-Parnass, Tikva. 2003. "Israel's Colonial Strategies to Destroy Palestinian Nationalism." *Race and Class* 45: 68–75.

———. 2011. *The False Prophets of Peace: Liberal Zionism and the Struggle for Palestine.* Chicago: Haymarket.

Human Rights Watch. 2008. "Flooding South Lebanon: Israel's Use of Cluster Munitions in Lebanon in July and August 2006." Vol. 20, no. 2.

Israeli Central Bureau of Statistics. 2010. Table 3: Population of Localities Numbering above 2,000 Residents.

Israel Statistical Yearbook. 2010. Jerusalem: Jerusalem Institute for Israel Studies. http://www.jiis.org/?cmd=statistic.424.

Israel Statistical Yearbook. 2012. Jerusalem: Jerusalem Institute for Israel Studies. http://www.jiis.org/?cmd=statistic.424.

Israeli Committee Against House Demolitions (ICAHD). 2012. "Demolishing Homes, Demolishing Peace." http://www.icahd.org/sites/default/files/Demolishing%20Homes%20Demolishing%20Peace_1.pdf.

Jad, Islah. 2010. "NGOs: Between Buzzwords and Social Movements." *Development in Practice* 17: 622–629.

Jad, Islah, Penny Johnson, and Rita Giacaman. 2000. "Gender and Citizenship under the Palestinian Authority." In *Gender and Justice in the Middle East*, edited by Suad Joseph, 137–157. Syracuse: Syracuse University Press.

Jiryis, Sabri. 1976. *The Arabs in Israel.* New York: Monthly Review Press.

Johnson, Penny. 2006. "Living Together in a Nation of Fragments." In *Living Palestine: Family Survival, Resistance, and Mobility under Occupation*, edited by Lisa Taraki, 51–102. Syracuse: Syracuse University Press.

Joseph, Suad. 1999. *Intimate Selving in Arab Families: Gender, Self, and Identity in Arab Families.* Syracuse: Syracuse University Press.

Kaminkar, Sarah. 1997. "For Arabs Only: Building Restrictions in East Jerusalem." *Journal of Palestine Studies* 26, no. 4: 5–16.

Kanaaneh, Rhoda. 2002. *Birthing the Nation: Strategies of Palestinian Women in Israel.* Berkeley: University of California Press.

Kark, Ruth. 1991. *Jerusalem Neighborhoods: Planning and Bylaws (1855–1930).* Jerusalem: Magnes.

———. 2001. *Jerusalem and Its Environs: Quarters, Neighborhoods, Villages, 1800–1948.* Detroit: Wayne State University Press.

Karmi, Ghada. 2002. *In Search of Fatima: A Palestinian Story.* London: Verso.

Kelley, Robin D. G. 1994. *Race Rebels: Culture, Politics, and the Black Working Class.* New York: Free Press.

Kendall, Henry. 1948. *Jerusalem: The City Plan, Preservation, and Development during the British Mandate, 1918–1948*, London: H. M. Stationery Office.

Khalidi, Rashid. 1997. *Palestinian Identity: the Construction of Modern National Consciousness*. New York: Columbia University Press.

———. 1999. "Transforming the Face of the Holy City: Political Messages in the Built Topography of Jerusalem." *Jerusalem Quarterly File* 2, no. 4: 21–29.

———. 2006. *The Iron Cage: The Story of the Palestinian Struggle for Statehood*. Boston: Beacon.

———. 2011. "Human Dignity in Jerusalem." *Jadaliyya*, July 5, 2011. www .jadaliyya.com/pages/index/2052/human-dignity-in-jerusalem.

Khalidi, Walid, ed. 1992. *All That Remains*. Washington, DC: Institute for Palestine Studies.

Kimmerling, Baruch. 2008. *Clash of Identities: Explorations in Israeli and Palestinian Societies*. New York: Columbia University Press.

Koenig Report. "Memorandum Proposal-Handling the Arabs of Israel." 1976. Reprinted in the *Journal of Palestine Studies* 6, no. 1: 190.

Kollek, Teddy. 1978. *For Jerusalem: A Life*. New York: Random House.

Kretzmer, David. 1990. *The Legal Status of the Arabs in Israel*. Boulder, CO: Westview.

Krystal, Nathan. 1999. "The Fall of the New City." In *Jerusalem 1948*, edited by Salim Tamari, 84–139. Washington, DC: Institute of Jerusalem Studies.

Kuttab, Eileen. 2005. "The Paradox of Women's Work." In *Living Palestine*, edited by Lisa Taraki, 231–274. Syracuse: Syracuse University Press.

Lazar, Karen. 1997. "A Feeling of Realistic Optimism: An Interview with Nadine Gordimer." *Salmagundi* 113 (Winter).

Lefebvre, Henri. 2003. *The Urban Revolution*. Minneapolis: University of Minnesota Press.

Levi, Primo. 1988. *The Drowned and the Saved*. New York: Simon & Schuster.

———. 2002. "Primo Levi: Begin Should Go." In *Primo Levi: The Voice of Memory Interviews 1961–1987*, edited by M. Belpoliti and R. Gordon. New York: New Press.

Lybarger, Loren. 2007. *Identity and Religion in Palestine: The Struggle between Islamism and Secularism in the Occupied Territories*. Princeton: Princeton University Press.

Mada al-Carmel. 2012. Personal Status Litigation for Palestinians in Israel: A Controversial Issue; *Jadal* Issue 16, December. http://mada-research.org/en /2012/12/19/jadal-issue-16-december-2012/. Access date February 30, 2013.

Magnes, Judah. 1983. *Palestine—Divided or United? The Case for a Bi-National Palestine before the United Nations*. Westport, CT: Greenwood.

Mahmoud, Saba. 2005. *Politics of Piety: The Islamic Revival and the Feminist Subject*. Princeton: Princeton University Press.

Makdisi, Saree. 2010. *Palestine Inside Out: An Everyday Occupation*. New York: W. W. Norton & Company.

Malinowski, Bronislaw. [1922] 2008. *Argonauts of the Western Pacific*. London: Dutton.

Malkki, Liisa. 1995. *Purity and Exile: Violence, Memory, and National Cosmology among Hutu Refugees in Tanzania*. Chicago: University of Chicago Press.

Mamdani, Mahmoud. 2004. *Good Muslim, Bad Muslim*. New York: Random House.

Mandela, Nelson. 1997. Address by President Nelson Mandela at the International Day of Solidarity with the Palestinian People. December 4. http://www.etools.co.za/anc/mandela/1997/sp971204b.html.

Marcus, George E., and Michael M. J. Fischer. 1986. *Anthropology as Cultural Critique: An Experimental Moment in the Human Sciences*. Chicago: University of Chicago Press.

Marx, Karl. 1881. "Letter to Nikolai Danielson, February 19." In *Marxists Internet Archive*, http://www.marxists.org/archive/marx/works/1881/letters/81_02_19.htm.

Marx, Karl, and Frederick Engels. 1848 [1967]. *The Communist Manifesto*. New York: Penguin.

———. 1960. *On Colonialism: Writings on India*. New York: Foreign Language Publishing House.

Masalha, Nur. 2007. *The Bible and Zionism: Invented Traditions, Archaeology and Post-Colonialism*. London: Zed.

Mauss, Marcel. 2007. "Body Techniques." In *Beyond the Body Proper: Reading the Anthropology of Material Life*, edited by Margaret Lock and Judith Farquhar, 50–68. Durham, NC: Duke University Press.

McCarthy, Justin. 1990. *The Population of Palestine: Population History and Statistics of the Late Ottoman Period and the Mandate*. New York: Columbia University Press.

McClintock, Anne. 1995a. *Imperial Leather: Race, Gender, and Sexuality in the Colonial Context*. Oxford: Routledge.

———. 1995b. "Postscript: The Angel of Progress." In *Imperial Leather: Race, Gender, and Sexuality in the Colonial Contest*, 391–396. Oxford: Routledge.

Meir, Golda. 1969. "Interview." *Sunday Times*, June 15.

Melville, Herman. 1876. *Clarel: A Poem and Pilgrimage to the Holy Land*. Evanston, IL: Northwestern University Press.

Memmi, Albert. 1965. *The Colonizer and the Colonized*. New York: Orion.

Mitchell, Timothy. 1988. *Colonizing Egypt*. Cambridge: Cambridge University Press.

———. 1991. "America's Egypt: Discourse of the Development Industry." *Middle East Report* 169 (March-April): 18–36.

———. 2002. *The Rule of Experts: Egypt, Techno-Politics, and Modernity*. Berkeley: University of California Press.

Moallem, Minoo. 2005. *Between Warrior Brother and Veiled Sister: Islamic Fundamentalism and the Politics of Patriarchy in Iran*. Berkeley: University of California Press.

Mohanty, Chandra, Ann Russo, and Lourdes Torres, eds. 1991. *Third World Women and the Politics of Feminism*. Bloomington: Indiana University Press.

Morris, Benny. 1997. *Israel's Border Wars, 1949–1956: Arab Infiltration, Israeli Retaliation, and the Countdown to the Suez War*. Oxford: Oxford University Press.

———. 2004. "Survival of the Fittest." Interview with Ari Shavit, *Ha'aretz*, 9 January. http://www.haaretz.com/survival-of-the-fittest-1.61345.

Muhammad, Ahmad Sheikh, Leena Abu-mukh Zoabi, Mtanes Shehadeh, Sami Miaari, Foad Moadi, and Liana Fahoum. 2012. *Reality of Arab Women in Israel*. Shefa-Amr: The Galilee Society.

Museum of Tolerance Web Site. 2012. http://www.wiesenthal.com/site/pp.asp?c=lsKWLbPJLnF&b=5505225.

Museum on the Seam. Promotional material from WEB site. 2013. http://shop.mots.org.il/about-the-museum.

Naber, Nadine. 2012. *Arab America: Gender, Cultural Politics, and Activism*. New York: New York University Press.

Nassar, Issam. 2006. *European Portrayals of Jerusalem: Religious Fascinations and Colonialist Imaginations*. Lewiston, NY: Edwin Mellen Press.

———. 2008. "Jerusalem in the Late Ottoman Period: Historical Writing and the Native Voice." In *Jerusalem: Idea and Reality*, edited by Tamar Mayer and Suleiman Ali Mourad, 205–222. New York: Routledge.

Nusseibeh, Sari. 2007. *Once Upon a Country: A Palestinian Life*. New York: Farrar.

Obenzinger, Hilton. 1999. *American Palestine: Melville, Twain, and the Holy Land Mania*. Princeton: Princeton University Press.

Olmert, Ehud. 1997. "I Am the Most Privileged Jew in the Universe: Interview with Ehud Olmert." *Middle East Quarterly* 4, no. 4: 65–73.

Omi, Michael, and Howard Winant. 1994. *Racial Formation in the United States: From the 1960s to the 1990s.* Oxford: Routledge.

Panourgiá, Neni, and Pavlos Kavouras. 2008. "Interview with Clifford Geertz." In *Ethnographica Moralia: Experiments in Interpretive Anthropology,* edited by Neni Panourgiá and George E. Marcus, 15–28. New York: Fordham University Press.

Pappe, Ilan. 2007. *The Ethnic Cleansing of Palestine.* Oxford: Oneworld.

Peteet, Julie. 1991. *Gender in Crisis.* New York: Columbia University Press.

———. 1994. "Male Gender and Rituals of Resistance in the Palestinian 'Intifada': A Cultural Politics of Violence." *American Ethnologist* 21, no. 1: 31–49.

———. 2005. *Landscape of Hope and Despair: Palestinian Refugee Camps.* Philadelphia: University of Pennsylvania Press.

Peters, F. E. 1990. *The Distant Shrine: The Islamic Centuries in Jerusalem.* New York: AMS.

Rabin, Yitzhak. 1979. *The Rabin Memoirs.* Boston: Little, Brown.

Ricca, Simone. 2007. *Reinventing Jerusalem: Israel's Reconstruction of the Jewish Quarter after 1967.* London: I. B. Tauris.

Rodinson, Maxine. 1973. *Israel: A Colonial-Settler State?* New York: Monad.

Rofel, Lisa. 1992. "Rethinking Modernity: Space and Factory Discipline in China." *Cultural Anthropology* 7, no. 1: 93–114.

Rome Statute of the International Criminal Court. 2002.

Rubinstein, Danny. 2001. "Who Owns the Western Wall?" *Ha'aretz,* January 2.

Said, Edward. 1992. "Palestine, Then and Now: An Exile's Journey through Israel and the Occupied Territories." *Harper's Magazine* (December): 47–55.

———. 1993. *Culture and Imperialism.* New York: Knopf.

———. 1995. "Projecting Jerusalem." *Journal of Palestine Studies* 25, no. 1: 5–14.

———. 1998a. "Palestine: Memory, Invention and Space." Keynote Address at the Birzeit Landscape Conference. November 12.

———. 1998b. "In Search of Palestine." BBC documentary film. Prod. Keith Bowers.

———. 1999. *Out of Place: A Memoir.* New York: Knopf.

Said, Edward, and Christopher Hitchens. 1989. *Blaming the Victims: Spurious Scholarship and the Palestinian Question.* London: Verso.

Salzinger, Leslie. 2003. *Genders in Production: Making Workers in Mexico's Global Factories.* Berkeley: University of California Press.

Samuel, Edwin. 1970. *A Lifetime in Jerusalem*. London: Transaction.

Sassen, Saskia. 1999. *Globalization and Its Discontents*. New York: New Press.

Sawalha, Aseel. 2011. *Reconstructing Beirut*. Austin: University of Texas Press.

Sayigh, Rosemary. 1985. *From Peasants to Revolutionaries*. London: Zed.

Schama, Simon. 1996. *Landscape and Memory*. New York: Vintage.

Scheper-Hughes, Nancy. 2004. "Violence Foretold: Reflections on 9/11." In *Violence in War and Peace: An Anthology*, edited by Nancy Scheper-Hughes and Philippe Bourgois, 224–226. Malden, MA: Blackwell.

Schlaim, Avi. 1988. *Collusion across the Jordan*. New York: Columbia University Press.

Schwenkel, Christina. 2006. "Recombinant History: Transnational Practices of Memory and Knowledge Production in Contemporary Vietnam." *Cultural Anthropology* 21, no. 1: 3–30.

Scott, James. 1990. *Domination and the Arts of Resistance: Hidden Transcripts*. New Haven: Yale University Press.

Segev, Tom. 1986. *1949: The First Israelis*. New York: Free Press.

———. 2001. *One Palestine, Complete: Jews and Arabs under the Mandate*. New York: Metropolitan.

Selig, Abe. 2010. "Fake Graves Cleared from Jerusalem Cemetery." *Jerusalem Post*, August 15. http://www.jpost.com/Israel/Fake-graves-cleared-from-Jlem -cemetery.

Sennett, Richard, and Jonathan Cobb. 1993. *The Hidden Injuries of Class*. New York: W. W. Norton.

Shafir, Gershon. 1989. *Land, Labor and the Origins of the Israeli-Palestinian Conflict, 1882–1914*. Cambridge: Cambridge University Press.

Shafir, Gershon, and Yoav Peled. 2002. *Being Israeli: The Dynamics of Multiple Citizenship*. Cambridge: Cambridge University Press.

Shahak, Israel, and Witold Jedlicki. 1991. "Lynch Mobs in Jerusalem." *Against the Current* (January/February): 3–6.

Shammas, Anton. 1997. "West Jerusalem: Falafel, Cultural Cannibalism and the Poetics of Palestinian Space." *An-Nahar Cultural Supplement*, Beirut, August 23.

Sharoni, Simona. 1995. *Gender and the Israeli-Palestinian Conflict: The Politics of Women's Resistance*. Syracuse: Syracuse University Press.

Shehadeh, Raja. 1988. *Occupier's Law: Israel and the West Bank*. Washington, DC: Institute for Palestine Studies.

Shihade, Magid. 2011. *Not Just a Soccer Game: Colonialism and Conflict among Palestinians in Israel*. Syracuse: Syracuse University Press.

Shipler, David. 1986. *Arab and Jew: Wounded Spirits in a Promised Land*. New York: Times Books.

Shohat, Ella. 1988. "Sephardim in Israel: Zionism from the Perspective of Its Jewish Victims." *Social Text*, nos. 19/20: 1–35.

Slyomovics, Susan. 1998. *The Object of Memory: Arab and Jew Narrate the Palestinian Village*. Philadelphia: University of Pennsylvania Press.

Smith, Andrea. 2005. *Conquest: Sexual Violence and American Indian Genocide*. Boston: South End.

Spivak, Gayatri. 1988. "Can the Subaltern Speak?" In *Marxism and the Interpretation of Culture*, edited by Cary Nelson and Laurence Grossberg, 271–313. Urbana-Champaign: University of Illinois Press.

Stack, Carol. 1974. *All Our Kin: Strategies for Survival in a Black Community*. New York: Basic.

Statistical Yearbook of Jerusalem. 2002–2003. Jerusalem: Jerusalem Institute for Israel Studies.

Stoler, Ann. 1995. *Race and the Education of Desire: Foucault's History of Sexuality and the Colonial Order of Things*. Durham, NC: Duke University Press.

———. 2002. *Carnal Knowledge and Imperial Power: Race and the Intimate in Colonial Rule*. Berkeley: University of California Press.

———. 2006. *Haunted by Empire: Geographies of Intimacy in North American History*. Durham, NC: Duke University Press.

Swedenburg, Ted. 1995. *Memories of Revolt: The 1936–1939 Rebellion and the Palestinian National Past*. Minneapolis: University of Minnesota Press.

Tabar, Linda, and Sari Hanafi. 2005. *The Emergence of a Palestinian Global Elite: Donors, International Organizations and Local NGOs*. Washington, DC: Institute for Palestine Studies.

Tamari, Salim, ed. 1999. *Jerusalem 1948*. Washington, DC: Institute of Jerusalem Studies.

———. 2009. *The Mountain and the Sea*. Berkeley: University of California Press.

Taraki, Lisa, ed. 2006a. *Living Palestine: Family Survival, Resistance, and Mobility under Occupation*. Syracuse: Syracuse University Press.

———. 2006b. "Introduction." In *Living Palestine: Family Survival, Resistance, and Mobility under Occupation*, edited by Lisa Taraki, xi–xxx. Syracuse: Syracuse University Press.

Taussig, Michael. 1991. *Shamanism, Colonialism, and the Wild Man: A Study in Terror and Healing.* Chicago: University of Chicago Press.

———. 1992. *The Nervous System.* New York: Routledge.

———.2006. *Walter Benjamin's Grave.* Chicago: University of Chicago Press.

Tibawi, Abdel Latif. 1978. *The Islamic Pious Foundations in Jerusalem.* London: Islamic Cultural Center.

Trouillot, Michel-Rolph. 1995. *Silencing the Past: Power and the Production of History.* New York: Beacon.

Tutu, Desmond. 2002. "Apartheid and the Holy Land." *The Guardian*, April 29, http://www.guardian.co.uk/world/2002/apr/29/comment.

Twain, Mark. 1869. *The Innocents Abroad: Or, the New Pilgrims' Progress.* London: Wordsworth.

United Nations General Assembly Resolution 194. 1948. 11 December.

United Nations Office for the Coordination of Humanitarian Affairs. 2011. "Bedouin Relocation: Threat of Displacement in the Jerusalem Periphery" (September).

United Nations Office for the Coordination of Humanitarian Affairs. 2012. http://www.unocha.org/ocha2012-13/opt.

United Nations Office for the Coordination of Humanitarian Affairs Occupied Palestinian Territory. 2012. "Movement and Access in the West Bank."

United Nations Security Council document. 1953. S/PV. 630, Appendix II, October 27. unispal.un.org/UNISPAL.NSF/0/017EEFB458011C9D05256722005E5499.

Usher, Graham. 1995. *Palestine in Crisis.* London: Pluto.

———. 1999. *Dispatches from Palestine: The Rise and Fall of the Oslo Peace Process.* London: Pluto.

Varzi, Roxanne. 2007. *Warring Souls: Youth, Media, and Martyrdom in Post-Revolutionary Iran.* Durham, NC, and London: Duke University Press.

Vidal, Gore. 1962. *Julian.* New York: Vintage.

Vitullo, Anita, Hilmi Araj, and Nader Said. 1998. *Women and Work in Palestine: A Briefing on the Situation of Women in the Employment Sector in Preparation for the International Labor Organization Mission.* Ramallah, Palestine: Development Studies Program.

Wasserstein, Bernard. 2008. *Divided Jerusalem: The Struggle for the Holy City.* New Haven: Yale University Press.

Whitlam, Keith. 1997. *The Invention of Ancient Israel.* London: Routledge.

Wiesel, Elie. 2010. "Open Letter to Barack Obama." *Washington Post*, April 16.

Yiftachel, Oren. 2006. *Ethnocracy: Land and Identity Politics in Israel/Palestine*. Philadelphia: University of Pennsylvania Press.

Zizek, Slavoj. 1994. "Introduction: The Spectre of Ideology." In *Mapping Ideology*, edited by Zizck, 1–32. London: Verso.

———. 2010. "Liberal Multiculturalism Masks an Old Barbarism with a Human Face." *The Guardian*, 3 October.

Index

273